PERSPECTIVES ON THE HISTORY OF ECONOMIC THOUGHT
VOLUME II

TWENTIETH-CENTURY ECONOMIC THOUGHT

Perspectives on the History of Economic Thought Volume II

Twentieth-Century Economic Thought

Selected Papers from the History of Economics Society Conference, 1987

Edited by
Donald A. Walker

Published for the History of Economics Society by
Edward Elgar

Published by
Edward Elgar Publishing Limited
Gower House
Croft Road
Aldershot
Hants GU11 3HR
England

Gower Publishing Company
Old Post Road
Brookfield
Vermont 05036
USA

British Library Cataloguing in Publication Data
Perspectives on the History of Economic Thought: selected papers
 from the History of Economics Society Conference, 1987.
 Vol. 2, Twentieth-century economic thought.
 1. Economics, to 1986
 I. Walker, Donald A. (Donald Anthony), *1934–* II. History of
 Economics Society
 330'.09

ISBN 1 85278 132 7

Printed and bound in Great Britain by
Anchor Press Ltd, Tiptree, Essex

Contents

Introduction
Donald A. Walker

The papers in the second volume of those selected from the papers given
at the 1987 meeting of the History of Economics Society are grouped
into three categories. The first group deals with the contributions of
economists who devoted much of their attention to the economic
policies of specific countries. In these papers we are given a sample of
how economic theories have been used in the formulation of practical
economic proposals. Jürgen Backhaus examines the work of Werner
Sombart on the business cycle. Sombart believed that each economy
behaves differently, and that therefore a special macroeconomic theory
must be developed for each economy. Backhaus shows how Sombart's
work on business cycles was related to his proposals for the reform of
Germany's economy, and indicates that Sombart played an important
role in advocating means of alleviating economic depression in Germany during the 1930s. Elizabeth Durbin explains the contributions of
British socialist economists who were active during the 1930s. She shows
how they developed a practical set of policy proposals for the Labour
Party and a non-Marxist economic theory of democratic socialism that
made considerable use of both microeconomic theory and Keynesian
ideas. She indicates how their work provided a rationale for British
government intervention after the Second World War and suggested
many elements of the specific policies that the Labour Party was to
follow. The third paper that takes up the theme of the reform of
national economies is by Heinz G. Grossekettler. He discusses the ideas
of a group of thinkers who were concerned with rebuilding the German
economy immediately after the Second World War. He gives a fascinat-
ing account of how economists of the Freiburg School took various ideas
from economic theory and notions about the proper way of doing things
from their cultural heritage to devise a framework of rules and
institutions for the German economy.

Part II is devoted to the ideas of John Maynard Keynes. Robert W.
Dimand performs a service by unearthing the reviews of Keynes'
Treatise on Money and putting them into an intelligible order. Dimand
provides us, at a time when it is often said that the *Treatise* was a failure

with Keynes' contemporaries, with a reminder of what an extremely enthusiastic reception it received from many important reviewers. He argues that the success of the work was crucial in preparing the way for the success of the *General Theory of Employment, Interest and Money*. Steven Pressman shows how Keynes' view on speculation changed, and how he ultimately reached the view that speculation should be discouraged by tax policies and prohibited in some respects by government regulation. Keynes' views on these matters take on heightened interest in the light of the recent volatility of securities markets. Ingo Barens takes the principal words of the title of his paper from the 'banana parable' that Keynes developed in the *Treatise*. In that parable, Barens argues, Keynes concluded that a market economy does not tend towards a full-employment long-run equilibrium. Keynes' thought on ways of solving the problem of unstable equilibrium, Barens contends, led him to the development of the concepts that were the foundation of the *General Theory of Employment, Interest and Money*. Robert W. Clower finds the origins of Keynes' *General Theory* in even earlier writings, namely those of Alfred Marshall. Keynes' aggregate analysis, Clower argues, has a close analogy to Marshall's short-run analysis of a competitive industry. Clower uses his model to contrast the Marshallian, Walrasian and Hicksian fix-price interpretations of Keynes' theory of effective demand. He concludes that the Marshallian interpretation is the only one that faithfully mirrors both the letter and the spirit of Keynes' argument. Christopher Marmé and Karl A. McDermott trace the development of the quantity theory of money in the work of Keynes from his earliest publication on the matter through to the *General Theory*. Unlike many writers, the authors argue that Keynes retained elements of the quantity theory in the *General Theory*. They show that he explicitly connected his ideas in that book with the quantity theory, but also that he abandoned the traditional version and modified and revitalized the elements that he retained.

Part III is comprised of four analyses of very modern economic topics. Hansjoerg Klausinger is concerned with some aspects of the history of neutral money. Friedrich von Hayek's analysis, Klausinger shows, ultimately becomes a comparison of the intertemporal equilibrium of a money and of a barter economy. Klausinger then turns to the writers of the neoclassical synthesis and the new classical economics, and maintains that neither of them has a conception of neutral money that is as fruitful as von Hayek's. M. M. G. Fase surveys monetarism in Holland. Modern debate on the topic in that country, he explains, was initiated in reaction to J. A. Schumpeter's criticisms of Keynes' views on money during the 1920s. Some of the leading Dutch economists believed in a neutral role for money, while others believed that monetary policy should be used actively to stabilize the general price level. Fase contends that the principal achievement of Dutch monetary policy was J. G. Koopman's theory of neutral money. He also discusses the contrasting view of M. W. Holtrop, President of the Netherlands Bank, who was concerned with inflationary and deflationary disturbances and with monetary equilibrium. Paul B. Trescott explains that there are two versions of the real-balance effect. Don Patinkin's is based on wealth; the other examines the disequilibrium real-balance effect. The latter, Trescott explains, is especially useful in analysing how monetary changes affect spending under various types of conditions. Trescott provides evidence that Keynes recognized the disequilibrium effect, and that Clark Warburton and Milton Friedman recognized links between the money stock and consumption. Shyam J. Kamath gives a great deal of information about the use in economics of the rational expectations hypothesis. He also subjects it to a methodological critique in which he evaluates the criticisms of the hypothesis. He judges the degree of success of the rational expectations revolution in regard to reinstating rationality into economic theory, in regard to its attempt to explain business cycles, and in regard to the formulation of economic policy.

Contributors

Jürgen Backhaus, Faculty of Economics and Business Administration, Rijksuniversiteit Limburg, Maastricht, The Netherlands

Ingo Barens, Department of Economics, Bergische Universitat, Federal Republic of Germany

Robert W. Clower, Department of Economics, University of South Carolina, Columbia, SC

Robert W. Dimand, Department of Economics, Brock University, St Catharines, Ontario, Canada

Elizabeth Durbin, Graduate School of Public Administration, New York University, Washington Square, NY

M. M. G. Fase, De Nederlandsche Bank N.V., Amsterdam, The Netherlands

Heinz G. Grossekettler, Department of Economics, University of Munster, Munster, Republic of Germany

Shyam J. Kamath, School of Business and Economics, Department of Economics, California State University, Hayward, CA

Hansjoerg Klausinger, Institute of Economic Theory and Policy, University of Economics, Vienna, Austria

Christopher Marmé, Department of Economics, University of Illinois at Urbana-Champaign, Champaign, IL

Karl A. McDermott, Department of Economics, Illinois State University, Normal, IL

Steven Pressman, Department of Economics and Finance, Monmouth College, West Long Branch, NJ

Paul B. Trescott, Department of Economics, Southern Illinois University at Carbondale, Carbondale, IL

PART I

ECONOMIC THOUGHT ON NATIONAL PROBLEMS

1 Werner Sombart's theory of the business cycle

Jürgen Backhaus

Werner Sombart is rightly known as the founder of *comparative economic systems* as a separate sub-discipline of economics with its own identifiable subject matter and methods (Sombart, 1930a). We do not think of him as an architect of macroeconomics. I should therefore explain what this chapter is about.

Today, Sombart's theory of the business cycle is of interest for two reasons. The economic historian will be interested in Sombart's role during the economic depression and Germany's 'Keynesian' recovery programme 1932–35. Sombart played a substantial part in pushing for these programmes, and in doing so he found himself opposed by the vast majority of German professors of economics. The historian of thought harbours a different interest. Sombart had set himself an ambitious task. Basing his work on Marx and Schmoller, he tried not only to reconcile but to complete the work of both. It is often said that his historical work was descriptive and speculative, but that he failed in the task of theorizing. This assessment was certainly neither his own nor that of his contemporaries (Schumpeter, 1927), hence, a reconstruction of his theory of the business cycle is called for. Sombart has indeed developed theoretical views on the business cycle[1] which were, on the one hand, fairly abstract, but on the other hand, not too abstract for the author to derive precise measures of economic policy. Hence, this chapter tries to answer two questions:

1. what is Sombart's theory of the business cycle?; and
2. what were the policy measures that Sombart derived from his theory, when he was asked in 1932 to comment on a specific programme and propose policy measures on the basis of his theoretical views?

A few biographical remarks may help answer these questions. Obviously, the best way to learn about Sombart is to reread his books and essays.[2] Next to Marx and Engels, Sombart was probably the most widely read German economist. His numerous books reached large

3

circulations and they continue to be reprinted.[3] Sombart was well placed from the outset. His father, a prominent Member of Parliament, was among the founders of the *'Verein für Socialpolitik'* (the German Economic Association) and a close friend of Schmoller's. In drawing on every accessible historical study, Sombart tried to arrive at an historically-based systems theory. His empirical method was secundary analysis. But Sombart differed substantially from all the other members of the historical school by emphasizing the importance of Marx. Not unlike Schumpeter, Sombart appreciated Marx's theoretical contribution, although this does not imply that he subscribed to Marxism. He differed from both Marx and Schmoller in his brilliant style, which had an artistic quality about it. He was able to present his findings in such a way that they were not only accessible to the interested layman, but were avidly read by a large public.[4]

In 1932, when the depression reached its nadir, Sombart had recently retired from his chair at the University of Berlin. That university was then Germany's most prominent academic institution, and he had just assumed the presidency of the *Verein für Socialpolitik*. Early in the same year, his colleague Wagemann had proposed a sweeping currency and credit reform[5] which had met with so much criticism, both nationally and internationally, that the government was forced to distance itself from the suggestion and reaffirm its determination to stick with its austerity policies. Probably organized by Stolper,[6] German professors of economics, in rare unanimity, protested against plans for credit-based employment policies. Apart from Wagemann, the only dissenting views could be heard from Röpke,[7] the Kiel group[8] and Sombart.

The term 'theory' as used in the title of this chapter, 'Sombart's Theory of the Business Cycle', raises the question what kind of a theory this historically working economist might have produced. We would not expect any of his work to be reprinted in the *Journal of Economic Theory* today, not least because it might prove inaccessible to contemporary theoreticians. Sombart anticipated this question, and he suggested an answer in the preface to the second edition of his first volume:[9]

> Today, some economists who are gifted with very special talents suggest a contradiction between the theoretical orientation of our science and those principal orientations of research that guided the historical school. This is in essence a somewhat traditional and arbitrary reduction of the term theory to the preoccupation with a well-defined set of problems, namely those problems, which turn on the preservation and development of the models developed by the classics of our discipline and which relate to the standard regularities of economic phenomena that have been derived through this process of abstraction.

The value of this theory, that is abstract and partial reasoning, is emphasized by no one more than by the author of this work. [He then gives a number of references to individual chapters. J.B.] But to believe that these abstractions and isolations make up all that belongs to that social science of economics, which up to now used to be called political economy, or to believe that engaging in those constructions is somehow a well-defined and separate part of this science, seems to me to be rather wrong.

Today it seems to be obvious that only the combination of both activities to one combining effort results in scientific work in economics. It is almost trivial to insist that theory and empirical work are like form and substance of the same subject matter. (I, pp. xiv–xv)

Schumpeter agreed with Sombart in his review of the latter's third volume (of *Modern Capitalism*), when he argued that:

a basic theoretical model is necessary for the representation of a historical process, that this set of economic principles tends to be further developed in conducting empirical research, and that due to the special character of the economic science and the nature of her subject, a 'general' explanation and research into some specific processes become two complementary aspects of the same task. Division of labour is certainly called for. As compared to this task, the other tasks of making empirical material available and sharpening the tools of our intellectual work – 'theory' according to Marshall – become subsidiary activities. (Schumpeter, 1927, p. 199)

What was true for Sombart's treatment of economic phenomena in general also applied to his theory of the business cycle. He explicitly stated (III,2, p. 568) that the fundamental causes of social activity are the motives of individuals who are endowed with a free will and can make choices. Hence, the business cycle had to be explained in terms of particular circumstances that made people act so as to bring about cyclical activity. His approach is thus surprisingly modern. Compare Olson's (1985) recent critique of modern macroeconomics: 'This makes it all the more puzzling that most of the explanations of macroeconomic and monetary problems that economists offer are not systematically derived from an analysis of the incentives facing the participant in the economy' (Olson, 1985, p. 631). The business cycle was not considered by Sombart to be a specific phenomenon that required a theory of its own. His theory of the business cycle is embedded in his encompassing theory of capitalism, of which the business cycle was considered an essential part.[10] His theory of the business cycle can thus not really be isolated from his systems theory of capitalism. Doing so does lead to certain misrepresentations, and the task of understanding is certainly not facilitated by the need to use contemporary terms which have different connotations from Sombart's. Yet, although Sombart's way of theorizing was so different from ours today, he was able to arrive at quite tangible conclusions in the crisis of 1932.

1

Sombart's is an historically-based systems theory of capitalism. The system develops in stages. Accordingly, the first volume of his *Capitalism* is devoted to pre-capitalist systems, the second to early capitalism, and the third to 'Hochkapitalismus', which may best be translated as 'mature' or high capitalism.[11] The period of mature capitalism extends over some 150 years up to the outbreak of the First World War (III, 1, p. xi). The period to follow was late capitalism. The distinction is important, since Sombart took the claim of the historical school seriously, that every economic system requires its own theoretical model. Again, this is in line with Olson's critique of modern macroeconomics: 'If . . . macroeconomic performance is also explained in large part by the pattern of incentives, then it should not be surprising if macroeconomic problems and performance were also different in different countries, regions and historical periods' (Olson, 1985, p. 634). This implies that the economic depression of the early 1930s required a theory derived from an analysis of late capitalism. We can therefore not expect to find a fully developed explanation of that crisis in the work on high capitalism. Consequently, when he was asked to comment on the Great Depression, he had to extend his analysis to the system of late capitalism (Sombart, 1932) and adapt his business cycle theory to that stage.

In principle, Sombart distinguishes between two types of business cycle, hence, there are two different types of theory of the cycle. The first type is more universal than the second. It may occur in any market system, whether it be a capitalist one or not. It is caused by some factor which results in a decline of market demand (a leftward shift of the demand curve) with supply essentially unchanged: a *glut* will result (II, 1, chs 16, 17). The second type of business cycle is a phenomenon typical of high capitalism. These cycles are caused on the supply side, and they are the consequence of capitalist expansion. Here, the crisis is caused endogenously, and the cycle is a normal phenomenon in the capitalist development process. Sombart pointed out that in late capitalism, containing the business cycle has become an objective of economic policy, and the cycle of expansion ceases to be a typical characteristic of the system.

Let us consider the two cycles in turn.

Cycles caused by insufficient demand
This cycle may be caused by any number of exogenous factors invariably resulting in a glut. Sombart's discussion is indicative of his entire approach. He takes one industry which he found well documented and

traces its development over several centuries. The industry chosen is the silk industry in the French city of Lyons, and the period of investigation 1605 to 1787 (II, 1, pp. 219–23). For this period and industry he identifies ten factors which he considers typical causes for the glut. These are:

1. laws against luxury
2. fashion
3. state-ordered mourning
4. new products
5. development of foreign industries
6. bad harvests
7. wars
8. widespread poverty
9. insufficient money supply
10. state commercial policy.

It is remarkable that of those ten causes, only no. 8 (insufficient demand due to low income) can be called a typically economic one. Another two (9 and 10) are connected to economic policy; while at best causes nos. 1 and 3 may be influenced by measures of economic policy as traditionally conceived.

While most of the causes of the cycle are exogenous, frequence and timing of the gluts are well determined by economic and institutional factors. Four factors are particularly important.

1. The depth and the breadth by which an economy is endowed with means of communication and transportation. The better this infrastructure, the more susceptible is the economy to exogenous shocks.
2. Military and economic warfare as well as commercial conflicts. Sombart is referring to the conflicts motivated by mercantilist economic policies. The more frequent or the more serious these conflicts, the more severe was their impact on demand and the ensuing glut.
3. Deficiencies in the state fiscal and commercial organization, notably (a) fiscal administration, (b) monetary constitution, (c) organization of credit, and (d) deficiencies in the organization of commerce and trade. The efficient organization of these institutions is clearly seen as an objective of economic policy. The less effective these policies are, the more susceptible is the system to exogenous shocks.
4. Migrations are emphasized.

It is characteristic of early capitalism that gluts caused by insufficient demand occur frequently, but they remain unsynchronized in time and place (II, 1, p. 225). Accordingly, as the capitalist system expands globally, it becomes more susceptible to ever more severe crises. The world economic depression of the 1930s is interpreted by Sombart as just one such crisis:

> How many misunderstandings could have been avoided had one not insisted on parallels between the current world crisis and the cycles of expansions that are characteristic for high capitalism. These parallels do not exist. The current crisis is a 'simple' demand induced glut of the kind we have been observing in the aftermath of every major war since the development of open market economies. The capitalist system as such has nothing to do with this crisis. (III, 2, p. 563).

The capitalist cycle caused by the organization of supply

The capitalist cycle is caused on the supply side. It is a typical characteristic of capitalist expansion, and it is as necessary as its duration is limited. At the centre of this theory stands the entrepreneur, who is the motor of capitalist expansion. The causes of the cycle must be seen in those stimuli which motivate the entrepreneur. Yet the conditions furthering entrepreneurial activity are conventional: (1) low interest rates, (2) low prices, and (3) low wages. The theory of interest Sombart proposes is somewhat unconventional. Saving in the sense of capital accumulation takes place within the enterprise during the upswing of the cycle. The role of the interest rate is played out in the capital markets, where share markets and bond markets are distinguished. In times of depression, corporations do not issue shares, savings must therefore be held as bonds, and bonds are not invested in new forms of production. Hence there is less productive activity and profits are lower; consequently the interest rate remains low (III, 2, pp. 569–70). In addition, and assuming that they will always be monetized by the central bank, Sombart invokes gold imports as an additional factor that has often depressed interest rates and served as a trigger of entrepreneurial activity. (In his policy conclusions in 1932 he consequently urged a departure from the gold standard.)

Apart from the availability of labour and capital at low rates, investment opportunities are important to stimulate entrepreneurship. These opportunities are further circumscribed. Entrepreneurial investment will lead to increases in production capacity when prices are expected to remain stable; more particularly, capacity will be increased for the production of durables 'which yield higher returns when prices remain constant' (p. 569); durables which will be used for the construction of long-term projects such as railways, roadways, plants and commercial buildings, i.e. investment projects that are capital intensive.

This circumscribes the sector where capitalist expansion will be focused. Still, expansion will only take place if entrepreneurs form expectations about new market opportunities (p. 571). Typical instances affecting the formation of such expectations are:

1. the development of new markets;
2. the reconstruction or renovation of the infrastructure of an economy, notably inventions and innovations;
3. good harvests which will lead to strengthened demand by the rural population; and
4. a general population increase causing e.g. new demand for housing. Again, we see that these factors are partly exogenous.

At the beginning of the cycle, several lags are important. Investment will start when wages and prices for raw materials and other inputs are low and expected to be stable, while product prices are (already) expected to rise. An increase in liquidity (*Kaufkraft*) will fuel this activity, where liquidity depends on:

1. 'the import of gold, which will already cause a rise in prices while the discount rate is still falling' (III, 2, p. 572);
2. an extension of credit; and
3. an increase in aggregate demand caused by a sectoral increase in production.

Sombart obviously has a multiplier process in mind. For the further development of the cycle the differentiation between two sectors is crucial. Production growth in the organic sector (agriculture, forestry, etc.) is limited, while in the mining and manufacturing sectors it is not. Hence it is there where acceleration will mainly take place. This scenario is given twice: in monetary and in real terms. In monetary terms, the manufacturing sector can expand where large stock-holding companies draw on their established bank credit and publicly guaranteed projects allow for large-scale issue of shares and bonds. In real terms, rapid expansion is possible since production is based on non-agricultural inputs such as coal, iron, bricks, etc. This circumscribes the expansionary sector fairly sharply as revolving around construction, reconstruction and drastic renovation. The expansion can last the longer, the more flexibly the organic sector supports the expansion. In this context, worker migration is also mentioned (II, 1, p. 576). For an explanation of the downturn, Sombart invokes a quasi-Marxian theory of disproportionality between sectors. The argument again is given in both monetary and real terms. In monetary terms, the system enters a liquidity crisis. There is a growing disproportionality between circulating and fixed capital, where the growth of circulating capital (i.e. the money supply) is determined by the supply of gold (III, 2, p. 578). In real terms, we have a growing disproportionality between the agricultural sector, which cannot keep pace with the growth of the manufacturing sector. Growth in the latter sector is thus restricted, and it is there where the depression sets in.

Sombart was at great pains to emphasize his view that the full cycle was a necessary condition for capitalist expansion. He collected data to show that during the crunch, productivity increases could be achieved. Likewise, the cyclicity of capitalist expansion contains wage increases and allows capital accumulation within the enterprises during the upswing, when product prices are already increasing ahead of wages (p. 584).

The thoroughly eclectic nature of Sombart's theory is so obvious that it need not be emphasized. When Volume III appeared in 1927, Schumpeter criticized Sombart, who had been among the first to push for business cycle research (Sombart, 1904), for not developing his theory sufficiently. Cycles of different length which may overlap do not in fact occur, and the role of the entrepreneur, while central, remains somewhat vague. On the other hand, the importance of gold may have been overemphasized. Schumpeter was particularly unhappy with the disproportionality theory, and suggested that the reader turn to the chapters on the stabilization of the cycle (Schumpeter, 1927, chapter 4). Indeed, Sombart suggested (III, 2, chapter 45) that the sharp cyclicity of economic development was a thing of the past. The more developed capitalist economies experience ever less severe cycles. The causes responsible for this development parallel those given earlier, namely a more rational monetary constitution which reduces the dependence of the economy on the gold supply, better data for forecasting market developments and lower population growth. (For the United States, he supplied data linking immigration with the business cycle.) According to Sombart, the dampening of the cycle will limit capitalist expansion. The more regular and the more regulated the capitalist economies become, the less capitalist they are, and the less spectacular will be their economic development.

At this point, it may be useful to compare Sombart's business cycle theories with those of other authors, first in general terms, and secondly with specific references to Wicksell and Schumpeter. Sometimes a distinction is drawn between those theories that consider the slump phase as an unavoidable precondition to moving the economy ahead to a new expansionary phase, and those that view the contraction of output as an undesirable episode to be postponed and, if possible, eliminated.[12]

Sombart falls into both categories. His cycle of capitalist expansion requires a contractionary period, because it is during that period that the economy experiences its major productivity boosts. His cycle caused by insufficient demand, on the other hand, serves no particular purpose. Its depth and effects can be contained by effective economic policies. Another way of distinguishing business cycle theories turns on whether the business cycle itself is fundamentally characterized and ultimately explained by the dynamics of relative prices, or whether the dynamics of macroeconomic aggregates provide the explanation. Again, Sombart's capitalist cycle falls into the first group, whereas the cycle caused by insufficient demand is more akin to the latter and certainly argued in aggregate terms.

Cycle theories in which relative prices have a significant role tend to recognize among the causes of the end of the expansionary phase an insufficient supply both of productive factors and of finished products. This production constraint would lead to a distortion of relative prices, compounding inefficiencies that the system runs up during the expansionary phase. Sombart's theory is also of this kind. The constraint imposed by the slowly growing organic sector on the system as a whole and upon the growth attainable in the manufacturing sector leads to an increase in the prices of the organic sector and most notably pushes up wages (labour is part of the organic sector). In order to contain these price increases, and notably in order to contain wages, the downturn has to occur.

Wicksell, in the appendix to the American edition of *Interest and Prices*, offers a cycle theory where the crisis comes about because the supply of circulating capital (stocks) needed to feed the production process and utilize labour and capacity becomes insufficient. The slump is then necessary because the resulting unemployment and relative price decline make it economical to build the stocks required for the next expansionary phase (Wicksell, 1965, p. 232). Sombart argues very similarly that, in the context of a gold standard economy, the gold supply cannot increase sufficiently to sustain a credit expansion that can keep pace with the ongoing investment process, i.e. the accumulation of embodied capital. Projects that have been started come to a standstill, capacity can no longer be fully utilized, and payment deadlines begin to be missed, further exacerbating the credit squeeze.

Finally, in comparison with Schumpeter, Sombart mentions technological innovations as one motor of capitalist expansion, but it is surprising that Sombart's expansionary process is strongly dependent on large government-financed projects. While Schumpeter gave full account of all manner of technological innovations and how they came about, in

Sombart's business cycle treatment the entrepreneur, rather surprisingly (see notably Sombart, 1913a), remains a pale and somewhat mechanical figure. Of course, we must admit, to Sombart's credit, that the entrepreneur, to this day, has not been satisfactorily integrated into economic theory. Schumpeter's and Sombart's theories are parallel in emphasizing how the downturn of the cycle enhances the productivity of the system as a whole (Schumpeter speaks of 'creative destruction'). Even with innovations continuing, in Schumpeter as in Sombart, the boom must reach a turning-point due to a lack of resources. According to both authors, the bottleneck is likely to occur in the organic sector, with workers pushing for greater wage demands. The slump serves to rearrange relative prices and reallocate resources.

2

As I mentioned earlier, Sombart also discussed stabilization of the cycle; he felt that capitalism had entered a period with less severe cyclical activity. This prompts the question about the future of capitalism which Sombart tried to elucidate in the monograph of that title (Sombart, 1932). He distinguished there between three logically possible scenarios that the future course of capitalism might take: continuation of the status quo, retrogression, and progression. The first scenario implied that the situation of 1932 could somehow be retained. He described the economic policies of his day as consisting of haphazard state intervention, state initiatives lacking coordination as they were made in response to pressures from special-interest groups, subsidies here, regulatory controls there, protection of farming and promotion of the export industries. This, of course, describes the situation of Germany in 1932, and Sombart was convinced that it was an untenable one. The second possibility involved a return to full capitalism, which was indeed implicitly favoured by the majority of German economists at that time. A return would have required above all sweeping changes in the legal structure – namely dismantling the regulatory state – in order to free the entrepreneurial spirit. Sombart rejected this idea too, because it had been rendered impossible by the very development of capitalism itself. The large conglomerated corporations, trusts and cartels had themselves created a system of rules which tended to obstruct entrepreneurial activity. In addition, the political interest groups had become too powerful to be ignored or overruled, and the sheer size of the capitalist corporation had made into a political unit what once could probably have been regarded as a private affair. In referring to the then recent bank collapse in Germany he noted that the failure of just one major bank had repercussions that the state could no longer ignore: 'No state can tolerate sovereign industrial duchies in its interior.' Thus having rejected the possibility of either retrogression or else the maintenance of the status quo, Sombart saw progression to a new economic order as the most likely outcome. His projection involved, on the one hand, a concerted approach to economic policy (a concept he called 'planning') and, on the other hand, a return to largely self-sufficient national economic development.

In talking about planning, Sombart was mainly interested in a coordination of the various political interventions into the economy to fit one common pattern, to harmonize the different legal developments, to use taxation as an instrument of fiscal policy, not merely as a method of revenue generation, and to do this on the basis of the traditional political system that guarantees individual liberties. As Sombart was anxious to point out, his approach to 'planning' would not bring about the introduction of any new policy instrument that was not already in use, rather, it was arguing for the integrated coordination of all these approaches that were already being practised that was his own contribution.

In this projection, Sombart in 1932 was describing what is commonplace today. The second element of his scenario, however, his rather critical view of free trade, which led him to emphasize (relative) autarky, is somewhat more puzzling. Sombart's argument is reminiscent of public policy debates in Europe and the United States today, but it has a special catch. He began by noting that development in the less developed countries was picking up, and that consequently domestic industries faced increasing competition from abroad. Foreign competitors were able to replicate productive processes which were once exclusive to the domestic sector, and they were able to do this at a lower level of wages and other input costs which reflected the artificially high input price level consequent to unionization and other forms of cartelization, the universal quest for security and fixed incomes. An export industry could, however, thrive only on the basis of continual innovation. This was no longer feasible owing to the changes in capitalism itself, which had stifled initiative and entrepreneurship. The argument is then simple and straightforward. If exports decline, imports have to be reduced as well. And this means that those products which are essential and which tend to be imported, notably primary (agricultural) products, have to be produced at home. This is why Sombart called for 'internal colonization', an increase in the agrarian population which would absorb most of the currently unemployed (1932). True to his two-sector scheme, Sombart wanted to strengthen the organic sector in order to compensate for the declining innovative strength of regulated capitalism.

These were the main threads of the argument Sombart made in 1932, and they form the background for his economic policy recommendations. Sombart's activities with respect to economic policy formed part of the work of an association called *Studiengesellschaft für Geld- und Kreditwirtschaft* (Study Group on Money and Credit) which had set itself the task of campaigning for a reform of the monetary constitution of Germany, in order to make credit-financed employment measures possible. The association was fairly small and composed of industrialists, bankers, economic journalists and several university professors, notably Sombart. The group had prepared a comprehensive employment programme which was so detailed that it could be implemented any day. This programme had first been offered to the Chancellor (the accompanying letter is dated 10 August 1932) and was later published (Dräger et al., 1932). On 29 February 1932 Sombart had presented his lecture on the future of capitalism, the gist of which I have just summarized and which was published in book form during the same year. In addition, the study group's programme was accompanied by a separate opinion on exports in which Sombart drew the practical conclusions from the 1932 study.[13] This export opinion develops criteria for successful employment measures, criteria that Sombart deduced from the general study.

In discussing this export opinion, I do not want to suggest that Sombart was the author of Germany's successful employment programmes between 1932 and 1935. Indeed, the author was Lautenbach. However, the latter was not uninfluenced by the substantial publicity which the study group generated, to which Sombart contributed quite effectively. The fact that Lautenbach, who was a theoretically-inclined economist working as a high-placed civil servant in the Finance Ministry, could carry the day with his suggestions is in itself remarkable. In my view, the extent to which such suggestions could become politically acceptable was not independent of the position major economists took on the matter. Sombart was beyond doubt the most effective persuader the economics profession counted among its ranks. His contribution to creating an atmosphere in which credit-financed employment programmes could become acceptable was thus potentially significant.

Sombart began his export opinion to the Chancellor by appropriately pointing out the political premises he was starting from. He was arguing for a concerted approach to economic policy (called 'planning'), thus distancing himself from both socialists and liberal non-interventionists.

He argued against policies aimed at autarky, but for policies that emphasized Germany's interests *vis-à-vis* her neighbours, notably in the reparations question. While distancing himself from autarky, he pleaded for policy measures designed to protect Germany's economic development from outside intervention. These protective measures included three types:

1. a moratorium on the external debt as far as payments on the principal are concerned, and a reduction of the interest rate by having the debt guaranteed by a potent international organization in order to do away with the risk premium;
2. protective measures against the dumping of foreign products on home markets, notably in agriculture; and
3. measures to ensure the continued inflow of raw materials.

Since Sombart foresaw trade wars, he argued for reciprocal trade arrangements, where necessary on a barter basis.

Given such a protective belt to allow for national German stimulation measures (in the absence of an international concerted action), he turned to a discussion of successful measures for creating employment. Again, he started with those that he rejected. First, he rejected a general deregulation of the economy which, while opening up new room for entrepreneurial initiatives, would not be much of a stimulus in the presence of depressed effective demand.[14] Secondly, he rejected policies of subsidizing private enterprises with the intention of stimulating employment. Thirdly, he rejected public employment programmes in so far as they were to be financed out of current tax revenues. This would only substitute state demand for private demand, without further stimulating employment consequences. Hence, he argued for credit-based employment programmes, which required not only a currency reform but also a reform of the monetary institutions. As in his other writings, he emphasized the constraining role of gold and argued for a departure from the gold standard.

Credit-based employment programmes were not popular with the general public in Germany. Memories of hyperinflation were still fresh, and risking a new inflation was politically unwise.[15] Sombart approached the problem of inflation by pointing out that baseless fears of inflation were not really unwelcome, since they would lead the way out of the liquidity trap by stimulating purchases of non-monetary assets.[16] The fear of inflation would be baseless, as long as the credit-financed government outlays led to an immediate increase in production. This is the central premise of Sombart's position, and the rest should follow smoothly.

Credit-financed government employment programmes must lead to immediate increases in production, and to improvements in the productivity of the economy. Hence, they must not be used for improvements of public services benefiting the consumer. On the basis of this reasoning, he argued against the electrification of the railway which would not lead to more than small improvements in speed and substitute readily available coal for more costly electricity. He argued against improvements in roads designed to stimulate long-haul trucking, since this would simply reduce capacity utilization of the railway. He argued against the construction of motorways, considering cars to be luxury items. Likewise, almost akin to Malthus, he argued against improvements in housing. As we saw when discussing his theory of the capitalist business cycle, the bottleneck of economic development in a capitalist system was considered to be the organic sector. Consequently, the measures Sombart favoured were all designed to improve the productivity of that sector, notably agriculture. The programme that the *Studiengesellschaft für Geld- und Kreditreform* had presented contained numerous such proposals, and hence he endorsed:

1. the settlement of entire new villages;[17]
2. strengthening of farmers' cooperatives in order to reduce the costs of production in agriculture;
3. draining of wetlands, improvement of grasslands and cultivation of wilderness areas, which would increase agricultural production by more than $12\frac{1}{2}$ million hectares (approximately 31 million acres);
4. construction of roads where this would lead to an improvement of productivity and better access to markets;
5. construction of canals under the same condition;
6. rationalization of agricultural production by improving the layout of farms, introducing new techniques of production and setting up new agricultural schools (winter schools).

All of these measures, Sombart pointed out proudly, could begin either immediately or with the beginning of the new season, and they would roughly absorb as many workers in the organic sector as were currently unemployed.

Finally, he added a special suggestion. Throughout his modern capitalism, Sombart kept emphasizing the importance of household production. At one point, he noted that, with increasing urbanization, the means for household production become increasingly scarce which leads to a reduction in welfare. Hence, he suggested that people who were unemployed should be given the option of taking on, rent-free, a smallholding just big enough to serve as the basis for modest family means.

If we compare Sombart's proposals with what actually happened, we find striking similarities. In doing so, we need to keep in mind that the German employment programmes were actually composed of several programmes. It is useful to distinguish two different phases: first, 1932–35, and second, 1935 onwards. During the first phase, there were four programmes – the Papen and Schleicher programmes completed before Hitler took power, and the two Reinhardt programmes conceived before he took power but endorsed by him. In 1934 after Schacht took over, a new economic era began, and it is this era which is normally and rightly associated with Nazi economic policies, aiming at full employment and rearmament. Schacht, immediately upon resuming his new function as minister, sacked the architect of the four earlier programmes, Wilhelm Lautenbach, and began to take credit for what had already been accomplished. It is the second phase which is also characterized by the technically ambitious projects, the large-scale construction of motorways and railways, and the new emphasis on steel, car and aircraft production.

As was pointed out above, Sombart, on theoretical grounds, staunchly opposed any emphasis on manufacturing, favouring the modernization of 'organic' agriculture. He had no sooner taken this position when he was bitterly attacked by the party press, which asserted, on the contrary, that modern technology was 'the birth of the Nordic spirit' and 'technology is the essential part of our culture'. Further, with respect to employment policy: 'German socialism is, first of all, a victory over technology: the final victory. We have to build our social order in such a way that technical progress does not turn against the people and put them out of work. Capitalism will fall by the wayside not despite, but as a consequence of, further progress in technological development.'[18]

The contrast could scarcely have been starker. While, according to the party line, the way to full employment was technology-oriented, Sombart had argued for an economic programme based on a thorough modernization of agriculture. In line with his proposals, much of what we find in the early employment programmes was indeed centred on Germany's underdeveloped agrarian provinces.

Summary and concluding remarks
In this chapter, I have shown how Sombart set about developing a systems theory of the business cycle. He insisted that for every different economic system, there must be a separate theory of macroeconomic

activity. Although his main effort lay in developing a theory of high capitalism, in the face of the world economic depression of 1929–32 he extended his work to include the regulated economy or 'late capitalism'. This systems theory, while fairly abstract, he was nevertheless able to rely on in drawing very specific economic policy conclusions in terms of criteria a credit-financed state-sponsored employment programme had to meet. Historically, there is a considerable correspondence between these proposals and German economic policy in the early 1930s.

I suggested (p. 3) that Sombart's theory of the business cycle is of interest for both economic historians and historians of economic thought. Economic historians stand to benefit from an understanding of Sombart's influential role in shaping a climate in which 'Keynesian' and theory-based economic policies could be implemented successfully well before the appearance of the *General Theory*. In particular, the specific features of the programmes are so strikingly different from standard macroeconomic policy measures as conceived today, aiming as they did at particular industries instead of at aggregate variables, that a closer study of the implementation might be useful today. As there is widespread concern that macroeconomic policies have lost their teeth, studies of the implementation of the successful policy experiments will probably have to assume great importance.

Historians of economic thought are interested in reconstructing the development of economic theory. The case of Sombart, once a towering figure in economics, is striking because his name has disappeared from economic theory literature. As we turn to the index pages of even the most erudite macroeconomics textbook today, we look for his name in vain. Likewise, Sombart has disappeared from the pages of comprehensive histories of economic analysis.[19] This is true even for Schumpeter's encyclopaedic *History of Economic Analysis*. There Sombart is discussed in a number of places, but usually alongside Max Weber in the context of his important (and usually underestimated) work on the methodology of economics. In the chapter on the historical school (which Schumpeter was unable to finish), he speaks of Sombart's peak achievement as the historical school and his outstanding performance as a scholar and teacher, but he does not substantiate his judgements. This substantiation is contained in a long essay (Schumpeter, 1927) which has remained inaccessible to the mainstream of economics due to language barriers.

One author stands out in stating explicitly why Sombart should not be considered as a contributor to economic theory. Mark Blaug, in the fourth edition of his *Economic Theory in Retrospect*, puts Marx, Schmoller, Sombart, Max Weber, Pareto and the Webbs in the camp of economic sociology (p. 710) which, true to the tradition established by Schumpeter, he wants to keep separate from economic theory. While one should not squabble with classifications as long as they serve to help us understand well-defined problems, we should be cautious before accepting classifications that might cut the discipline off from important developments. While Schumpeter considered economic sociology an important area of economics, Blaug is (quite justifiably) critical of attempts to replace economic theory with economic sociology. This has not happened and is unlikely to happen unless new theories can be developed from economic sociology that are able to beat the old theories (p. 711). Students of Sombart are unlikely to be satisfied with Blaug's explanation for his absence in modern expositions of economic theory. Sombart indeed had an historically-based systems theory of capitalism to offer with which he was able to embrace a wide variety of phenomona that cannot readily be handled in standard economic models today. That these efforts were not always satisfactory is evident from the discussion of his theory of business cycles offered in this chapter. And the need for a theory that can, for instance, explain the effects of family structures, demographic changes or migration on macroeconomic activity is still present in the economics profession.[20]

Notes

1. This was not lost on careful readers, such as Knut Wicksell (1978), *Lectures in Political Economy*, vol. 2, p. 209.
2. The biographical information that can be found in textbooks and encyclopaedias is often misleading. This is true of the treatments in Blaug's *Who's Who*, the textbook by Spiegel or the *International Encyclopaedia of the Social Sciences*, where Jürgen Kuczynski wrote the entry. A notable exception is the piece by Schefold in the *New Palgrave*.
3. This is true of his main work, *Der moderne Kapitalismus*, but also of separate studies, such as *Luxury and Capitalism* (New York, 1938; Ann Arbor 1976). Even those books that are currently out of print are readily accessible in secondhand bookshops. The only exception is Sombart's last book, *Vom Menschen,* which (in 1938) he was allowed to publish only under severe restrictions.
4. Today, the form of his work no longer facilitates a wider circulation. Sombart put his research in voluminous books and he expected his reader not only to have lots of spare time, but also to be in command of a handful of modern and classic languages. His student and translator Mortimer Epstein provided two outstanding translations in English.
5. Wagemann, in addition to being a professor in the economics department of the University of Berlin, also served as the President of the Central Office of Statistics; in addition, he presided over the private Business Cycle Research Institute which he had himself founded.
6. Compare Carl Landauer, Ludwig Albert Hahn and Gustav Stolper (1932), 'Anti Wagemann: Drei Kritiken', *Der Deutsche Volkswirt*, Berlin.
7. Röpke had collaborated with Lautenbach in preparing the Braun's commission reports. See Wilhelm Röpke (1933), 'Trends in German Business Cycle Policy', *Economic Journal*, September.
8. See also the contributions in the Löwe Festschrift (1984) *Beschäftigung, Verteilung*

und Konjunktur: zur politischen Ökonomik der modernen Gesellschaft, ed. Harald Hagemann and Heinz D. Kurz (Presse- und Informationsamt of the University of Bremen.)

9. References to his modern capitalism are given by Roman volume number, Arabic book number, followed by the page number. The trilogy has three volumes of two books each.

10. In a formulation that is typical for his style, he called the business cycle 'the breath of the monster' (*der Atem des Ungeheuers*) (III, 2, 564), and the 'monster' was of course high capitalism. This expression should not lead one to premature conclusions about Sombart's own attitude towards capitalism. This attitude was quite ambivalent. In a similar context, he speaks of the 'admirable construction' (*Wunderbau*) of high capitalism (III, 2, 583).

11. Mitchell translates the term as high capitalism. See Wesley C. Mitchell (1929), 'Sombarts Hochkapitalismus', *Quarterly Journal of Economics*, Vol. 43, pp. 303–23.

12. The following comparison follows the outline given by Gianluigi Mengarelli in the Bresciani Turroni Festschrift (1986), 'Business Cycle Theory and Structural Changes in the 1970s', *Review of Economic Conditions in Italy* no. 3, pp. 455–83.

13. This export opinion was not published. It is contained in the files of the Chancellor, Bundesarchiv Koblenz, Reichskanzlei R431–2045, Folio.1 'Bekämpfung der Arbeitslosigkeit durch Arbeitsbeschaffung'.

14. This is my rendition of the ambiguous term 'Kaufkraft'; the original sentence reads 'Es wird erstens nicht zu erwarten sein, dass bloss durch eine Befreiung der privaten Unternehmerschaft von ihren Lasten und Bindungen und ein dadurch gewecktes Vertrauen eine Belebung des Marktes eintreten würde, da die Verringerung der Kaufkraft sich überall als das reale Hindernis dieser Belebung entgegenstellt.'

15. When in 1933 Hitler became Chancellor, he was equally concerned that the credit-based employment programmes, over which he presided, might have inflationary effects. Having received reassuring advice from the civil servants in the Finance ministry, he left the policies intact and later took credit for their success.

16. He did not use the term 'liquidity trap', but was referring to the same situation. The original reads 'Die *Furcht vor einer Inflation* kann – abgesehen von einem leicht zu behebenden Run auf die Banken – nur zu einer Flucht in die Sachwerte führen. Eine derartige Wirkung brauchte aber keinerlei über volkswirtschaftliche Folgen zu haben. Im Gegenteil: sie kann ein Mittel zur Belebung des Marktes werden. Damit würde aber gleichzeitig einem anderen Übelstande abgeholfen werden, der schwer auf unsere Volkswirtschaft lastet: die gehorteten Notenbeträge werden automatisch herausgeholt und dem Verkehr zurückgegeben werden'. (p. 4).

17. This would take place either on government land or on the land of bankrupt agricultural estates which were then available cheaply and in large numbers.

18. *Der völkische Beobachter*, no. 287, 5. October 1934, S. 2. The original text reads: 'Für uns dagegen ist die moderne Technik Geburt nordischen Geistes . . . Die Technik ist der wesentliche Faktor unserer Kultur . . . Deutscher Sozialismus bedeutet zuerst einmal den Sieg über die Technik: den Durchbruchssieg. Wir müssen unsere Sozialordnung so gestalten, dass der technische Fortschritt sich nicht gegen den Menschen wendet und ihn auf die Strasse setzt, sondern unmittelbar seine Lebenshaltung verbessert. Der Kapitalismus wird dabei zwar zum Teufel gehen: gerade durch die Weiterentwicklung der Technik.'

19. See also note 2 above. While his name may occasionally surface, a serious discussion of his theoretical contributions to economics is lacking.

20. See Gary S. Becker, 'Family Economics and Macro-economic Behaviour' (AEA Presidential Address 1987, forthcoming).

References
Backhaus, J. (1985), 'Keynesianism in Germany', in T. Lawson and H. Pesaran (eds), *Keynes' Economics: Methodological Issues*, pp. 209–53.

Becker, G. S. *Family Economics and Macro-Economic Behaviour*. (AEA Presidential Address 1987, forthcoming).
Blaug, M. (1985) *Economic Theory in Retrospect* (Cambridge University Press).
Brocke, B. von (1987), *Sombarts Moderner Kapitalismus: Materialen zur Kritik und Rezeption*, Munich: Deutscher Taschenbuch Verlag.
Dräger, H. (1932), '*Arbeitsbeschaffung durch produktive Kreditschöpfung: Ein Beitrag zur Frage der Wirtschaftsbelebung durch das sogenannte Federgeld*. München: Eher.
Dräger, H. et al. (1933), '*Arbeitsbeschaffung: Eine Gemeinschaftsarbeit.*' Berlin: Reimar Hobbing.
Hagemann, H. and Kurz, H. D. (eds) (1984), Löwe Festschrift *Beschäftigung, Verteilung und Konjunktur: zur politischen Ökonomik der modernen Gesellschaft*, Bremen (Presse- und Informationsamt of the University of Bremen).
Landauer, C., Hahn, L. A. and Stolper, G. (1932), 'Anti Wagemann: Drei Kritiken', Berlin, *Der Deutsche Volkswirt*.
Mengarelli, G. (1986), 'Business cycle theory and structural changes in the 1970s', in the Bresciani Turroni Festschrift, *Review of Economic Conditions in Italy*, no. 3, pp. 455–83.
Mitchell, W. C. (1929), 'Sombarts Hochkapitalismus', *Quarterly Journal of Economics*, Vol. 43, pp. 303–23.
Olson, M. (1985), 'Microeconomic incentives and macroeconomic decline', *Weltwirtschaftliches Archiv* 70, pp. 631–45.
Röpke, W. (1933), 'Trends in German business cycle policy', *Economic Journal*, September 1933.
Schefold, B. and Reich, H. (1987), 'Werner Sombart', in *New Palgrave: A Dictionary of Economic Theory and Doctrine*, London: Macmillan.
Schumpeter, J. A. (1911), *Theorie der wirtschaftlichen Entwicklung*.
Schumpeter, J. A. (1927), 'Sombarts Dritter Band', *Schmollers Jahrbuch für Gesetzgebung, Verwaltung und Volkswirtschaft im Deutschen Reiche 51*, pp. 349–69.
Schumpeter, J. A. (1939), *Business Cycles: A Theoretical, Historical, and Statistical Analysis of the Capitalist Process*, New York, London: MacGraw-Hill.
Sombart, W. (1888), *Über Pacht- und Lohnverhältnisse in der römischen Campagna*, PhD. dissertation, Berlin.
Sombart, W. (1884), 'Zur Kritik des ökonomischen Systems von Karl Marx', *Archiv für soziale Gesetzgebung und Statistik*, Vol. 7, pp. 555–94.
Sombart, W. (1896), *Sozialismus und soziale Bewegungen im 19. Jahrhundert*, Jena, Gustav Fischer (*Socialism and the Social Movement*), London, Dent. New York, Dutton, 1909. 10th edn: *Der proletarische Sozialismus (Marxismus)*, 1924.
Sombart, W. (1902), *Der moderne Kapitalismus: Historisch-systematische Darstellung des gesamteuropäischen Wirtschaftslebens von seinen Anfängen bis zur Gegenwart*, 2 volumes, Leipzig. 2nd edn., 3 volumes, Munich and Leipzig: Duncker & Humblot, 1916–1927.
Sombart, W. (1903), *Die deutsche Volkswirtschaft im neunzehnten Jahrhundert*, Berlin: Georg Bondi.
Sombart, W. (1904), 'Zur Systematik der Wirtschaftskrise', *Archiv für Sozialwissenschaft und Sozialpolitik*, Band 19, pp. 1–21.
Sombart, W. (1909), *Das Lebenswerk von Karl Marx*, Jena, Gustav Fischer.
Sombart, W. (1911), *Die Juden und das Wirtschaftsleben*, Leipzig: Duncker & Humblot (*The Jews and Modern Capitalism*, London: T.F. Unwin, 1913).
Sombart, W. (1912), *Die Zukunft der Juden*, Leipzig: Duncker & Humblot.
Sombart, W. (1913a), *Der Bourgeois: Zur Geistesgeschichte des modernen Wirtschaftsmenschen*, Munich and Leipzig: Duncker & Humblot. (tr. and ed. by M. Epstein as '*The Quintessence of Capitalism: A Study of the History and Psychology of the Modern Business Man*, New York: Dutton, 1915).
Sombart, W. (1913b), *Studien zur Entwicklungsgeschichte des modernen Kapitalismus*, Munich and Leipzig: Duncker & Humblot. Vol. I: *Luxus und Kapitalismus*, (tr. into English as a report under the auspices of the Works Progress Administration and the

Department of Social Science, Columbia University, Project number 465–97–3–81).
Vol. II: *Krieg und Kapitalismus*.

Sombart, W. (1915), *Händler und Helden. Patriotische Besinnungen*, Munich and Leipzig: Duncker & Humblot.

Sombart, W. (1929), 'Economic Theory and Economic History', *The Economic History Review 2*, pp. 1–19.

Sombart, W. (1930a), 'Capitalism', *Encyclopaedia of the Social Sciences*, Vol. III, pp. 195–208.

Sombart, W. (1930b), *Die drei Nationalökonomien*, Munich and Leipzig: Duncker & Humblot.

Sombart, W. (1932), *Die Zukunft des Kapitalismus*, Berlin: Buchholz & Weisswange.

Sombart, W. (1933), 'Zum Problem der Arbeitsbeschaffung', *Die Wirtschaftswende*, special issue, no. 2.

Sombart, W. (1934), *Deutscher Sozialismus*, Berlin: Buchholz & Weisswange. (tr. and ed. by Karl F. Geiser as '*A New Social Philosophy*', Princeton University Press, Oxford University Press, 1937).

Sombart, W. (1936) *Soziologie: Was sie ist und was sie sein soll*, Sitzungsberichte der Preussischen Akademie der Wissenschaften, Berlin.

Sombart, W. (1938), '*Vom Menschen. Versuch einer geistwissenschaftlichen Antropologie.*' Berlin: Buchholz & Weisswange.

Veblen, Th.B. (1902–3), Book Review: 'Der Moderne Kapitalismus' by Werner Sombart, *Journal of Political Economy 11*, pp. 300–305.

Wagemann, E. (1932), *Geld- und Kreditreform*, Reimar Hobbing, Berlin.

Weippert, G. (1953), *Werner Sombarts Gestaltidee des Wirtschaftssystems*, Göttingen: Vandenhoeck & Ruprecht.

Wicksell, K. (1965), *Interest and Prices*, New York: August, Kelley.

Wicksell, K. (1978), *Lectures in Political Economy II*, Fairfield, NJ: Kelley.

2 The economics of democratic socialism after fifty years

Elizabeth Durbin

Fifty years ago the Labour Party adopted *Labour's Immediate Programme* at its 1937 annual conference. The heart of the economic programme contained a practical set of institutional reforms, which would ensure central control over the forces determining money supply, exchange rates and investment. There were detailed proposals to expand the public sector significantly through the nationalization of the railways, coal and electricity, as well as new social services. Although official economic policy remained fairly orthodox, unofficial committee positions ensured that Keynesian policies to deal with unemployment were eventually adopted. Further confidential reports provided the leaders with detailed plans to cope with negative banking, business or speculative reactions to their financial policies. This platform became the basis of the Party's 1945 election manifesto, of the Labour government's postwar legislation, and consequently of the British version of the mixed economy.

This achievement was a far cry from the complete disarray the Labour Party faced in the early 1930s. The second Labour government elected in 1929 had been unable to deal with the collapsing domestic and international markets, nor to introduce any significant steps towards socialism. The Chancellor of the Exchequer, Philip Snowden, remained a stern upholder of free trade, balanced budgets and the Treasury view, never doubting the orthodox methods for managing the economy. After a series of financial and political crises, the cabinet split in August 1931. The Prime Minister, Ramsay MacDonald, formed a coalition National government with Liberal and Tory members, and completely crushed his erstwhile comrades in the October election.

Economic science was in a similar state of disarray with economists offering completely conflicting diagnoses and solutions to the overwhelming unemployment problem. Orthodox economists, such as Professor Lionel Robbins and F.A. Hayek at the London School of Economics, looked to the self-correcting mechanisms of competitive market forces as the cure; they argued against 'inflationary' expansion and in favour of cutting public expenditures to balance the budget. Keynes was pressing ever more forcefully for expansionary monetary policies, building on theoretical work started with D.H. Robertson in the late 1920s. Other economists, such as Piero Sraffa, were also questioning the Marshallian theory of the firm at the microeconomic level. The 1930s, the years of high theory, witnessed the two revolutions which made economic science seem relevant once more, and which laid the groundwork for the postwar consensus on the macro- and micro-justifications for government intervention.

In March 1931, G.D.H. Cole founded the New Fabian Research Bureau (NFRB); he laid out a systematic research programme to investigate practical questions of policy and institutional reform for the Labour Party. Hugh Dalton, as chairman of the Finance and Trade Subcommittee of the Labour Party's National Executive Policy Committee, masterminded the translation of policy into legislative proposals. Beginning in 1931, he consulted regularly with a group of 'experts' on London's money markets, who called themselves the XYZ Club, and after 1932 he relied increasingly on the New Fabian economists for research memoranda. Hugh Gaitskell and Evan Durbin led the new generation of young socialist economists; together they thrashed out both a strategy to accomplish the Party's aims and a coherent political and economic rationale for its position. Their political contributions still remain influential statements of the revisionist case for Britain (Jay, 1937; Durbin, 1940). But their economic contributions were more scattered in professional articles, in research memoranda and in confidential reports. Durbin's notes for his promised book, 'The Economics of Democratic Socialism', unfinished at his death in 1948, were literally lost for almost thirty years.

For socialists who seek to replace the capitalist system, economics must always hold a central place in their analysis. In Britain, Fabian democratic socialists rejected what Shaw called the 'insurrectionary economics' of Marx (Durbin, 1984). Instead, successive generations adapted the existing tools of orthodox economics to articulate the socialist alternative. The early Fabians based their belief in socialism on the neoclassical analysis of unearned rents accruing to the factors of production, which, they believed, justified the collective ownership of the means of production. In the 1920s Dalton added arguments for progressive taxation and educational reform based upon Pigovian social welfare arguments for redistribution. Neoclassical economics provided their grounds for rejecting Marxist economics and their case against capitalism.

However, the economic dimensions of the socialist alternative were not as clearly articulated. Socialists believed in planning, and in the 1920s the Webbs delineated a detailed structure of boards and commissions to run the economy through a Social Parliament. But orthodox economics provided no solutions for Britain's unemployment problems and little justification for these elaborate administrative controls. Thus, the Webbian concept of planning stressed administrative efficiency rather than economic criteria; their view was that socialism was 'about property'. The 1931 crisis reinforced the pressure for immediate takeover of the economy and re-animated Marxist interpretations of capitalism's collapse. John Strachey, the most articulate exponent of the coming class struggle in Britain, left the Labour Party and did not rejoin until 1940 when the work of Keynes and the New Fabians convinced him 'that a way through did exist' (Thomas, 1973).

The central contribution of the 1930s was to articulate both a feasible economic programme and a non-Marxist economic rationale for socialism based on the new economics and its appropriate use in the new socialist state (Durbin, 1985). The New Fabian economists set out to explore the role of economic theory, as well as the practical problems of policy and institutional reform. Even before the collapse of the second Labour government, Durbin convened a committee to study 'the relation between banks, the provision of credit, the price level and industrial fluctuations' in a socialist economy; and Gaitskell organized another committee on the theory of socialist economic policy, which for the first time discussed the problems of efficient allocation and growth. They were soon embroiled in the broader professional controversies and making their own contributions to the revolutionary literature. By the late 1930s they had spelled out their version of the economics of democratic socialism in theory and in practice, in which they rejected both Snowden's orthodoxy and the Webbian version of planning.

Much of this intellectual ferment has been forgotten, as the triumphant success of the Keynesian revolution within the profession and its institutionalization after the war eclipsed earlier controversies and swept aside all doubts and caveats. But is there any more to it than interesting chapters in the history of the Labour Party and footnotes to the history of economic thought? The purpose of this chapter is to evaluate these economic contributions with the benefit of hindsight and to summarize the important lessons for the theory and practice of economics by democratic socialists.

In many regards the contributions made by the democratic socialist economists fifty years ago were so fundamental that they seem platitudinous today; as Gaitskell noted of Hugh Dalton's contributions 'that is the fate of the pioneer' (Gaitskell, 1955). From the extraordinary efforts of time and energy that went into countless committees, conferences and discussion groups, three distinct but interrelated activities can be unravelled. First, there was the development of an economic theory of democratic socialism. Second, there was the articulation of an appropriate political strategy to introduce socialism and to spell out its economic component. Finally, there was its translation into appropriate institutional reforms to ensure the implementation of socialist economic policy. By the end of the 1930s there was substantial agreement on all three components. Nevertheless, there remained significant differences among these non-Marxist socialists, which in important ways presaged the subsequent fragmentation of British progressives.

1. Economic theory and democratic socialism

The theoretical work began in the NFRB committees chaired by Gaitskell and Durbin. In the socialist economic policy committee they worked on the economic principles in the socialist state and their theoretical implications for planning with H.D. Dickinson, who has since been credited with first introducing the concept of marginal cost pricing. In early 1934 the committee summarized their conclusions in a report to the Labour Party (Durbin, 1934). They argued that to be fully efficient, any economic system must meet three criteria: (1) it must ensure full employment of labour and capital; (2) it must provide investment for new technology; and (3) it must adjust production to the needs and tastes of the public (the last a problem 'often neglected in current Socialist discussions'). Socialist planning would have to meet these criteria and pursue three critical policy goals, the use of monetary policy to cure unemployment *before* extending the public sector, the establishment of the necessary controls for banking, finance and basic industries, and finally 'a clear and unambiguous equalization programme'. Thus, for the first time, economic efficiency was used as one criterion for evaluating the success of socialism. In addition, short-term and long-term macroeconomic policies were separated from microeconomic problems of allocation, and the principles of consumers' sovereignty in product markets and marginal cost pricing in nationalized industries were established. The committee was specifically opposed to subsidizing consumer goods except for 'a limited number of social services'.

In further professional work Dickinson and Durbin went on to demonstrate that the market system by definition could neither price collective goods nor reflect the true social value of externalities, and, therefore, it could not determine the appropriate allocation of resources for their production (Dickinson, 1930, 1933, 1935; Durbin, 1935b, 1937). They also incorporated the new economics of imperfect competition associated with Joan Robinson to restate their objections to the existing system, which they termed 'monopoly capitalism'. A planning authority would be able to correct these deficiencies, and it should use the principles of optimal allocation to guide its decisions.

Meanwhile, in the industrial fluctuations committee the burning questions of unemployment theory and policy were thrashed out between the new Keynesians, James Meade, Colin Clark and Roy Harrod, and the more cautious Durbin and Gaitskell, who had been strongly influenced by Hayek's work on business cycles. Beginning in 1929 these two had been hard at work refuting simple underconsumption models, such as Major Douglas's social credit scheme, which was very popular among Labour supporters; they argued that such models misrepresented the role of monetary policy in the socialist state. They believed that the central macroeconomic task of socialist policy must be the cure of capitalism's trade fluctuations, for which Hayek's theories seemed more appropriate. However, by 1933 James Meade had convinced them that expansionary policies were the cure for unemployment, and by 1935 they had also accepted the use of deficit finance. Meade also converted Douglas Jay, whose 1937 book was the first to propose that Keynesian fiscal and monetary measures to control output and employment be explicitly incorporated as part of socialist planning methods.

In the mid-1930s the democratic socialists all took part in the great planning debates, which followed the attack on collectivist planning launched by Hayek (1935). Oskar Lange and Abba Lerner are best known for demolishing the Austrian case and for proving that the central planning of resource allocation and income distribution would not cause the allocative chaos which their critics charged (Lerner, 1934, 1937; Lange, 1938). In these so-called competitive solutions, which built on the work of Dickinson and Durbin, the socialist state would allow consumer preferences to set prices for private goods and for labour services through the market, thus explicitly rejecting the totally collectivist state posited by Hayek and von Mises. Socialist central planning would supplant the capitalist market as the integrator of household and production decisions, and it would actually improve allocative efficiency through its planning powers where the market failed. These microeconomic arguments for planning, together with Keynesian macroeconomics, became the more generalized conception of the economic role of government after the war.

2. An economic strategy for the Labour Party

In late 1934 Durbin and Gaitskell organized a private discussion group to work out the necessary components of political and economic strategy 'to set up a Socialist community by democratic methods' (Durbin, 1935c). Durbin later defined three conditions which any democratic socialist programme must meet: (1) it must include a transfer of a substantial increase in the economic power of government; (2) it must not provoke the opponents of socialism to appeal to force or frighten them into uncontrollable financial panic; and (3) it must retain the loyalty of a large proportion of its political supporters (Durbin, 1935d). The group distinguished four kinds of social and economic measures: (1) ameliorative measures to help certain groups, such as the aged, the young and the unemployed; (2) power measures to transfer economic power 'to the Government and to Society'; (3) prosperity measures to reduce unemployment and to promote growth; and (4) egalitarian measures to establish economic and social equality. They also clarified immediate, medium-term and long-term goals. In the short run it would be essential to prevent financial panic and to reduce unemployment. But the main task of the next Labour government would be to gain control of the 'commanding heights of the economy', that is, the financial system, a limited number of basic industries and an effective national investment programme. The second stage would complete this transition, as the long-term goals of central planning machinery and the full range of social programmes would be put in place. In a 1935 report to the Party's policy committee, the group recommended that finance, transport, coal, power, and iron and steel should be nationalized; they also urged the priority of 'power' measures over the 'ameliorative' and 'egalitarian' measures to change the economic and social order.

The detailed work of translating the theoretical insights and strategic concerns into a practical programme preoccupied the New Fabian economists and the XYZ club working for Dalton's committee throughout the 1930s. In the early years the discussions and memoranda centred on expansionary policies and the danger of capital flight. In Cambridge, Colin Clark organized a group of NFRB sympathizers, who included Gilbert Shove, Lionel Elvin and Joan Robinson, to discuss problems of capital supply and the form of the National Investment Board. In Oxford, James Meade organized a similar group with Roy Harrod, Robert Hall and Redvers Opie; between 1933 and 1934 he sent a series of important memoranda to Dalton's committee about the financial policy necessary 'to avoid economic chaos and unemployment' during the transition to socialism. He advocated Keynesian cheap money and budget deficits to deal with unemployment, and fluctuating exchange rates to protect the domestic market. In a significant break from the Labour Party's traditional means of state ownership, he stressed only those reforms essential to carrying out these policies: 'It cannot be too strongly emphasized that in the financial sphere that it is not so much administrative machinery and ownership of existing organization which needs altering, as their financial policy' (Meade, 1933).

In continuing work on financial panic, Dalton asked the XYZ club to summarize the research findings before the 1935 election, while Durbin and Berry furnished two long memoranda on the nationalization of the English banking system. They concluded, first, that no new powers were necessary to control internal and external panic. Second, nationalization of the Bank of England and the formation of the National Investment Board were sufficient to pursue expansionary policies by orthodox means. Third, only less orthodox and more powerful methods for curing unemployment required new financial machinery. Nationalization of the joint-stock banks was one way to accomplish the last goal; however, Berry and Durbin pointed out that even this would not be necessary, if the government had the power to guarantee advances.

In pointed contrast to Dalton, Meade and others, Durbin and Gaitskell had agreed with radical left-wingers that the government must control the direction of short-term credit through public ownership of banks. In 1932, at the height of radical pressure, the Party had voted to nationalize the joint-stock banks. However, Durbin modified his views somewhat in light of the National Government's experience with a cheap money policy in the early 1930s (Durbin, 1935a). In December 1936 he wrote to Dalton that he no longer believed that the joint-stock banks would have to be nationalized. The next year this proposal was purposely omitted from *Labour's Immediate Programme*. It is likely that *The General Theory* had convinced Durbin that the problem of implementation had shifted from commercial banks to the central bank and the government by identifying total investment and business expectations as the crucial variables.

3. Different economic rationales for democratic socialism
By the late 1930s there was substantial agreement among democratic socialist economists on the economic rationale for the socialist state. A mixed economy was the essential characteristic of the socialist economy, not simply a short-run necessity for the transitional stage. They all believed that the economic role of the market was crucial for both economic and political reasons. Politically, the market allowed individuals the freedom to choose their own jobs and to choose how they

wanted to spend their income; these freedoms were precisely the characteristics which distinguished democratic socialism from the Marxist varieties, which these socialists totally rejected on economic and political grounds. Economically, the market was the most efficient means to allocate resources to meet these goals. It was also the most efficient way to provide entrepreneurs with the incentives to innovate and to invest, which were essential to the growth of the economy. But they also believed that there were deep and inherent faults with the capitalist system which only socialist planning could remove. Thus, government planning was necessary to ensure full employment using fiscal and monetary instruments, to allocate resources between the public and private sectors and between industries efficiently, and to redistribute income and wealth.

Nevertheless, there were also significant differences in theoretical approach, which are more apparent now than they were at the time, and which represent different visions of the new socialist society. The more centrist position sought full employment, less inequality and more opportunity, and rested upon the newly emerging mainstream case for intervention. In the 1930s this group supported the Party's platform of nationalization and financial control; but, once this was accomplished, it later became clear that this was as far as they would go. James Meade articulated this view in the pre-war years, and has contributed to its further elaboration throughout his life.

G.D.H. Cole was the non-Marxist furthest to the left in the 1930s; he remained 'an unrepentant believer in guild socialism' (Cole, 1935, 1938). His aim was to revolutionize social power relationships through the public ownership of industry and the active participation of workers in economic decision-making. He proposed central planning machinery along the lines laid down by the Webbs; a representative planning authority would draw up the national plan with advice from a national planning commission, which coordinated the plans drawn up by industry boards, government departments, import and export control boards, and so on. He tried to build a new socialist economics which explicitly merged efficiency criteria and his own socialist values in both macro- and microeconomic policy. He completely rejected the centrist position and neoclassical economics, which he thought confused socialism with state economic planning and produced 'a diluted socialist doctrine which was little more than Keynesian Liberalism with frills' (Cole, 1950).

Firmly rejecting both Webbian administrative models and guild socialist visions, Durbin and Gaitskell represented a third option. They recognized the need for short-term demand management, but as

Gaitskell had declared as early as 1932: 'Prosperity as an aim is important. . . . But it must be stated emphatically, it is not the distinguishing characteristic of the Socialist ideal' (Gaitskell, 1933). Thus, they insisted that supply-side problems of capital formation and public sector efficiency must be tackled as the essential core of socialist planning. Furthermore, Durbin remained sceptical of the use of expansionary fiscal and monetary policy to maintain balanced growth in the long run. When *The General Theory* was published in 1936, he wrote to Keynes about his fear of its eventual inflationary effects, and 'the continuous dilemma between allowing the movement to gain further impetus or checking it . . . and if the movement is checked the disappointment of expectations is the crisis and produces the depression' (Keynes, 1979). Although Durbin was not satisfied with his own investment models, he was optimistic that a socialist government armed with the appropriate financial controls could maintain stable non-inflationary growth by encouraging investment in capital goods while controlling consumption by raising taxes (Durbin, 1933, revised). His theoretical position was closest to D.H. Robertson's, as they both worked on the problem of how to maintain capital formation and long-term economic stability (Durbin, 1986). They accepted that expansion could solve short-term unemployment, but they were convinced that it could cause sectoral imbalances and actually increase instability in the long run; and they believed that *The General Theory* did not provide an explanation of the trade cycle nor deal with the problems of different factor elasticities and discontinuities in the investment process.

Durbin also had some serious reservations about aspects of the market socialist solution to the allocation problem. He agreed with Hayek about the practical impossibility of implementing massive equational systems, upon which Lange's Walrasian system depended. But he was concerned that Lerner's marginal cost pricing rule, which was based on Marshallian partial analysis, was also impractical. He advocated average cost pricing for two reasons: (1) the marginal cost rule reduced the decision of managers to 'empty formularies' with serious consequences on the incentives to press for efficiency at the plant level; (2) the average cost rule was necessary to cover fixed capital and maintenance costs and avoided the complications of choosing the appropriate time frame to calculate marginal costs. He also argued that Lerner avoided the very real difficulties of operating a mixed economy, if nationalized industries were suffering serious losses, and he worried about fiscal responsibility, accountability and bureaucratic red tape (Durbin, 1949).

Indeed, while Durbin and Gaitskell had been the first to incorporate efficiency criteria as an integral part of the planning process, they were also concerned with the moral, political, social and psychological dimensions of planning theory. Furthermore, they believed that socialist planning would surpass capitalism's economic record, and that it would also expand personal liberty. Durbin saw planning as a method for solving economic problems, the counterpart of democracy as a method for solving political problems; it was 'a way of life', 'a principle of administration', but *never* 'an inflexible budget of production'. Thus, he attacked Hayek's mistaken view of planning in his review of *The Road to Serfdom* (Durbin, 1945). He also found Hayek 'guilty of a strange inconsistency about personal liberty'. Hayek defined political freedom as 'freedom from the arbitrary power of other men, release from the ties which left the individual no choice but obedience to the orders of a superior to whom he was attached'. While he deplored its absence in the political sphere, he did not recognize that its absence in the economic sphere, in employer/employee relations, could mean exactly the same thing. In any case, as Durbin pointed out elsewhere, the exercise of political freedoms in many countries had led the voters to introduce much of the legislation limiting market forces to which Hayek was so opposed (Durbin, 1940).

In a speech shortly after Durbin's death, Gaitskell defined socialism as a reaction to the three evils of capitalism: inequality, insecurity and inefficiency (Gaitskell, 1949). In the unpublished notes for his book on 'The Economics of Democratic Socialism', Durbin reviewed the familiar macro- and micro-needs for planning; but he also greatly expanded the usual economic criteria to include training, selection and the incentives of managers and workers to be efficient at the plant level, because he thought that organization and motivation were inseparable and must be addressed systematically in the planning process. Since the early 1930s he and Gaitskell had struggled with the problem of trade unions, workers' control and wage-setting in the socialist state. He now concluded that planned economies would need to pay 'according to ability', and that the direct election of workers would not solve discipline in the workplace. He believed in comprehensive consultation, expanded works councils, and even some workers' involvement in 'the normal conduct of discipline'. However, he was adamant that on all cost matters of common social concern, such as wages, hours and the mobility of labour, 'the last word must remain with the representative of society – not with the representative of the Worker – because the interests of Society are more important – and because people cannot be expected to discipline themselves in the immediate way that is necessary.' Finally, on the question of the central planning mechanism, Durbin believed it was crucial to set it up right away, in order to prevent nationalized industries from establishing their own syndicated power. The Supreme Economic Authority should be responsible for macroeconomic policy and the coordination of industrial and financial policy.

4. The economics of democratic socialism after 1945

After the war the theoretical base for the economics of democratic socialism in Britain merged with the mainstream case for intervention. In a short book commissioned by the Fabian Society, Sir W. Arthur Lewis argued that there were many ways to plan the economy, which were not inconsistent with socialism; 'socialism is about equality', not about property, nor about the state (Lewis, 1948). Thus, he implicitly rejected the Durbin/Gaitskell notion that only socialism could operate the economy efficiently and democratically, even though one might still think only a socialist government would. He believed that the crucial issue was whether the government should operate 'through the price mechanism or in supersession of it'; the real choice was between 'planning by inducement, and planning by direction'. He thought that Britain needed some of both; while reiterating the market socialist case for free consumer goods and labour markets, he argued that demand was not sacred and should be manipulated in the aggregate and in specific markets to achieve policy goals.

In the early 1950s the Fabian Society began to rethink the way forward, now that the main components of the first stage to socialism were in place. In *New Fabian Essays*, the essayists were all agreed that the British version of the mixed economy was a permanent Fabian accomplishment, and that the Tories would not dismantle the welfare state nor renege on full employment (Cole and Crossman, 1952). Marxian prognostications about the demise of capitalism were couched in Keynesian terms, and the unanimous support for the United States and opposition to the Soviet Union reflected a high point of faith in the political and economic virtues of the modified market system in Britain. However, these Fabians were still united in their dissatisfaction with that system. Despite enormous gains, substantial inequities remained and new problems of bureaucratic power and labour/management relations had emerged. Although most of the essayists were vague about 'the exact shape' of their equality goal, Tony Crosland was explicit that more nationalization, more free social services, more controls and more direct taxation were *not* the directions to go. In an important shift, many democratic socialists had not only come to believe in the mixed economy, but to accept its current structural form.

Later, Crosland spelled out his ideas on planning in what he called 'post-capitalist society' (Crosland, 1955). He believed not only that its 'essential role' was Keynesian economic management, but that the techniques were no longer controversial nor the preserve of any one party. He disagreed with some planning specifics, particularly pricing policies in nationalized industries which had led to under-investment in the public sector, but he did not elaborate upon nor question the use of mainstream economic criteria under socialism. British socialist economists were in general agreement on the centrality of macroeconomic policy, and many of them were in the forefront of developing the theory and practice of Keynesianism. One of the very few dissenters was G.D.H. Cole, who was less interested in broad aggregates; he maintained his concerns with structural problems and the relationship of workers to the decision-making process.

Although many eminent socialist economists have advised successive Labour governments and leaders and made their own contributions to economic theory, there have been no systematic attempts to rethink the economics of democratic socialism from first principles. However, Labour governments have made a number of efforts to improve the institutional framework for making economic decisions in Britain. The postwar government took giant steps in expanding the public sector and in establishing the central machinery for demand management, but it has been judged a failure at instituting more general mechanisms for allocating resources for improving industrial efficiency and for managing relations between employers and workers in the public interest, the kind of supply-side planning which Durbin had in mind. It must be said that at the time the legacy of wartime controls appeared to give the government all the necessary powers to perform those functions. Writing in 1948 Durbin noted that the government had been able 'to control the use of foreign exchange and raw materials with the allocation of foodstuffs, building resources and money for long-term capital expenditure', while removing controls over the direction of labour (Durbin, 1948). However, the unpopularity of these controls, the lack of any central planning authority and thirteen years of Tory rule subsequently revealed that the only permanent accomplishment was the power of the Treasury and the Bank of England to control fiscal and monetary policy. In a recent book comparing British and French methods of governing the economy, Peter Hall has concluded that subsequent attempts to introduce 'a more dirigiste industrial policy' through the Department of Economic Affairs between 1964 and 1970 and to institute a formal incomes policy in the 1970s foundered on Britain's bias towards tripartite authorities, the structure of industrial capital financing and the Treasury's preoccupation with public expenditure control (Hall, 1986).

Conclusions

The essential contribution of the Fabian economists of the 1930s was to think through the theory and the practice of economic policy in a democratic socialist state from first principles. In a process completed in the 1950s they brought the British Labour Party into the mainstream of economic thinking, and at the same time they helped to transform economic thinking about the appropriate macroeconomic and microeconomic roles for government intervention. Driven by the Party's need for a practical economic programme to meet its goals, they outlined a policy synthesis which pre-dated its subsequent theoretical analogue, the so-called neoclassical synthesis.

In some respects the 1980s have witnessed the re-emergence of conditions not dissimilar to the early 1930s. Economic science is in disarray at both the macro- and the micro-levels in its ability to provide clear-cut and agreed guidance on economic policies. In Britain, the Left is in political disarray, and its fragmentation on economic policy reflects the different visions of democratic socialism outlined above. With James Meade as one of its advisers, the Social Democratic Party propounds the centrist position with its reliance on modern adaptations of mainstream economics and its proposals for fixing the current system by maintaining full employment and helping the less fortunate. Within the Labour Party but to the left, the heirs of G.D.H. Cole press for more elaborate controls and planning machinery and are committed to more workers' participation. In between the Party's leadership is once again struggling to articulate a feasible economic programme, but has yet to engage in the kind of fundamental rethinking undertaken fifty years ago. In particular, the Left lacks a coherent supply-side economics relating fiscal and monetary policies to fluctuations in capital formation and to sectoral imbalances of the kind which Durbin was advocating; and it has failed to set up the permanent planning machinery he had in mind.

The experiences of the 1930s reveal some useful lessons for systematic thinking about economic policy. First, the intense discussions of the Fabian economists underscore the importance of rigorous economic theorizing to clarify the purposes and the methods of economic policies. Second, their detailed work for the Labour Party demonstrates the need to master the details of the institutions responsible for carrying out policies, to assess feasible strategies and to design the necessary reforms that ensure successful implementation. Third, the Fabian economists were also clear that institutional reform has its own limitations; without appropriate economic policies political control of decision-making can be meaningless. Workable economic programmes and policies require careful study of the interplay between causal explanations, institutional structures and administrative principles.

Finally, the most important lesson may be the example which these socialist economists set for later generations. In spite of depressing economic conditions, frustrating lack of power and growing fears of war fifty years ago, they maintained an optimistic faith that they could make the world a better place. They believed in the Labour Party, they believed in democratic processes, they believed in government, *and* they believed in economics as a science able to yield workable solutions to deal with problems in an organized and rational way. In thinking through the economics of democratic socialism, British socialist economists demonstrated how to integrate economic principles, political strategy and social vision, in order to come up with coherent policies and practical reforms. In the process they helped to revolutionize economic science.

References
Cole, G. D. H. (1935), *Principles of Economic Planning*, London: Macmillan.
Cole, G. D. H. (1938), *The Machinery of Socialist Planning*, London: Hogarth Press.
Cole, G. D. H. (1950), *Socialist Economics*, London: Gollancz.
Cole, M. and Crossman, R. H. S. (eds) (1952), *New Fabian Essays*, London: J. M. Dent.
Crosland, C. A. R. (1955), *The Future of Socialism*, London: Jonathan Cape.
Dickinson, H. D. (1930) 'The economic basis of socialism', *Political Quarterly*, Vol. 1, No. 4.
Dickinson, H. D. (1933) 'Price formation in a socialist community', *Economic Journal*, Vol. 43.
Dickinson, H. D. (1935), 'The failure of economic individualism', in G. D. H. Cole, (ed.), *Studies in Capital and Investment*, London: Gollancz.
Durbin, Elizabeth (1984), 'Fabian socialism and economic science', in Pimlott, B. (ed.) *Fabian Essays in Socialist Thought*, London: Gower.
Durbin, Elizabeth (1985), *New Jerusalems: The Labour Party and the Economics of Democratic Socialism*, London: Routledge and Kegan Paul.
Durbin, Elizabeth (1986), 'A supply-side critique of *The General Theory:* unpublished correspondence between D. H. Robertson and E. F. M. Durbin in the 1930s', unpublished paper, History of Economics Society Conference, Barnard College.
Durbin, E. F. M. (1933), *Socialist Credit Policy*, New Fabian Research Bureau, Pamphlet No. 15, London; revised, No. 26, 1935.
Durbin, E. F. M. (1934), 'Memorandum on the principles of socialist planning', Labour Party Subcommittee, Policy No. 197, unpublished typescript.
Durbin, E. F. M. (1935a), *The Problem of Credit Policy*, London: Chapman and Hall.
Durbin, E. F. M. (1935b), 'The social significance of the Theory of Value', *Economic Journal*, Vol. 45.
Durbin, E. F. M. (1935c), 'Labour Party policy', unpublished typescript.
Durbin, E. F. M. (1935d), 'Democracy and socialism in Great Britain', *Political Quarterly*, Vol. 6.
Durbin, E. F. M. (1936), 'Economic calculus in a planned economy', *Economic Journal*, Vol. 46.

Durbin, E. F. M. (1937), 'A note on Mr. Lerner's "dynamical propositions" ', *Economic Journal*, Vol. 47.

Durbin, E. F. M. (1940), *The Politics of Democratic Socialism*, London: Routledge and Kegan Paul.

Durbin, E. F. M. (1945), 'Professor Hayek on economic planning', *Economic Journal*, Vol. 55.

Durbin, E. F. M. (1948), 'The economic problems facing the Labour government', in D. Munro, (ed.), *Socialism: The British Way*, London: Essential Books.

Durbin, E. F. M. (1949), *Problems of Economic Planning*, London: Routledge and Kegan Paul.

Gaitskell, H. T. N. (1933), 'Socialism and wage policy', unpublished manuscript, Fabian Papers, Nuffield College, Oxford.

Gaitskell, H. (1949), 'The economics of democratic socialism', unpublished typescript.

Gaitskell, H. (1955), 'The ideological development of democratic socialism in Great Britain', *Socialist International Information*, Vol. V, Nos 52–53.

Hall, P. (1986), *Governing the Economy: The Politics of State Intervention in Britain and France*, Cambridge: Polity Press.

Hayek, F. A. (ed.) (1935), *Collectivist Economic Planning*, London: Routledge.

Jay, D. (1937) *The Socialist Case*, London: Gollancz.

Keynes, J. M. (1979) *The Collected Writings of John Maynard Keynes*, ed. Donald Moggridge, Macmillan/Cambridge University Press, Vol. 29.

Lange, O. (1938) *On the Economic Theory of Socialism*, Minneapolis: University of Minnesota Press.

Lavoie, D. (1985) *Rivalry and Central Planning: The Socialist Calculation Debate Reconsidered*, New York: Cambridge University Press.

Lerner, A. P. (1934) 'Economic theory and socialist economy', *Review of Economic Studies*, Vol. 2.

Lerner, A. P. (1937) 'Statics and dynamics in socialist economics', *Economic Journal*, Vol. 47.

Meade, J. (1933) 'Financial policy of a socialist government during the transition to socialism', Labour Party, Constitutional Committee, Policy No. 189, unpublished typescript.

Thomas, H. (1973) *John Strachey*, London and New York: Harper & Row.

3 On designing an economic order. The contributions of the Freiburg School

Heinz G. Grossekettler[1]

1. Introduction and overview

Imagine that someone were to give you the task of developing the economic institutions for a modern industrial state from scratch. One could designate this organizational problem the 'framework and rule-making': one must create all the institutions which define the property rights of the individual economic units and the rules for their interaction; in other words, one must create the limitations on economic behaviour of individuals, enterprises, associations and regional groupings. How would one approach such a task? You might reply that such an imagination would be senseless; for economic institutions are not designed on a drawing-board from scratch but rather develop gradually in the course of history and as answers to various challenges. This is a reasonable answer under normal circumstances. But there are exceptions, and some of them have occurred in our century: Lenin, for example, had to develop a set of rules of operation for the economic administration of his socialist state, and resistance groups in the Third Reich planned a transition from the Nazi economic system (a form of capitalistic central planning) to a free market economy.

The Freiburg School was a group of German neo-liberal economists and jurists who saw a need to develop such a transition, at first because they were dissatisfied with the economic order existing at that time but later more and more because they saw the necessity of designing a new system in the resistance to Hitler and as part of the preparation for the postwar period. Their basic outlook strongly resembled that of the Chicago School; they worked out a programme in the 1930s and 1940s for the introduction, establishment and adaptation of an economic order mainly directed by economic competition and they tried politically to implement their concept in Germany in the 1950s. Their model, called 'Ordoliberal', is characterized by interaction between economic and legal elements. The economic part sets the goals the institutions have to support; the legal part is saddled with the task to shape these institutions

38

in accordance with these goals.

Section 2.1 introduces the founders and proponents of the Freiburg School and describes the circumstances surrounding its genesis. One can question whether it is *always* appropriate to begin a discussion on the history of theory in this way, e.g. Stigler (1965, pp. 16ff.) argues that contemporary history plays little role in the development of economic theory. But we shall see that in this particular case neither the genesis nor the implementation of the Ordoliberal programme would be comprehensible without knowledge of contemporary events. Section 2.2 is devoted to the presentation of the economic doctrine of the Freiburg School, and section 2.3 shows how its members thought they might incorporate their views into law and how they hoped to get political acceptance. In section 3 I shall show Ordoliberalism's place in the history of economic thought. I shall sketch the differences between this school and other forms of liberalism as well as show the relationship to Catholic and Protestant theories of society and to the 'New Institutionalism' as it is presented in Property Rights Theory, in Transactions Cost Economics, and in particular in Constitutional Economics. In section 4 I shall evaluate the success of the School and pass judgement on it, and in section 5 I shall summarize the main achievements and sketch where I personally think there are opportunities for further development.

2. The genesis and programme of the Freiburg School

2.1. The founders and history of the founding

The main founders of the Freiburg School were Walter Eucken and Franz Boehm. Walter Eucken (1891–1950) was the son of the philosopher and Nobel prize winner Rudolph Eucken. He began his academic work under the influence of the early Historical School.[2] He soon changed course, in his book on German monetary policy (Eucken, 1923), in which he criticized the lack of a theoretical foundation for policy as partially responsible for the hyperinflation after World War I. Eucken, who in the meantime had left Berlin to accept professorships first in Tübingen (1925) and then in Freiburg (1927), continued his work in a paper on the crisis of capitalism (Eucken, 1932). He attacked the influence of representatives of interest groups on a state which was weak because it had taken on too many responsibilities. He felt that politicians formulated policies lacking a theoretical basis and without having theoretically analysed the facts of history; that they rather depended on untested and naive *ad hoc* theories and the expectation that a strong political will could always achieve its goals. It was here that Eucken first showed what later would become so typical of his work: the emphasis on the connections between political and economic order

(Lenel, 1987a, p. 6). The main message was that personal and political freedom could only be realized in a free market economy and not in a centrally planned economy (Eucken, 1975, pp. 304ff.).

Eucken showed himself to be a capable analyst in *Capital Theory (Kapitaltheoretische Untersuchungen*, 1954) first published in 1934.[3] It was there that he first considered – probably influenced by Wicksell – the problem of an economic order. Wicksell, whom Eucken had studied thoroughly while preparing his book on capital theory, wanted to progress from theoretical analysis via applied analysis. This would be an analysis of how economy would function with given institutions, and would then consider institutional reforms (Uhr, 1960, pp. 29ff.). This kind of thinking could have sparked Eucken's idea (or could have reinforced it) to look consciously and from a sound theoretical basis for an institutional framework which brings order to economic processes in a liberal atmosphere. The systematic search for such an institutional framework and the dissatisfaction with the economic policy of the Weimar Republic on the one hand and with that of the Third Reich on the other, characterize the two main works of Eucken: *Foundations of Economics (Grundlagen der Nationaloekonomie*, 1965), first published in 1940, and *Principles of Economic Policy (Grundsätze der Wirtschaftspolitik*, 1975), published posthumously in 1952. These efforts make it clear that Eucken was becoming more and more opposed to the ruling powers in Hitler's Germany and that he was developing a natural affinity for lawyers, who were trying to put together an 'economic constitution', i.e. a code of laws pertaining to industry and trade.[4]

This brings us to Franz Boehm (1895–1977), a professor of law who started his career as a specialist for cartels in the Ministry of Economics in 1925. One result of this activity was his book *Competition Versus Monopoly Abuse (Wettbewerb und Monopolkampf*, 1933), in which the main question of his life work was raised: the question of the function of law in social order and the question of the relationship between private power and the state's system of laws.[5] He received his doctorate in 1932 and his 'habilitation' (post-doctoral degree) in Freiburg in 1933 and stayed there until 1936 as an assistant professor. In 1937 he accepted a full professorship in Jena but in the same year was dismissed because he had protested the persecution of the Jews. Until the end of the war he was unemployed and had a close relationship with Gördeler's resistance group. In 1945 he became professor and president of the University of Freiburg and shortly afterwards he was appointed Minister of Culture in the State of Hesse. In 1952 he was at the head of the German delegation at the negotiations for reparations with Israel.[6] From 1953 until 1965 he was a CDU (the Conservative Party) delegate to the Bundestag and in this function was one of the writers of the German law against restraints on competition. His book *Economic Order as Historical Task and Achievement of Legal Creativity (Die Ordnung der Wirtschaft als geschichtliche Aufgabe und rechtsschöpferische Leistung*, 1937) was of great importance for the Ordoliberal movement. This was the first book in a series which was published by F. Boehm, W. Eucken and H. Grossmann-Doerth, a Freiburg professor of civil and commercial law. One can consider the publication of this book the birthdate of the School.[7]

Later, Boehm (1957) described how the cooperation of the nucleus of the Freiburg School came into being. In the beginning Grossmann-Doerth noticed how business used contracts containing their general conditions of business to exploit their economic power and proposed that this 'law', created by business itself, required looking into by the government. At the same time Boehm, as was already mentioned, was engaged in the study of the power of cartels. Thus both raised the question of how such forms of private 'law-making' could be reconciled with the economic steering functions of civil law. This was the point that Eucken took up. He asked himself how one could protect an efficiently functioning price system. Boehm (1957, p. 99) summarized it this way: 'the question which we were all concerned with was, if we state it narrowly, the question of private power in a free society. That led by necessity to the further questions of what order is like in a free economy, . . . what kinds . . . of economic order exist, . . . and what kinds of disorder could exist in an economy . . .'

After they had noticed that they were working on similar problems, they started holding seminars together. Here the lawyers learned to appreciate the function of the price system and the economists became aware of the importance of a framework of legal institutions, which have to be established so that a price system can function in a satisfactory manner. We can see how these seminars functioned in an example given by Böhm (1957, p. 111). The question was to what extent man can be free if his behaviour is determined by the price system. The lawyer would say, said Boehm, that either the price mechanism works, in which case there is no *free* economy, or the price mechanism does not work, in which case you have *no* workable economic system. From this discussion in the seminar the view emerged that the influence of prices on the individual economic plans was a kind of plebiscite, a constantly repeated economic balloting. Here nobody is dependent on the will of another *individual* (that would mean a lack of freedom); but simply *all* men are subject to the same *impersonal* directing system formed by the price system. The proposition that all men are subject only to the law, which is the institutional basis of the price system, then seems the only possibility of defining 'freedom for all' and of having freedom in a world in which goods are scarce and coercion as a means of distribution has to be rejected.[8]

The group was soon widened to include a number of other economists. We should mention C. von Dietze and A. Lampe. These two men were also closely associated with the Gördeler resistance group and were working on plans for the reconstruction of the German economy after the planned *coup* against Hitler and the end of the war.[9] I have mentioned these works and the group's connection with the resistance because that helps explain the great influence of the Ordoliberals on economic life in post war Germany. I shall return to this later, but let me say here that the academics who accomplished the transformation of these ideas into politics in the post war period, were L. Erhard (1897–1977) and A. Müller-Armack (1901–1978). After the war the former became the German Minister of Economics (1949–1963), Chancellor (1963–1966) and the political father of the *Wirtschaftswunder* (economic miracle); the latter was first a professor of economics in Münster and in Cologne and then became Erhard's adviser and undersecretary. Strictly speaking, neither can be called a member of the Freiburg School in the narrow sense, but they were both closely associated with it and they were as essential for its influence in post-war Germany as was the 'Erwin von Beckerath group', another group associated with the resistance and a cell from which came a number of academic advisers to the Federal Republic's Ministry of Economics.

Other members of the School in Freiburg itself were mentioned by Boehm (1957, pp. 95, 99ff.): K. P. Hensel, R. Johns, K. F. Maier, F. W. Meyer, F. A. Lutz and B. Pfister. As non-resident associated members he lists: H. Gestrich, A. Rüstow, L. Miksch, H. von Stackelberg and O. Veit, and as related thinkers with whom they had, wherever possible, contacts he lists: C. Antoni, L. Einaudi, A. Hahn, F. A. von Hayek, F. H. Knight, L. von Mises, W. Röpke and J. Rüff. I have limited my mentioning of younger members of the School to H. O. Lenel and H. Willgerodt. They have long been the editors of the yearbook, *ORDO*, which was founded by W. Eucken and F. Boehm in 1948 and became the discussion platform of the School. A reader on the Freiburg School in the broader sense will be found in W. Stützel et al. (1981).

2.2 The Ordoliberal programme
2.2.1 The problem of conceiving an economic order
Until now I have used the term 'economic order' in a relatively vague way and have not explained why the members of the Freiburg School call themselves

'Ordoliberals'. I shall now clear this up and talk about the programme of the School. We can refer to a famous paper by H. C. Simons (1948) and call the Ordoliberal programme 'a positive programme for a free and socially aware market competition'. The members of the Freiburg School were neo-liberals. One usually calls any school of thought 'neo-liberal' if it wants to preserve the well-established parts of *laissez-faire* economics but at the same time would like to make it more 'humane' and 'tame' it by means of policies dealing with competition, business cycles and the social aspects of society. Ordoliberalism combines these basic goals with a clear, positive-action programme of economic policy and for the legal and political establishment of that policy. That also explains its name: 'ordo' in Latin refers to a 'natural' order in contrast to 'ordinatio' which refers to an order imposed from outside. The morpheme 'ordo' in the term 'Ordoliberalism', in one sense, is to be understood as the 'ordre naturel' used by the physiocrat, P. F. Mercier de la Rivière (1767) with relation to the adaptation to human nature; in another sense, however, it is different from the concept of the physiocrats as well as from the views of classical theory and some modern thinkers, for example von Hayek: The Ordoliberals do not believe that 'ordo' or 'ordre naturel' would come about if the state merely refrains from action and does not insist on establishing an 'ordinatio' or 'ordre positif' which could only be enforced by coercion. No, the Ordoliberals believe that in order to have 'ordo', the state must play an active role which includes the use of coercion and other legal means to establish and preserve the right kind of legal framework for the economy.

The second part of the name 'Ordoliberal' is to be understood in its normal sense and has a direct connection to the classical economists' attitude towards economic policy. 'Liberal' is meant in the usual Continental sense of the word and would be translated into American-English as 'Libertarian'. But here, too, there is a difference to the way the classical economists used the word: 'The "invisible hand" works within the institutions which reconcile individual and public interests, but does not create those institutions' (Eucken, 1975, pp. 359ff.).

The word 'institutions' just mentioned leads us to the concept of 'economic order'. Eucken (1965, p. 51) defined the term as 'the totality of all limitations within which the economic process functions at any given time on a day to day basis'. Thus we have to interpret the word 'economic order' as a framework, or speaking in terms of models, we should understand it as 'totality of constraints' which decision-makers in economic life have to take into consideration in maximizing their utility. The economic order is, therefore, the totality of all institutional constraints which place limits on the freedom of movement of subjects in the economy. Such constraints are necessary to coordinate the actions of the economic units. So one can say that the economic order of a country is a mechanism to coordinate the actions of the economic units by means of institutional constraints (Moeller, 1983, p. 7). An important part of these limitations are the laws ruling. This part, which we can call the legal framework of the economy (Ordoliberals use the term 'economic constitution'), has to be the starting point of a conscious creation of an economic order which harmonizes individual and public interests or – technically expressed – produces incentive compatibility.

One can use the term 'economic order' for various limited social-economic systems and in that way refer to certain types of order which occur in these systems or prevail. If we are looking at entire economies, we have orders in the sense of comparative economic systems; if we are looking at markets, we can talk about economic morphology of markets; if we are thinking about enterprises, we take the approach of comparative institutional frameworks (Williamson, 1985, pp. 213ff.); and if we differentiate among various forms of creation and functions of money, we get various kinds of monetary orders.

Eucken considers the differentiation of economic systems, the morphology of markets, and the monetary systems as being very important for the conscious shaping of economic systems. Eucken (1965, pp. 78ff.) uses two classification variables in order to differentiate between *economic systems* derived from the answers to the following two questions: Who writes economic plans in the country? How distinct is the division of labour? If the economic plan is written by a leader or by a central administration, then we have a planned economy. Depending on the degree of division of labour, this can be 'simple' – then there are a number of independent economic units in the country which usually are tributary to a classical minimal–state/prince – or complex – then it requires a special apparatus for administration (centrally planned economy). A market economy contrasts with these two forms of centrally planned economies in that it has many partial plans, and therefore the problem of coordination of these partial plans comes up. If the degree of division of labour is small, i.e. only few exchanges take place among independent units, the market economy can be a barter system; otherwise it has to be a money economy, and in that case questions must be raised about the economic order of the money system.

At the level of *markets* Eucken (1965, pp. 91ff.) distinguishes mainly between the markets which are open or closed and whether units in the market have to adjust to the prevailing price, or whether they run the market process and can set prices according to their interests and goals.

These basic forms then are further differentiated depending on the degree of control over the market. *Vollständige Konkurrenz* is considered the best form of market. The English translation of this German expression, 'perfect competition', has a very definite technical meaning in the standard economic theory, and this is not what the Freiburg School understands by *vollständige Konkurrenz*. Their interpretation of the term is more dynamic but at the same time less restrictive. Similar to D. A. Walker's (1986, pp. 5ff.) presentation of the dynamic aspects of the Walras system and its implications for the role of entrepreneurs, the Ordoliberals refer to market *processes*, the unhindered process of *approaching* long-term equilibria (which may, nevertheless, alter their position due to external shocks). They do not refer to particular *states* of equilibria. In this respect, the lack of power to sell constantly at prices above marginal costs is of vital importance to the functioning of this process. For it is the marginal cost prices which 'make possible an unbiased exchange of information [about scarcities] from the factors of production to the consumers and in the other direction' and have the effect that the economy functions indirectly as 'an automatic calculating machine' processing data which never would have been available if men had had to do the evaluating and reckoning consciously (von Stackelberg, 1949, p. 197). At the same time, the powerlessness just mentioned is simply an expression of the absence of three problems: the conscious underutilization of a *given* capacity and the conscious neglect or prevention of *expansion* of capacity as well as the conscious and continued prevention of adaptation of new technology so that prices can be kept at an artificially high level.[10] When one considers a market with strong market positions on the demand side, one could add a provision to the Ordoliberal definition of *vollständige Konkurrenz* that there be a prohibition of the strategy of making suppliers deliberately dependent. Because all of this is incompatible with the term 'perfect competition', I use the term 'free competition'.[11]

I have already emphasized that the Freiburg School considered the shaping of an economic order to be a *positive task* of government. But how did the School expect the government to coordinate and regulate all of the sundry elements of a vast economic order and which elements should be 'ordered' in the first place (i.e. considered as part of the framework)? Taking into account the number of legal details to be regulated, for example, for the protection of labour or concerning the corporation's liability to render account, how should one determine what should be done and what should not? The Ordoliberals would use a method we have known since Adam Smith (Book V, Part 2, *Principles of Taxation*). They suggest principles for establishing the basic framework and for making regular decisions about economic policy and they formulate criteria for the choice of instruments needed; they discuss the problems which would occur in transforming these principles into law and ask which tasks must be mastered if the establishment of order is to be politically feasible. I shall now turn to these areas.

2.2.2 Principles of economic policy   As I said, the principles which are to be discussed are to serve as the basis for constructing the legal framework of an economy and to serve as guidelines for political decisions. One would have to proceed in various ways depending on each country's customs and historical situation, but the goal worth reaching is unambiguous: it is a freely competitive order which provides for a workable price system and makes it possible for plans which have been worked out independently in a market economy with a highly developed division of labour to be adequately coordinated (Eucken, 1975, pp. 250ff.).[12] In realizing this goal, the experience which we have had in various industrial countries at various stages of history and with various systems of direction, should be analysed and evaluated in the light of economic theory: 'We can and should leave the stage of speculation and enter the stage of economic policy based on experience' (Eucken, 1949, pp. 1ff.). The principles which have to be deduced should not be based on natural rights, dogmatic laws or be of a philosophical nature (ibid., p. 290), but rather, they should have a theoretical and empirical foundation. According to Eucken (ibid., p. 252) they should serve the same function for the political economist as the laws of statics do for the architect. In other words, an economic policy guided by sound principles should replace random interventionism and naive *ad hoc* experiments (Chr. Watrin, 1985, s. 158).

One can distinguish four groups of principles:

1. The *necessary* elements of competition (*basic structurizing* principles). Since these aim at the formation of the framework of the economic process and particularly at the activity of the *legislative power*, one can refer to them as 'order policy in the narrow sense' (Tuchtfeldt, 1957, p. 52).
2. No misdirected developments in the economic process should take place. These *regulating* principles are mainly directed towards the *executive* and related to the permanent controlling of market and circulation processes in the framework of the so-called *Ablaufpolitik* or *Prozeßpolitik*, i.e. day-to-day administrative policy (ibid.).
3. Precepts which could not be formulated in forms of (ultimate) principles by the beginning of the 1950s because more experience

was needed before one could do so. Eucken wrote them up only in the form of questions. I propose we call them '*potential additional principles*', a rather uncommon formulation in the literature.

4. A group of principles dealing with the behaviour of the state in its own domain. These are the *principles of state*.

Anyone who has lived for a long time in a market economy – say, an American – will consider the basic structurizing principles perhaps somewhat abstract or artificially constructed. One must keep in mind that they were written in an historical situation in which most of the large cities in Germany were 80 per cent or more destroyed and in which all living space, clothes, food and jobs were assigned to people by public officials.[13] The transformation of such an economy into a market economy was not an abstract problem but a very concrete and difficult one.

In order to avoid misunderstandings, one must emphasize that the principles apply to the whole economic policy. They certainly have various levels of relevance for individual areas of law but must be observed everywhere. Indeed, each ministry should have a department where one would test whether the part of the law for which the ministry is responsible is compatible with the basic structurizing, regulatory and additional principles and those of state. Aspects of competition policy should not only be observed in anti-trust law but also in company and tax law, environmental protection, and when drafting consumer protection policies. Economic policy may *not* be only partially pursued (Eucken, 1975, pp. 304ff.). For example, company concentration should not be fought openly by means of anti-trust law, while at the same time it would benefit from tax law regulations (Eucken, 1947, s. 84).

All of these principles are listed in Table 3.1. They were discussed thoroughly by Eucken (1949, 1975). I can only sketch them briefly in this chapter.

The fundamental principle requires positive action on the part of government to make free competition possible, so that the accounting done by individual participants in the economy can be harmonized through competitive prices, and the economic process of the total economy can be run in a meaningful way.[14] There should not only be a law against cartels (negative policy) but an active (positive) policy should ensure that all kinds of barriers to trade and movement of resources are turned down so that monopoly markets develop by means of entries into competitive markets.

Price stability is to be given priority because unexpected price changes

Table 3.1   *Principles of economic policy*

1. Basic structurizing principles[1]

1.1   The fundamental principal of comprehensive striving for competitive prices

1.2   Principle of the primacy of price stability

1.3   Principle of keeping markets open

1.4   Principle of preference to private (instead of public) property rights as a means for the allocation of economic power freely to dispose

1.5   Principle of the right to enter into contracts in conformity with competition

1.6   Principle of avoidance of limits on liability (if possible) and the concordance of power freely to dispose and liability

1.7   Principle of predictability and regularity of economic policy

2. Regulating principles[2]

2.1   Principle of containment and correction of market power

2.2   Principle of a redistribution of income with regard to justness under consideration of the effect on investment

2.3   Principle of the correction of external effects

2.4   Principle of the correction of anomalous supply reactions

3. Potential additional principles[3]

3.1   Principle of avoiding isolated treatment of measures and of integration of competition order, legislation, jurisdiction, and administration

3.2   Principle of moderation in business cycle measures

3.3   Principle of encouragement of self-help

4. Principles of the state itself[4]

4.1   Principle of the limitation of the power of interest groups

4.2   Principle of giving preference to the lowest instance[5] for accepting new tasks and that of the priority of order policy over day-to-day policy

Sources: 1.   W. Eucken (1975), pp. 254–91.
2.   Ibid., pp. 291–304.
3.   Ibid., pp. 304–24.
4.   Ibid., pp. 325–8, 348.
5.   The lowest instance principle (in German called *Subsidiaritätsprinzip*) means that a community of a higher order (e.g. the municipality) should take care of a problem when (but only when) a 'lower instance' (e.g. the family) cannot manage it.

distort economic calculations and because inflation has a negative effect on competition and leads to disproportions in the structure of productive capacities and to a non-transparent redistribution of income. The money system should function as *automatically* as possible because people cannot stand up to special interest groups; it should balance out savings and investment and thus even out the business cycles. It should also be predictable and regular in order to create a climate friendly to long-term investment. Eucken (1975, pp. 261ff.) favoured the Graham Plan for a commodity reserve currency which is similar to a gold-backed currency, but instead of *one* commodity, gold, a market basket of commodities would be used.

The principle of keeping markets open does not simply require the proclamation of the freedom of trade and choice of profession but an active programme of fighting all barriers to trade and the movement of factors of production; this applies both at home and to international trade. Wherever temporarily limited monopoly rights such as patents are functional, institutes like those that issue licences should be established. Private restraints on business should be principally forbidden.

Private property would be encouraged, although socialist market economies are conceivable and similar systems exist, e.g. in Yugoslavia and Hungary. Reference should be made to the fact that private property automatically causes the 'command over the factors of production' to flow to the most successful entrepreneurs. It is only then that a latent ability becomes visible: a subtle intuition the lack of which in too large firms Williamson (1985, pp. 131ff.) describes as 'incentive limits of firms' when given the explanation of the limits of the concentration processes. At the same time it should be emphasized that private property is only definitely desirable in connection with competition and stable money because only then could exploitation be avoided.

The *freedom to enter into contracts* is naturally a prerequisite for any competition. Under certain circumstances, however, it can be ineffective and may even kill competition: If serfdom is repealed and the former master is the only person who has a demand for labour and who is a supplier of land for lease in the area the situation of the formally free farm hands and tenant farmers would change little in spite of the right to enter contracts freely. In the same way, if one forms cartels, competition can be prevented by contract. Therefore, Eucken requires that freedom to enter contracts should be tied to competition and he wanted to forbid its misuse as a means of limiting competition. Unavoidable monopolies should be obliged to do business with willing customers and be publicly regulated.

Liability is the complement to making profits; it prevents fraud, and, as private property, should have the effect that the control of the factors of production moves to the most successful entrepreneurs. That is why the Ordoliberals look very sceptically at any tendency of laws to place limitations on liability.

Regularity and predictability of economic policy improve the climate for investment and help install the faith needed for *long-term* investment. In addition, according to Eucken (1975, p. 289), they reduce the process of concentration, as far as it is due to efforts for more security in large concerns.

The regulating principles result from the idea that deficiencies remain, even if the basic structurizing principles are transformed into reality in the best possible way. Therefore, there must be continuous correction by the administration in the context of a day to day administrative policy:

- a constant control and correction of unavoidable market power by a 'monopoly office', which steps in wherever symptoms of market power are observed from the *outside* but only then (Eucken, 1975, p. 295);[15]
- a constant adjustment of the distribution of income by means of a progressive tax system which of course should not endanger the propensity to invest (ibid., pp. 300f.);
- a correction of external effects (above all in environmental law and health protection for workers);[16] and
- a correction of anomalous supply reactions (ibid., pp. 302ff.).

The *potential additional criteria*, as I already said, have not been fully set out. Eucken (1975, pp. 304ff.) emphasized that there is no point in pursuing the realization of principles only in some partial areas and to violate them in others. Anyone who tries to avoid concentration by means of anti-trust laws but at the same time produces an incentive for concentration by means of tax or company law should not be surprised if his economic policy remains ineffective. If one applied the basic structurizing and regulating principles, one could do away with a lot that keeps politicians of today busy. This holds true particularly in the case of *business cycle policy* which could apparently be limited to truly exceptional situations, and *social policy* which could concentrate on individual hardships and on government to promote self-help activities (ibid., pp. 318f.).

Now we turn to the *principles of the state itself*. Here Eucken (1975, pp. 325ff.) emphasizes that the growth in governmental activity corresponds with a loss of its authority because the representatives of special interests would have – as one would say today – more incentive for 'rent seeking' (ibid., p. 328). In order to prevent this, the state must consciously attempt to limit the power of the representatives of special interest groups (ibid., p. 334); it must concentrate on the order policy, and must be hesitant to take on new tasks (ibid., p. 336). In any way, it would be wrong to think that the state would be able to do better without exception in all those cases which can only be done unsatisfactorily by the market (ibid., pp. 330f.).

2.2.3 Conformity criteria for assessing individual measures   The competition framework can be understood as Kant's Categorical Imperative for competition in concrete form (Eucken, 1975, pp. 365ff.). According to the Categorical Imperative, the individual is morally bound always to act so that his own rules of conduct could at the same time always count as the principles of a general system of law. However, for the individual it is almost impossible to see what sort of economic activity fits in with the economic activities of others and is suitable for a realization of the general good. The competition framework helps by arranging the incentives so that all individuals act according to their own interests and can at the same time assume that the interests of others are also being respected and that the general welfare is being maximized. Those who want to live in the economic sphere according to the Categorical Imperative must therefore commit themselves to the realization of the competition framework. For all those having political influence this means: 'In drafting legislation, be sure to realize the framework of competition'; then (and only then) does it follow for the 'normal citizen' that his behaviour should be guided by the simple principle: 'Act according to the spirit of law (here in particular of the economic constitution).'

If you want to realize the framework for competition, or if you wish to assess an individual measure (e.g. a bill or a regulatory activity) in the light of the Ordoliberal guidelines, Eucken's principles can be used as a checklist. But the task of assessing a proposed measure of economic policy will be less complex when applying a method of testing that I have presented in Table 3.2. It cannot be found in this form in the writings of the Ordoliberals and, by referring to Rawls, it also goes beyond the thinking of the core of the School.[17] But this method here shows that one *can* work with Eucken's principles, as well as how to do so. In addition, it takes into consideration three further criteria proposed by the Ordo circle and its associates: those of the conformity of an instrument

Table 3.2   Step-by-step system for assessing economic measures

1. Legitimation of the Goal of the Measures in Terms of Contract Theory

1.1 Step 1 = hypothetical justification: Does it seem plausible that enlightened citizens in a Rawls-type contract situation – i.e. with the impartiality of an arbitrator and under the 'veil of ignorance' as concerns personal consequences – would agree with the aim of the measures?

1.2 Step 2 = reference to conclusive behaviour: Does the world of experience indicate that the aim under discussion would be shared by the majority of enlightened and impartial citizens and that infringements would be seen as a social nuisance?

1.3 Partial result 1: If the partial result is positive, it should be recorded and one should test further; if the result is negative, one should proceed only under the proviso that the aim would presumably only help particular interest groups and not the community as a whole.

2. Economic Legitimation of the Form of the Measures

2.1 Instrumental vector: finding out what conceivable instruments could be used for realizing the aim.

2.2 Testing instruments for effectiveness (= conformity to goals): Does measure X pull in the right direction to help to achieve the given goal and is X the sort of measure with which, quantitatively speaking, a satisfactory degree of goal fulfilment can be reached?

2.3 Elimination step 1: Ineffective means are dropped from further testing.

2.4 Testing of the various instruments for necessity (= conformity of the order): Does the measure X involve

● infringements of the individual's freedom of action or
● additional power for official instances (graded according to the lowest instance principle) or
● related effects which would interfere with the functioning of the market mechanism or
● come in conflict with any other of Eucken's principles?

Is the extent of the lack of conformity to the system limited to the minimum necessary for achieving the given goal and does it turn out to be impossible to reduce disturbances by reshaping measure X (minimum degree of disturbance of the system necessary for goal fulfilment)?

2.5 Elimination step 2: Rejecting all instruments except those with the absolute minimum degree of disturbance of the system necessary for goal fulfilment.

2.6 Testing for (cost) appropriateness (= cost-effectiveness): With the measure selected, is the benefit from realizing the goal in reasonable proportion to the production and transaction costs of all kinds connected with the use of the instrument? In difficult cases this test must be carried out with the help of cost-benefit or cost-effectiveness analysis.

2.7 Partial result 2: presentation of the test results for all instruments in the form of a matrix showing instruments and criteria and concluding description of the instrument finally chosen.

● to its goal (the appropriateness of means with its end),
● to the working of the market mechanism, and
● to the competition order as a whole.

The call for market conformity comes originally from Röpke (1942, pp. 252ff.) and requires that economic measures should respect the conditions for the automatic functioning of the market. For example, fixed prices do not meet the criterion of market conformity. Müller-Armack (1966, p. 246) in particular then adopted this requirement and directly combined it with the obvious one of conformity to the goal pursued. The criterion of conformity to the order (or system) goes back to Thalheim (1955, pp. 577ff.) and distinguishes various degrees of conformity to the total concept of the competition system. Tuchtfeldt (1957) gives an overall view of the most important parts of the debate on conformity.

Table 3.2 shows how, with the help of the conformity criteria, Eucken's principles can be incorporated in a step-by-step system for the methodical assessment of economic measures that can be used as a matter of routine in politics, administration and justice.

According to this plan, to assess a measure you start by examining its aim. In view of the inadequacies of the formation of public opinion, as investigated in the public choice literature, and especially against the background of the Capture Theory (as we should say today), two questions are asked to establish whether the aim is in the general interest. The first question makes use of a purely hypothetical idea of a social contract; the second one refers to empirical indicators which tell us whether the hypotheses formulated in answer to the first question have proved to be valid. In general, the problem of evaluating aims should thus be taken out of the area of non-commital personal statements and raised to the level of positive hypotheses about aims of common interest, these hypotheses being to some extent testable.[18]

All this may sound somewhat complicated, and I shall, therefore, give an *example* to illustrate it. Let us suppose that measures to aid farmers are to be discussed. The aim may be defined as follows: 'Medium scale farmers are to be permanently supported by the state.'[19] One could hardly imagine that such an aim would be made part of a Rawls-type social contract (negation of question 1.1); apart from this, at least in Germany there are currently expressions of dissatisfaction indicating that the aim is unacceptable (negation of question 1.2). Consequently, measures intended to realize *this* aim would have failed the double test described. On the other hand, if the goal had been to specify *general* conditions (such as a radical structural or regional crisis) under which groups affected (*all* groups, not just farmers) could if necessary be subsidized for a limited period, and had these conditions been operationalized by valid indicators, the double test would probably have been passed.

It has been mentioned that the form of assessing aims proposed here goes beyond the Ordoliberal literature. None the less, regarding its substance it is in accordance with the Ordoliberal concept, merely presenting it in a more modern manner. I have emphasized that Eucken had been particularly influenced by Kant, he has himself explicitly referred to the Categorical Imperative (cf. above, p. 51). In addition, the ideas of the Historical School and especially Schmoller had gripped him; a School believing (not solely, but to a certain extent) in the ethical ideals of institutions (J. Herbst, 1965, p. 143). The difference between my presentation and Ordoliberal terminology can be reduced to the fact that they did not develop a *formalized* testing procedure. In a more global manner they stated 'the will towards a socially and ethical inspired order' and expected 'social matters to be arranged in the spirit of freedom' (Eucken, 1975, p. 370). In contrast, the proposed 'double test' shows how specific problems can be decided upon in accordance with the global Ordoliberal spirit, and thus with 'dignity of man'. In other words, the 'double test' indicates how positive hypotheses can be tested on the way enlightened individuals would organize their society under the veil of ignorance.

The second part of the testing procedure follows the Ordoliberal literature more closely. It is devoted to the assessment of measures for the achievement of given goals. The steps of this part should be immediately clear. If a price and wage freeze were to be suggested as a way of achieving price stability, one would have to turn it down because of proven *ineffectiveness*.[20] In terms of the above introduced example on agricultural policy: If (as happens within the EC) minimum prices for agricultural products together with state purchases and storage depots are proposed, this measure would have to be rejected because of *insufficient conformity to the economic order*. In contrast, temporary subsidies which are proved to be tied to restructuring measures could be regarded as a means whose degree of disturbance of the economic system is the minimum necessary for the realization of the goal. But this measure would also fail the test of *(cost) appropriateness* if the proposed subsidies amount too high, if the intended organization for carrying it out is inefficient, or if the induced negative side effects amount to an intolerable degree. Particularly when assessing the (cost) appropriateness the 'fundamental principle of economic policy' (Eucken, 1975, p. 221) has to be observed, namely that each measure has to be analysed in three respects: in respect to its *immediate* momentum on economic order and process of economic adjustments, in respect to the induced *tendencies to changes* of the economic order and in respect to its *repercussions* on other orders.

Here I have shown how the Eucken principles and the results of the Ordoliberals' discussion on conformity can in practice be applied to the assessment of concrete economic measures. I shall now leave the discussion of the content of the Ordoliberal programme and turn to the solutions that have been suggested for the legal and political problems of implementing the programme.

2.3 Ideas on legal and political implementation

Only those who, *sit venia verbo*, still believe in Santa Claus could allow themselves the luxury of hoping that, once the economists had done their work and drawn up guidelines for a functioning economic order, well-meaning politicians would put it into effect. The Ordoliberals were not so naïve, nor could they be: after all, Eucken and Boehm in particular had themselves analysed the 'capturing' of the state by multitudinous interests (*die Interessenhaufen*) (Boehm, 1950, p. xxxvi). But then, how is the new economic order to be realized? Three questions must be answered:

● What technical problems of law arise when economic ideas are put into the language of legislators?
● How can one impart to administrative civil servants who have generally received only a legal education, to the judges, and to the people, the minimum knowledge of economics needed to understand the functioning of an economic system and thus avoid the wrong judgements that so often result from an intuitive approach to justice?[21]
● How can one create the political willingness to realize the framework for competition?

Within the scope of this chapter I am naturally unable to discuss these questions in depth, and I shall have to restrict myself to referring to the essentials of Ordoliberal thought and to the literature.

The question about the technical problems of law is much more important than appears at first sight. 'It is a question of . . . a practical case of whether [and possibly how] the language of economists can be translated into the language of the law' (Partsch, 1954, p. 24). For example, there are considerable problems in interpreting the freedom of trade, the freedom of contract and the freedom of association so that both the idea of the rule of law and Eucken's principles are respected.

On the one hand, indicators are needed which will lead to operational legal concepts,[22] and on the other hand, the tendency of lawyers to consider only what is said in court must be held in check. For example, if contracts between manufacturers and dealers are treated in this way, the parties to the dispute will very easily reach agreement at the expense of third parties – in this case, the consumers.

A further technical problem of implementing the desired economic order into law becomes evident if one distinguishes three parts of the legal code: the part which creates the conditions for the establishment of markets (for example, clearly defined property rights), the part which, as it were, comes into existence within the economy itself and then goes to the state to be regulated (for example, regulations of futures markets), and a third part whose connection with market and circulation processes is not obvious and has disappeared from the consciousness of at least many jurists.[23] For example, German labour law continues to develop out of the interplay between large associations and judges regardless of its consequences for the economy; and in sport, culture and welfare, economic questions are often overlaid and befogged with ideological considerations. It is especially in this third part that there is the additional difficulty that necessity of testing decisions for their conformity to the economic order is by no means recognized, although legal formulations such as 'just and equitable', 'socially acceptable' or 'immoral' are potentially most disruptive for the economic system (Eucken, 1965, p. 241).

In Ordoliberal circles, the predominant idea for solving the technical problem of law is the same as for the second of the above questions, concerning the elimination of inadequate knowledge. This is the call for a basic training in economics for lawyers, for a basic legal training for economists, and for a deliberate cooperation between professors of law and professors of economics (Willgerodt, 1985). In addition, there should be more widespread use of explanations of economic aims as an aid to the interpretation of laws (for example, in preambles). There is also the desire to have more independent organizations with clearly defined tasks (an example is the Bundesbank [West German Federal Bank]); in Ordo circles the idea of 'constitutional brakes' on the state was looked on with favour, as was to some extent the notion of having a declaration of the aims of the state in the constitution (Moeschel, 1985, p. 42). Implicit in all this is the idea that a nation should be as willing to enter into rational commitment for the sake of its long-term welfare as private individuals are. With respect to Eucken's principles this means that they should be incorporated into law in order to ensure that politicians pursue policies in conformity with the economic order even if incentives would have suggested them to take a different line of action. Whether all these suggestions, which have been no more than outlined here, will help or whether there will perhaps have to be a systematically developed jurisprudence both economic and legal, is a question that I shall leave unanswered here.

The third problem listed above (that of producing the political willingness to create the framework for competition) is treated by Eucken (1975, pp. 325ff.) as a question of the 'regulating powers'. He comes to the conclusion that, in the last analysis, only science could produce a corresponding willingness by influencing the students who will later be among the leaders of the nation and – possibly as journalists – will also contribute to the formation of public opinion.[24] In this he is in agreement not only with the tradition of German Idealistic philosophy, now almost 300 years old, but also with the well-known quotation from Keynes (1936, p. 383) about the world being ruled by the ideas of philosophers and economists – with an author with whom he has little else in common.[25]

However, the Ordoliberals were not content with this hope alone: they also endeavoured to make the population and the bureaucracy understand their ideas and so to influence the politicians indirectly to bring about the framework for competition and to treat the representatives of interest groups with reserve. The Ordoliberal School had great influence at West German universities, especially in the 1950s and 1960s, and also tried to popularize its ideas (Welter, 1953). In this, Ordoliberals were – and still are – supported by the *Frankfurter Allgemeine Zeitung*, one of Germany's leading national newspapers. The *Frankfurter Allgemeine Zeitung* is supported financially by a foundation and is politically independent but it is not impartial as regards schools of economic thought.[26] Moreover, in the *Neue Züricher Zeitung*, the 'paper of European Liberalism', the group always had an organ sympathetic to them.[27]

3. The place of Ordoliberalism in the history of economics

For purposes of classification, one usually first takes the wider generic term covering several related phenomena (*genus proximus*) and then develops criteria to distinguish the phenomenon in question from those related to it (*differencia specifica*).

Following this procedure, Ordoliberalism's place in the history of economics can be defined in three ways:

● First, as *a theory of economic policy*, i.e. the totality of the shared ideas of the members of a school of thought in relation to the goals, means and agents (responsible authorities) for administering economic policy, and the way they can be assigned to one another.

● Second, as *a system of people* linked to each other by the transfer of ideas, especially as reflected in teacher–student relationships.

● Third, as a doctrine which stresses the importance of institutions and which is consequently connected with other *institutionalistic schools*.

I shall first turn to Ordoliberalism as a *theory of economic policy*. As suggested by the name, this is one of the theories which regard the freedom of the individual as a paramount aim and which have a lot in common with classical liberalism, especially as expressed by Adam Smith. But how does Ordoliberalism differ from other liberal theories? I shall start with *classical liberalism* and its theoretical position, as represented in particular with Hayek today. The Ordoliberals claim that the classical liberals, with their *laissez-faire* concept, ignored the power of private citizens over other private citizens and the fact that the state can be 'captured' by those who wield private power.[28]

Unlike the classical liberal economists, the Ordoliberals think that private citizens should be given every economic freedom except the freedom to make up the rules of play and, in particular, the form of the market and the monetary system. This should be the preserve of a constitutional state tied to a suitable economic order (Eucken, 1975, p. 246). In this context Eucken quotes E. F. Heckscher (1932, pp. 448ff.), who described the way in which industrialization would have taken place in a mercantilist society instead of in a liberal market economy as follows: 'The old method would have tried to erect a dam to check the upheavals. The new, victorious method gave them a free run. In consequence, the upheavals took place with a violence without parallel in the earlier economic history of mankind. A third way would have been neither to arrest the developments nor to leave them unregulated, but to steer them into orderly paths.' This third way would have been that of Ordoliberalism.[29]

This brings me to a standpoint taken by Hayek and his followers (some of them in Freiburg *today*). Hayek (1967) worked out his views particularly clearly for the Tokyo Conference of the Mont Pélérin Society in July 1966. He called for a *spontaneous* order such as one that would evolve in a common law society in which there are only *per se* prohibitions (ibid., p. 33). Altogether, these prohibitions should satisfy the requirements of the Categorical Imperative and thus be compatible with incentives and without inherent contradiction (ibid., p. 21); however, they would exclude all kinds of day-to-day political intervention and rule-of-reason consideration, and, above all, the regulation of monopolies (ibid., p. 31f.). Although it is not explicitly expressed, as Hayek sees it the Ordoliberals thus come close to a line of thought which Hayek calls Constructivism, a tradition which he defines in terms of names such as Voltaire, Rousseau, and Condorcet (ibid., p. 11). In contrast, Lenel (1987b, pp. 7ff.) and Willgerodt (1985, p. 32), referring to Boehm and Eucken, argue that an economic order must be deliberately formed. According to them, it is not clear how, from law which is created and interpreted in ignorance of its economic functions, there should grow 'spontaneously' (whatever that means) an economic order which would meet Hayek's own requirements in regard to compatibility of incentives. In addition, in other respects Hayek's ideas are so imprecise that one does not know how to assess individual economic measures (not only those of competition policy) with their help – unlike the use that can be made of Eucken's principles shown in section 2.2.3.

The Ordoliberals have a great deal in common with the Chicago School. Above all this holds true for the 'Old Chicago School'[30] and particularly for H. C. Simons (1948) who is cited by Eucken (1975, p. 255) as a significant forerunner together with Boehm (1933) and Miksch (1947). But there are also differences:[31] In Chicago it is assumed that market processes rapidly lead to a genuine Pareto optimum almost everywhere (Reder, 1982, p. 11). This is a *positive* assertion but it can no more be tested empirically than its opposite. In this context, the Ordoliberals have somewhat different priorities: They call for free competition in *their* sense (not necessarily the same thing as Pareto optimality), and they regard this aim as a *norm* for wide sectors of the economy which is not 'automatically' realized and must be organized (Eucken, 1947, pp. 75ff.). Apart from this, the Chicago School is convinced that there is a strong tendency for competition to *establish* itself, so that at the most only a very moderate anti-trust policy is necessary (Stigler, 1968, p. 297). In contrast, Ordoliberals are inclined to the view that there is an inherent self-destructive tendency within competition (Eucken, 1947, pp. 77f.). This dissent may be the result of differences of experience: America was and remains a very large market, whereas Europe for a long time consisted of many small markets which, at least with a protectionist foreign trade policy (which was long the rule), could relatively easily be monopolized or cartelized. There are other differences between the Ordoliberals and the Chicago School: the Ordoliberals are more sensitive to the political power of large companies (similarly more justifiable in a small country than in a large one); and they have other goals apart from that of the efficient allocation of resources (e.g. a just distribution of income).

At this point I shall turn to the relationship between the Ordoliberals and the social teaching of the Catholics and Protestants. Here one must first stress that both Churches make ethical demands, based on natural law, to individual human beings in their economic activity: individuals should contain their egotism and act with a sense of community. In contrast, as I hope to have brought out at the beginning of section 2.2.3, Ordoliberalism tries to minimize those ethical demands and to transfer them to a higher level: once the proper framework of competition has been established, individuals need only respect the law because the ethical requirements have already been taken into consideration when the laws were drafted. From the standpoint of Ordoliberalism, however, whose founders were committed Christians, it is admittedly a Christian duty for those with political influence to press for the realization of the competition system. But even this should be made easier: by means of a constitution political power should be restricted so as to comply with the competition order. In this manner, economic development is to be programmed in a way that morality, that 'scarcest of all goods in short supply, (von Nell-Breuning), is needed as little as possible and people 'are less led into temptation' (Boehm).[31]

A second difference between Ordoliberal and Christian teaching is that the social teaching of the Churches is less detailed than that of the Ordoliberal programme, and emphasizes personal participation with dignity and solidarity (Rauscher, 1977, pp. 49f.). In the view of the Churches, only *extreme* economic systems are thus excluded – for example, a pure *laissez-faire* system without social security, or a centrally directed economy without freedom of choice as concerns consumption and employment. In consequence, their principles do not clash with those of the Ordoliberals; at the same time, the areas covered are admittedly by no means the same. In practice, because of the participation principle, both Churches are better disposed towards worker participation and the trade unions than are the Ordoliberals. In any case, discussion in specialized circles within the Churches has been greatly enriched by Ordoliberalism.[33]

I shall now proceed to the classification of the Ordoliberals in a *system of people* linked by the mutual exchange of ideas. The key words here are Liberalism, the Historical School and Institutionalism. Table 3.3 schematizes an overview of personal influences between important members of each School. It documents in particular Freiburg's relations to the Historical School and to the Chicago School, respectively.[34] If the thesis is accepted, that at least via the philosophical theories of J. Dewey and H. Spencer there exists a connection between American Institutionalism and the Chicago School, then 'Freiburg' and 'Chicago' do have a

Table 3.3 Personal Influences

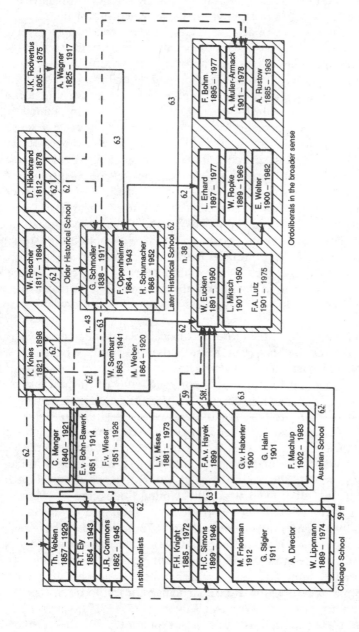

= strong influence on/teacher -student-relation ━━━▶ = strong mutual influence - - - -▶ = less important influence

[·] = number of page listing reference which document influences between the different schools

[n.] = number of note listing such a reference

common historical link as well as personal connections in more recent times. In addition to this rather loose connection there may have existed direct contacts between the two Schools, which, unfortunately, I have not been able to trace back from Germany. Spencer, by the way, has had a strong influence on Schmoller and Oppenheimer, too.

The *common historical link* between the schools was Karl Knies (1821–1898), together with Roscher and Hildebrand founder of the Older Historical School. Knies emphasized the necessity of a nation-wide infrastructure of institutions. On the one hand, in Heidelberg he taught Boehm-Bawerk and Wieser, which makes him in a sense the forefather of Hayek; and on the other hand, he also taught R. T. Ely (1854–1943).[35] The latter contributed a great deal to the transfer of economic ideas and proposals on how to set up institutions from Germany to America (J. Herbst, 1965, pp. 134ff.) – consider his 'Wisconsin Idea' of a scientific preparation of reform programmes discussed by Herbst (ibid., pp. 175ff.) – and he was one of the founders of the *American Economic Association* (1885). An important student of Ely was in turn J. R. Commons (1862–1945), through whom there are further connections which I shall go into later.[36] In any case, we see that 'Ely's new school teaching constituted a direct link between German historical economics and twentieth century institutional economics' (Coats, 1968, p. 34).

In Germany, out of the Older Historical School which merely worked out the connections between classical theories and the historical development and particularly stressed the importance of national institutions, the Later Historical School emerged, whose principal representatives were Schmoller, Brentano, Bücher, Knapp and Schanz. This School had a more reserved attitude towards classical economics, had a strong ethical emphasis, and endeavoured to convert their insights in the field of historical sociology into immediate political reforms. Their leading thinker, G. von Schmoller (1838–1917), was strongly influenced by Knies and Roscher and achieved a dominant position in Germany similar to that of F. Taussig in the United States and A. Marshall in Great Britain.[37] With other professors interested in social policy (especially Wagner and Brentano), in 1872 he founded the *Verein für Socialpolitik* (the German Economic Association), which Ely to some extent saw as the model for the *American Economic Association* (today it is more the other way round).[38] Schmoller, on his part, had a number of students, two of whom are of particular interest to us and for both of whom he had, together with A. Wagner (1835–1917), supervised their doctoral theses as well as their theses submitted for the certificate of habilitation, namely H. Schumacher (1868–1952), already mentioned above (note 1) who then supervised Eucken's doctoral thesis,[39] and F. Oppenheimer (1864–1943) who then supervised Erhard's doctoral thesis.[40] Others, too, claimed Schmoller to be their teacher: W. Sombart and M. Weber (H. Herkner, 1924, p. 9). Both of them, on their part, had a great influence on Müller-Armack, in particular regarding his sociological works. Thus, from the Older Historical School, and especially from Knies, there come three 'personal bridges of ideas' (indicated in Table 3.3 by broad lines): one to the American Institutional economists, one to the Austrian School and Hayek, and one to the Ordoliberals and to Eucken and Erhard in particular.

A *new 'bridge of people'* for the exchange of ideas was built in the 1930s and extended after World War II. The decisive event was the appearance of W. Lippmann's *Good Society* (1937). This book aroused great interest and led to a *Colloque Walter Lippmann* in Paris in 1938 (Duerr, 1954, p. 10). Many of the Liberals who took part in the Colloquium later met again in the Mont Pélérin Society, founded in 1947. Amongst them were both Eucken and Hayek the latter has taught in both Chicago and Freiburg. From Chicago, among others F. H. Knight and M. Friedman joined the foundation meeting (W. Seuß, 1987).[41] In his book, Lippmann expressed views similar to Hayek's and criticized 'designing a new *society*' (1937, pp. 362ff.). As I have already said, the Ordoliberals agreed on the rejection of a planned *society*; however, they did not want the economic *constitution* (the 'institutional skeleton') to grow without a plan, influenced by intervention on particular points and by group interests. They wanted it to be *fashioned* according to the model provided by the institutional framework for competition. To use a metaphor: They did not want the *game* to be planned, only the *rules*. But since this 'planning of the rules' requires economic expertise, it is, in Eucken's view (1947, pp. 81ff.), the responsibility of science to advance suitable proposals and by educating future leaders to ensure their long-term implementation.

As a third way of classifying Ordoliberalism, I have mentioned its *institutional aspect* (p. 58 above). The concepts relevant in this context are institutionalism, the Property Rights Theory, Transaction Cost Economics and Constitutional Economics; the human link is J. R. Commons. Here I do not wish to claim that Ordoliberalism was the forerunner of the 'New Institutionalism', of the Property Rights approach, of the Transaction Cost Economics or of the Constitutional Economics approach, or that they actually founded on Ordoliberalism. This is not the case for the simple reason, that Ordoliberalism was widely unheard of in America. My thesis is rather modest: I maintain that thinking in terms of institutions is a basic element of all these approaches.

As regards the *Property Rights approach*, this is made clear by a comparison of H. Demsetz's account of the beginnings of private property in the form of hunting areas and game among the Labrador Indians (1967) with A. Wagner's (1984) description of the beginnings of private property in the form of farmsteads and land among Germanic tribes (W. Meyer, 1983, pp. 4ff.). Both authors conclude that it was advantageous for the whole society to develop or change property rights (without neglecting transaction costs) so as to internalize disadvantages for the whole economy resulting from external effects: One had to accept the costs of enforcing law but it had the advantage that the owners did what was necessary to preserve wildlife and maintain the fertility of the soil – in contrast to the state of 'primitive communism'. Due to this remarkable correlation W. Meyer (op. cit., p. 6) thus speaks of a 'Demsetz–Wagner Principle' when referring to the onset of private property. As already mentioned, Wagner as well as Schmoller was an 'intellectual forefather' of Eucken. From this we see that the Property Rights approach and Ordoliberalism had 'common ancestors' in the form of the institutionalism of the German Historical School.[42] Another common feature of both approaches is the conviction that legal regulations to a large extent frame the course of economic processes. But there are differences, too, regarding the problem of how an economically satisfactory legal framework evolves. Most advocates of the Property Rights approach argue, that such a legal framework will automatically (spontaneously) come about, whereas the Ordoliberals maintain that it has to be consciously created, subjecting economic consequences of particular measures to a rational assessment, similar to the one presented in Table 3.2.

The relation to *Transaction Cost Economics* is less straightforward. On the one hand, the abovementioned bond between American Institutionalism (especially the versions promulgated by J. R. Commons and W. C. Mitchel) and the German Historical School is to be named (Hutchison, 1984, pp. 21ff.). On the other hand, the exponents of 'New Institutionalism' themselves pointed out these connections. For example. Williamson (1985, p. 3) refers to Commons who was mentioned above as an indirect link.

The connections just mentioned lead to 'old' Institutionalism. 'New' Institutionalism (of which Transaction Cost Economics is a part) stresses the idea that the analysis of the effects of institutions requires a set of solid theoretical tools. Hereby a link to Ordoliberalism becomes visible: Transaction Cost Economics and Ordoliberalism not only correlate regarding a general institution-matter-thinking but also when calling for a sound theoretical basis. That is why I am personally inclined to relate Ordoliberalism to 'New' Institutionalism in this sense, even though it has emerged much earlier. But there are differences to Transaction Cost Economics as well: Proponents of the latter are – in contrast to Ordoliberals – particularly predisposed towards a business-oriented and organizational way of looking at matters: The problem of 'market or hierarchy' is analysed with respect to the costs of transactions. These, however, were not explicitly taken into account by the Ordoliberals but rather treated, in accordance with neoclassical tradition, as 'frictions of change' not to be of any relevance to a long-term analysis. Therefore, Transaction Cost Economics leave out from discussion a number of basic problems of economic policy dealt with by Ordoliberals and confine themselves to stressing that there are also macroeconomic effects of the microeconomic organization of the firm and that they are of relevance to anti-trust law. Therefore, their views of the role of competition law diverge gradually. On the one hand, the proponents of Transaction Cost Economics are inclined to the belief (expressed by Williamson, 1975, pp. 258ff.; 1985, pp. 365ff.) that cooperation and concentration as well as any form 'between market and hierarchy' can be applied much more extensively than has been suggested by the (neoclassical) production theory, not only from a firm's but also from society's point of view. They do not, however, recommend an extension as broad as that propagated by some members of the 'New' Chicago School, a view deemed a little extreme in European eyes and hinting at the character of Pangloss in Voltaire's *Candide ou l'optimisme* (Borchert and Grossekettler, 1985, pp. 165f.). On the other hand, the founders of Ordoliberalism always shared fully the neoclassical point of view, as do their successors even today. In consequence, they call for a much more hard-line anti-trust policy. If, however, Williamson's theory would prove to be valid, it could be embedded in the Ordoliberal philosophy without uprooting the core of the Ordoliberal theory.

The term 'Old Institutionalism' refers to economists claiming themselves to carry forward the tradition of Veblen, Ely and Commons or to those sympathatic to the *New School of Social Research*. Both groups have in common with Ordoliberals the institution matter thinking. Unlike them, however, they have a less libertarian way of looking at matters. For example, Ordoliberals – in contrast to American Institutionalists such as Galbraith – totally disapprove of price controls and similar *ad hoc* interventions by government authorities (in order to realize 'national goals', e.g. in form of growth programmes).[43] Instead, they concentrate on the *conditions* for development, i.e. in particular on order policy in the narrow sense and thus on the legal framework within which people are to make their free decisions. Not 'social planning' à la Clark but 'framework planning' à la Simons is their motto,[44] not the employment of governmental measures to achieve centrally set goals, binding upon each individual (positive planning) but an unreserved attitude towards all individual ends and means not contrary to certain prohibitions or minimum standards required (negative planning) is called for.[45]

The final subspecies of the Institutionalistic School to be mentioned here, the *Constitutional Choice Approach*, has a close relation to Ordoliberalism, a relation so close that indeed direct personal contacts could be expected. No such contact, however, has become known to me. I can only formulate the following hypothesis: As I have mentioned above (p. 40), Eucken has thoroughly studied Wicksell in advance to his *Kapitaltheoretische Untersuchungen,* thus having been inspired to or at least reinforced in his reflections on order policy. Wicksell, for his part, has been influential to one of the founders and protagonists of the Constitutional Choice Approach, J. M. Buchanan. The latter has translated Wicksell's (1962) *New Principle of Just Taxation* from German into English and has repeatedly confessed to Wicksell's ideas, last and above all in his lecture delivered when he received the Nobel Prize in Stockholm. A clue hinting at the validity of my above hypothesis can be found in Vanberg (1987): Vanberg, on the one hand, documents the close relationship between the approaches of Ordoliberalism and Constitutional Choice, on the other hand he points to an important difference in their principal line of thought. While proponents of the Constitutional Choice Approach concentrate on devising checks to tame the power of politicians and the state (referred to as 'leviathan'), Ordoliberals emphasize the taming of private power. Wicksell has presented his reflections in particular in his *Studies in the Theory of Finance (Finanztheoretische Untersuchungen*, 1896), and naturally Buchanan, researching in public finance, has followed Wicksell's line of thinking. In contrast, Eucken has – if my hypothesis holds true – rather followed the thought pattern of Wicksell's *Lectures (Vorlesungen,* 1913/1922), and at the same time he was impressed the particular situation to be found in pre-war-Germany, characterized by 'the rule of cartels'. This and Boehm's influence on him may have provoked Eucken to give priority to the taming of private power. But whether this hypothesis holds true or not: it can be said today that

Constitutional Economics and Ordoliberalism to a certain extent complement one another and that 'there are certainly sufficient affinities to allow for a faithful dialogue between the tradition of 'Ordungstheorie' and the yet emerging paradigm of "Constitutional Economics"' (Vanberg, 1987, p. 23).

4. Evaluation and criticism of the School

I shall now turn to the successes and failures of the School, in particular to its influence on German economic policy and to the teaching at universities.[46] As indicated in several places, the Ordoliberals had a remarkable influence in the 1950s and 1960s in universities and ministries, in Parliament and even on the formulation of the Treaties of Rome, the legal foundation of the European Community (Moeschel, 1987, p. 1). The question must be asked whether this speaks for the correctness of the long-term strategy of implementation which I described in section 2.3. The answer must be no, but mainly because the time from the end of the war until it succeeded was too short for such a strategy. The success of the Ordoliberals was rather to be attributed to the historical circumstances, which were closely associated with the name of Erhard: he was the 'political entrepreneur', working with the results of his own research and inspired by the ideas of Boehm, Eucken and Müller-Armack, who became the catalyst of the 'Social Market Economy' in politics. He was a promotor not only convinced of his mission, but also equipped with the tools of power to make it become reality.

Erhard, a student of F. Oppenheimer (1864–1947) who called himself a 'libertarian socialist' (V. Laitenberger, 1986, p. 16), worked from 1928 in the Nürnberg Institute for Economic Observation *(Institut für Wirtschaftsbeobachtung)* run by W. Vershofen, a market researcher. His antipathy towards the Nazi Party prevented Erhard from having a career in university teaching (Willenborg, 1979, p. 245), and, due to his *Weltanschauung,* his refusal to enter the German Worker's Front (Deutsche Arbeitsfront), a Nazi organization which had taken the place of the disbanded trade unions, led to his dismissal in 1942 (L. Herbst, 1982, p. 383). Personal animosities inside the Institute, however, also played a role here (Laitenberger, 1986, p. 34). Erhard founded the Institute for Industrial Research *(Institut für Industrieforschung)* in response (L. Herbst, 1982, pp. 383f.). Important German industrialists and representatives of the *Reichsgruppe Industrie* as well as representatives of planning offices were among his clients and correspondents (ibid., pp. 385ff.). The main area of his activity concerned the preparation for industrial changeover after the war (actively pursued by industry though this was forbidden) and also the problem of state-funded debt (ibid., p. 389).

This background explains why the Americans whose 'discovery' Erhard has called himself (1962, p. 8), appointed him Minister of Economics in Bavaria immediately after the war and later designated him, then an honorary professor at the University of Munich, a member of the Special Department for Money and Credit (*Sonderstelle Geld und Kredit*) in order to prepare the imminent currency reform (Willenborg, 1979, p. 245). On the one hand, Erhard was an expert with a clean record and with connections to industry as well as to former resistance groups. On the other hand, he had good relations with academics, especially to Ordoliberals and to the Erwin von Beckerath group (*Arbeitsgruppe Erwin von Beckerath*), which was influenced by Ordoliberalism. Müller-Armack, who had worked on liberal reform plans and had access to a wide variety of industrialists and researchers, became a trusted adviser.

Erhard, who was not a member of any political party, was elected Director of Economic Management in 1948 with help of the Free Democrats (then a Liberal Conservative party); the Christian Democratic Union (CDU), which he later joined, had strong reservations about this (Ambrosius, 1977, p. 156). In this way he attained a similar status to that of a Minister of Economics in the precursor of the Federal Republic and was commissioned to carry out the currency reform.[47] He was supported by Miksch, a member of the Freiburg School and Social Democrat who ran a department in the *Verwaltung für Wirtschaft* (directed by Erhard); they used the opportunity of the currency reform to release a number of important price controls, although this was disapproved of by the then suspicious Americans (Ambrosius, 1977, pp. 171–94).

The success of this start into a market economy strengthened Erhard's position, as did his connection with the CDU, which he later joined. It turned out to be politically very helpful that Müller-Armack, in contrast to the Ordoliberals in the narrow sense, placed more value on a supplementary social and business cycle policy than Eucken and linked the term 'social market economy' with this programme. In this way a framework which was acceptable to the labour wing of the CDU was brought into being[48] although the vagueness of the term 'social' threw a suspicious light on this economic programme in the eyes of the Ordoliberals in the narrow sense.[49]

All this shows that the great influence of the Ordoliberals on German economic policy, the resulting need for public officials who had been trained in the thinking of this school, and also the position of this school in the universities, were mainly determined by the historical situation. The success of its ideas helped it achieve more support among the people and civil servants than its strategy for implementation ever would have.[50] At the same time, one should not underestimate the long-term influence of this strategy. The people who had been trained at that time would have seen to it that the economic 'fashions' would be followed more moderately in Germany than in other countries and that, therefore, a regular development should be observed (Hutchison, 1981, pp. 166ff.).

One could ask two questions:

1. How far has the Ordoliberal *implementation strategy* (explained in section 2.3) proved successful in reaching the pursued economic order, in the light of the experiences made so far?
2. How have their *concepts for economic policy* been judged by academics?

I can say little in such a theoretical chapter on the history of economics to answer these questions, particularly because there has been insufficient debate in the literature on this subject.

One answer to be found in the literature to the first question (estimating the strategy's success) was that the Ordoliberals did not have an implementation strategy.[51] I refuted this in section 2.3. The basic idea of the Ordoliberals is that it is not enough to try to influence *today's* politicians, for they tend to cling to the convictions they have arrived at when they were young and, moreover, are inclined to an opportunistic bowing to the prevailing *Zeitgeist*. For this reason Ordoliberals want to call public attention to their economic order and also try to influence tertiary education so that politicians, civil servants and journalists of *tomorrow* will follow this programme in the future. In addition, to pursue policies complying with the market economy should not just be a 'moral duty' for politicians, but should lie in their own vested interests: Not only the 'push' of conscience but also the 'pull' of public opinion is to pave the way for the competition order. Finally, Ordoliberals strive for the transformation of the concepts of economics into legal language. These approaches might not amount to a sophisticated theory, but other schools do not have a more detailed one either. It is very difficult to evaluate this theory because, as I have explained, several exceptional historical circumstances contributed to its success. The decline in influence of the school after the mid-1960s can be partially explained by the wide scale of acceptance of the Keynesian theory which also attracted young German intellectuals; on the other hand, I agree with Olson (1982, pp. 75ff.) that the special interest groups became stronger than they were immediately after the war. Symptomatic of this resurgence is the fact that the passing of the law against restraints on competition was delayed for years and that Boehm was practically excluded from the final discussions with the representatives of industry (Mestmäcker, 1985, p. 49). In addition to that, I have the impression that ideas in the academic world often lose their appeal simply because they have become established.

As far as the second question (academic judgement on the concept for economic policy) is concerned, it can be said that the academic evaluation of *goals* in particular has been very controversial among German economists. There are those who, like Nawroth (1961), have in some ways a different view of the ends of a social economy. In this context, however, particularly those economists are to be mentioned, who accept politicians as 'machines for the setting of society's goals' and tend to confine themselves either to 'unpolitical' (*wertfreie*) positive research efforts or to a mere research into instruments and their deliberate effects as well as side-effects. Thus, anyone thinking this way would, expressed in terms of the above example concerning agricultural policy, be content to determine the minimum transaction cost alternative and point to potential side-effects, if the aim were to guarantee particular professions a regular subsidy. The Ordoliberal concept, in contrast, requires on top of that an evaluation of the aims to be pursued by given measures, particularly in respect of their general acceptance. Thereby, the politician's potential field of action will be diminished. Thus, a certain proposed action may only then be carried out in future, if politicians 'ascend to higher levels' in the hierarchy of means and ends in order to find a generally accepted aim compatible with some form of subsidy (or any other proposal), an aim which has, perhaps, so far not been seen. On this basis, then, measures are to be selected conforming to this generally accepted aim as well as to the economic order. In this context, order policy in the narrow sense (i.e. in form of general laws) will usually be given priority over a policy of specific and detailed regulations. Citing the example on agricultural policy again, this means investigating the legitimacy of the aims of the proposed subsidies. If the result of such an investigation pointed to deficiencies in the economic constitution, suitable measures should be designed according to the formula given in Table 3.2. In our example, a *general* law concerning subsidies would probably be drafted, regulating what kind of circumstances allow the use of subsidies and how they will be paid. The economists confining themselves to an 'instrumental view' reject limiting the politicians' setting of goals because they consider it a question of politics and thus outside the domain of science.

I do not share this opinion and believe the representatives of such views have their eyes closed to the results of public-choice research on distortions in the process of forming political opinion. It is my conviction that we can ascertain situations which will be declared a 'social nuisance' by *all* people not concerned and that the research into ways of avoiding such nuisances will, eventually, render results which will serve as a sound basis for economic action, just like a medical diagnosis of a disease serving as a sound foundation for the doctor's treatment of a patient. In accordance with Ordoliberalism, I maintain that economists have not completed their job when they have explained the functioning of the price mechanism. In addition they should win the public over to the cause of realizing conditions under which this functioning proves satisfactory. The founders of Ordoliberalism faced a number of social nuisances at their time: the formation of cartels and trusts, the resulting domination of markets and, eventually, of political decisions. They openly propagated the abolition of such an accumulation of power in private hands and advanced proposals for the way out. In my opinion this is a legitimate way of acting, even for a scientist, under the condition that the norms strived for are clearly laid out.

A second point of criticism was advanced by W. J. Samuels when discussing this paper at Harvard. The distinction between a 'frame' to be shaped in a way fostering the public good and free acts of free individuals within this frame sounds good, he maintains, but is ultimately an empty, and not an operational formula. This argument had not yet been discussed in Ordoliberal circles. Personally, I do not believe it to be adequate. The 'frame' of a competition order is formed by laws and by government agencies working on the basis of laws. Before passing them, however, these laws have, according to the Ordoliberal concept, to be subjected to the test presented in Table 3.2. Let us, for example, start with a rudimentary capitalist economy, the frame of which consists only of freedom of contract, of trade and choice of profession as well as consumers' sovereignty and the protection of private property, all of them being constitutionally guaranteed. Soon, we shall notice market deficiencies, such as the absence of anti-trust or patent law. So now, by applying the procedure of Table 3.2, we have to design a counter-measure, thereby completing the frame on our way to a satisfactory competition order. Once we have arrived at such a satisfactory competition order, we can talk about a maximization of freedom under *necessary* constraints (Grossekettler, 1984, pp. 37ff.): 'maximization of freedom' because individuals are now enabled to maximize their net utility by using all chances open to them, and 'under necessary constraints' because the legal frame ensures that all goals in common interest (e.g. in respect of collective goods and external effects) are pursued at least up to a certain minimum standard. In this way, the procedure of Table 3.2. can be characterized as a method of operationalization, i.e. a method to obtain an explanation of what is to be part of the 'frame'. It is a system of consciously set criteria to select among different schemes of shaping the social order and to ensure thereby an evolutionary process open to future experiences and developments, whose primary objective is the realization of the well-being of all individuals. It is the conscious setting of these criteria that marks the difference to the Liberals such as von Hayek who tend to rely on a system of law evolving spontaneously.

There are, however, two points of criticism implicitly included in Samuels' argument which seem justifiable to me. First, he refers to the fact that the procedure of Table 3.2 as such cannot be traced back to the literature written by the first generation of Ordoliberals, merely the cornerstones may be found there in a rather vague and rudimentary form.[52] Secondly, he remarks that the implementation of the competition order will be impeded by politicians who, naturally, are inclined to introduce laws serving only partial interests and refrain from tackling any reforms of potential inconvenience to themselves. My answer to this criticism is, first, that indeed there was a gap in the Ordoliberal literature, but the fact that there were no problems in filling this gap in drafting Table 3.2 proves the Ordoliberal ideas to be fundamental. Secondly, though it may not usually be the case that politicians act as true statesmen, we should not rule out the possibility completely. Have there not been laws passed [e.g. the law concerning the West German Federal Bank (*Deutsches Bundesbankgesetz*) and the *Gramm–Rudman Act*] documenting what I have just said? And has it not been proved in the past that an informed public can achieve a lot in this respect?

A third point of criticism, mentioned by J. C. O'Brien, is, in a way, related to what has just been discussed: Is it not true that people tend to focus on their individual goals, thereby neglecting the goals of common interest in day-to-day behaviour? Consequently, would not the political process then fail to employ a procedure such as the one presented in Table 3.2? When looking at the world of today, one may wholeheartedly agree with the view expressed here. But does that necessarily imply our inability to embody Ordoliberal principles in the laws forming the economic constitution? And will this procedure not rule out an exclusively individual behaviour at the expense of common interests? And have not the two laws just mentioned prove that politicians are in principle capable of accomplishing such a deed?

A further criticism of the Ordoliberals is that they did not elaborate sufficiently the transformation of their principles into operational definitions in the language of law. There is indeed a lot that has to be done here, because employable schemes amending the economic order must be formulated in a way that is legally applicable (Moeschel, 1987, p. 16). Above all, the concept of *vollständige Konkurrenz* (free competition) has been a problem. This is all the more true because structures and behaviour typically change in the course of market development. Perhaps one could make better progress if one avoided structural and behavioural criteria and were to develop instead observable indicators for the evaluation of the success of market *processes* in the coordination of plans. These processes are to aid the performing of the market functions, which have already been implicitly suggested by Eucken (1947, pp. 81f.). I mention here the process of the market clearance by functional variation of prices, the process of balancing the rates of return on capital by variation of capacity, and the process of continuous development of products and production techniques; an indicator valid for judging the quality of performance regarding the process of clearance of markets would be, for example, the rate of reducing queues.[53] But not only in the sector of anti-trust policy, is there a lack of clear ideas of how to apply the Ordoliberal principles, above all social policy and the structuring of public administration and finance.[54]

A fifth and final point of criticism has been proposed. Theories founded on empirical science must be open to attempts of falsification, and the replacement of falsified theories by theories having proved valid so far constitutes scientific progress. Considering this fact, is it not wrong, this criticism contends, to adjust the economic constitution to the state of the art, knowing that this may shortly be outdated? This, too, has not been discussed in Ordoliberal literature. But I think there is an answer. Although I concede that constitutions should be the calm eye at the centre of the hurricane of political development, they nevertheless must allow for the transitoriness of our knowledge and therefore have to be shaped in a way which leaves them open to revisions in the light of generally agreed future changes in our perception of how we should manage our affairs. This, by the way, not only applies with respect to our economic findings but above all to those in natural science and technical engineering.

5. Summary and outlook
I have described in this chapter the genesis and membership of the Freiburg School, the basic concepts of its programme (Ordoliberalism),

its political strategy for implementation of its policy, and the place of the School in the history of economic thought. The Ordoliberals developed guidelines based on economic theory for the creation and preservation of an economic order and for a system of laws to support that order. Their doctrine is closely related to that of the Chicago School and to the Constitutional Economics Approach, moreover it turned out to have common characteristics with American Institutionalism, and to the Historical School in Germany. The followers of this School had a theory for the transformation of economic knowledge into a planned system of institutions and institutional change. I discussed whether the theory of how to change institutions has proved successful or not in the case of the Federal Republic of Germany. I concluded that the question could not be answered definitively because too many contemporary factors prevailed at the time we were talking about.

The Ordoliberals were criticized for not refraining from expressing an opinion on goals and their compatibility with the 'competition order'. Moreover, the definition of the 'frame' was said to be vague. It was contended that the belief in the occurrence of a true competition order is nothing but wishful thinking. The problem of tying economic orders too firmly to the economic state of the art was mentioned. These points of criticism have been discussed and at least modified. The weak points of the development of the Ordoliberal conception lie in the insufficient transformation of economic guidelines into legal language and the inadequately specified operational criteria needed for judicial decisions. Of particular prominence in this connection are the problems which are connected with the concept of 'free competition'. Efforts are being made to develop the Ordoliberal concepts further. These efforts should concentrate on the construction and testing of operationally defined indicators, on making the model more dynamic, and on additional principles and institutional suggestions for the structurizing and managing of the public sector itself and for social policy in the wider sense.

Notes
1. I am indebted to Prof. H. O. Lenel, Prof. W. Moeschel and Prof. V. Vanberg for having made available to me manuscripts of forthcoming works on similar topics, and to my assistants M. Koch, Th. Krämer, J. Scheube, R. Schulte, and G. Schwarzner for their help and criticism.
2. With respect to the teachings and writings of Walter Eucken's cf. T. W. Hutchison (1981, pp. 155ff.), W. A. Joehr (1950), H. O. Lenel (1987a), F. A. Lutz (1961), and J. W. N. Watkins (1952). Lenel and Lutz are students of Eucken. The supervisor of Eucken's doctoral dissertation was Hermann Schumacher, a member of the Later Historical School, to whom I will return.
3. The titles of German books and quotes in German have been translated into English.

One can tell from the bibliography whether the original was written in German or in English.

4. Eucken's *moral* rejection of the Hitler regime can be seen in his cooperation with the resistance (see below); his rejection *in economic terms* was expressed in his paper (at that time a very courageous act) *Competition as an Underlying Principle of Economic 'Constitution' (Wettbewerb als Grundprinzip der Wirtschaftsverfassung*, 1942) and in *Theory of the Centrally Administered Economy* (1948).

5. For Boehm's life and work cf. H. Sauermann and E. J. Mestmaecker (1975) as well as *In the Beginning (In der Stunde Null*, 1979) and *Law and Morals in a Free Society (Recht und Gesittung in einer freien Gesellschaft*, 1985).

6. Cf. the personal portrayals by Nahum Goldmann and Felix E. Shinnar in Sauermann – Mestmaecker (1975, pp. 23ff., 29ff.).

7. Three more books in this series appeared shortly afterwards: H. Gestrich (1936), F. Lutz (1936) and L. Miksch (1937). The books started a lively discussion (H. Moeller, 1939, with further references).

8. Boehm refers to F. A. von Hayek (1953) and to the fact that this impressive point of view, especially for lawyers, was only to be elaborated in detail later (namely in 1953) and that it was the economist von Hayek, who did it. One should also mention here that although von Hayek was close to the Freiburg School, he differed from it in at least one major point; more about this later.

9. Carl Friedrich Gördeler (1884–1945) was the leader of the non-communist resistance to Hitler and had already been designated as Hitler's successor by this group. After C. Graf Schenk von Stauffenberg's (1907–1944) attempt to assassinate Hitler on 20 July 1944, Goerdeler was executed as was Stauffenberg. Some members of the Freiburg group who had worked with Goerdeler due to indignation about the persecution of the Jews, were arrested in connection with the attempted assassination of Hitler; they were saved a much worse fate though, mostly due to the end of the war, which soon followed. Lampe, however, died in 1948 from the effects of his imprisonment in a concentration camp. Cf. *In the Beginning (In der Stunde Null*, 1979) and Chr. Blumenberg-Lampe (1973) and (1986). (Chr. Blumenberg-Lampe is A. Lampe's daughter.) Cf. also the collection of materials on the German resistance (Weisenborn, 1981) by Ricarda Huch (Boehm's mother-in-law, a well-known author of poems and stories). With regard to von Dietze it should be particularly noted that he inspired the disbandment of the *Verein für Socialpolitik* (the scientific association of German economists) during the Third Reich in protest to attempts of administrational encroachments (Helmstädter, 1987, p. 159).

10. This definition cannot be found in the literature. It can only be inferred from the use of language in the School, especially in the work of Boehm and Miksch, and from additional work done in the 1950s and 1960s. See Borchert and Grossekettler (1985, pp. 134ff.) and E. -W. F. Duerr (1954, pp. 75ff. and pp. 152ff.).

11. One could also use the expression 'unrestrained competition', but it might have a negative connotation. H. M. Oliver (1960, p. 137) used 'complete competition' in a very informative review for the same reasons I do. Riha (1985, p. 201) used the same expression in his impressive book *German Political Economy*. I would like to avoid this expression, however, because the use of the term 'complete' as a collocation with 'competition' has caused a lot of confusion among German-speaking economists. If one understood by the terms 'perfect' or 'complete' competition in Gideonse's sense (1953, p. 168) merely the lack of friction in the movement of the factors of production and in the adjustment of prices, then these terms would be very close to the term used by the Freiburg School. However, this is usually not the case.

12. Because free competition was required to prevail the Ordoliberals called the economy they were trying to achieve 'Wettbewerbsordnung'. Cf. Eucken (1949; 1975, p. 240). This expression should be literally translated as 'competition order' or as 'competitive order'. One should note that this is an abbreviation for 'an economic system in which the decentralized, individual decisions are coordinated by competitive market processes'. The expression 'Soziale Marktwirtschaft' which is used to

describe the economy of the Federal Republic of Germany, as I shall show later, only appeared later, originating in politics. It would be literally translated as 'social market economy'; H. C. Wallich (1955, p. 114) translated it more adequately as 'socially conscious free market economy'.

13. To gain an impression of the situation, cf., for example, N. Balabkin's (1964, pp. 103 ff.) account of 'food rationing' or 'Das Parlament' (1987).

14. Cf. Eucken (1975, pp. 254 ff., 301).

15. H. Alsmoeller (1982, pp. 80ff.) listed the indicators of market power which one can find in Ordoliberal writings. L. Miksch (1947, p. 36) required a 'special economic law' for areas which neither have nor can have free competition; this law was to go beyond the 'general economic law' and to regulate the method of constant adjustments.

16. Lenel (1987a, p. 26) points out quite rightly that when one believes that environmental protection was only recognized in the 1960s and 1970s, one shows a weakness in knowledge of the literature.

17. The basic idea of the table is, however, to be found in Boehm (1950, p. xxxiii), though admittedly in much less detail and not in the form of a table.

18. The basic features of this double test can be traced back to Kant (Homann, 1985, with further references), whose influence on Eucken was particularly great.

19. This aim is hypothetical for illustration purposes. However, real-life agricultural policies in the European Community (and similarly in the USA) come close to such an aim. Cf. in this context C. Avery (1987).

20. If instruments are proposed that are clearly ineffective as regards the declared goal, the declared goal is often only an excuse. The real aim is then different – in our example, perhaps to calm public discontent and to create the false impression of firm leadership until the next general election.

21. For example, if prices rise in times of great shortage and fall in times of plenty, many people will intuitively see this as reprehensible 'pickpocketing'. It could easily be shown by public opinion surveys that this attitude is very common. It results from ignorance or an underestimation of the guiding function of prices, and it also encourages political intervention that is equally wrong from the point of view of the economic order.

22. Cf. Eucken (1975, pp. 248f.) and in the same sense Gideonse (1953, p. 173, with further references).

23. Cf. the very similar distinction in Lachmann (1963), who speaks of 'external' institutions (those imposed on the economy by the state), 'internal' ones (those that come into existence within the private sector of the economy) and 'neutral' ones, these last being neither 'internal' nor 'external'.

24. Cf. Boehm (1950, pp. lxiiif.) and Eucken (1947, pp. 54ff.).

25. Cf. Hutchison (1981, p. 155) and J. Herbst (1965, p. 175). Herbst points particularly to Americans who had similar ideas and had been trained in Germany. Later, the resistance movement followed a related idea when stating that the population should be informed about economic matters and thus be immunized against erroneous opinions and ideologies. See the moving farewell letter written by Gördeler shortly before his execution, 'Thoughts of a Man Condemned to Death' (Gördeler, 1944). This view also resulted from the fact that Hitler had managed to get the population on his side with (short-term) economic successes, which impressed the outside world as well: 'Hitler . . . had already found how to cure unemployment before Keynes had finished explaining why it had occurred' (Robinson, 1972, p. 8).

26. Cf. *Frankfurter Allgemeine Zeitung* (1983, p. 55); and J. Eick (1985, p. 71).

27. Cf. the remarkable publication to mark the 200th anniversary of the *Neue Züricher Zeitung* (1979, eds. Linder, Helbling and Buetler).

28. Cf. Boehm (1950, especially pp. liiff.).

29. I doubt whether the accusation of too extreme a *laissez-faire* is justified in the case of Smith in particular. One must bear in mind that Smith was primarily writing *against* mercantilism and was thus putting forward what were above all counterproposals. If

he had managed to write his planned book on 'Government', the Ordoliberals would presumably not have been able to reach such a clear verdict. This also seems to be the view of Hutchison (1981, p. 163) who writes: 'the distinctive Freiburg contribution, with its concern for the legal and institutional order, is much closest, methodologically, to the original Glasgow source of Adam Smith.'

30. With respect to the Chicago School and particularly the classification of an old and a new branch, cf. W. J. Samuels (1976).

31. For the characteristics of the Chicago School, see especially W. J. Samuels (1976), M. W. Reder (1982), the further literature given by Borchert and Grossekettler (1985, pp. 161ff.) and the recent I. Schmidt and J. B. Rittaler (1986), which is highly critical but not always convincing.

32. O. von Nell-Breuning (1975, pp. 469f.), long adviser to the Pope in economic matters, uses the above formulation in a report of a discussion between himself and Boehm, which clearly ended on a most conciliatory tone.

33. This can also be seen in the relevant German textbooks, for example N. Monzel (1967) or H. Weber (1970). A detailed criticism of Ordoliberalism from the Catholic point of view can be found in E. E. Nawroth (1961). He is a Dominican and prominent representative of the Catholic doctrine on social affairs. I cannot explain in depth this discussion. Understandable for a Catholic, Nawroth founds his arguments on the medieval (and in particular scholastic) *disputatio de universalibus (Universalienstreit)*. From his 'realistic' (Thomist) platform he rejects Ockham's 'nominalism' which, he believes, is propagated by Eucken. Disregarding the basic points of view towards the *disputatio de universalibus* will Ordoliberalists and representatives of the Catholic Church be able to agree on specific economic goals in most cases.

34. The table shows only the most important connections and contains only those names relevant to a stream of ideas between different schools. In other words, not all members of a particular school are mentioned. The numbers appearing with arrows and schools indicate the page number or note (marked with an n) in this chapter where cues to further references are given.

35. Concerning the relation of Knies to Boehm-Bawerk/Wieser, cf. C. Brinkmann (1956, p. 136); concerning the relation of Knies to Ely, cf. A. W. Coats (1968, p. 33). Boehm-Bawerk, on his part, was von Mises' teacher, students of whom were, among others, von Haberler, Halm, Machlup, Morgenstern and von Hayek (M. N. Rothbard, 1968, p. 380).

36. Cf. J. Dorfmann (1968, p. 22). Commons has made himself acquainted with German literature, above all with Wagner's *Textbook on Political Economy* (*Lehrbuch der Politischen Oekonomie*). Cf. L. G. Harter (1962, p. 215).

37. Schmoller has written his doctoral thesis (a prized paper induced by C. von Schütz) on the economic views prevailing in Germany at the time of the reformation, published in the *Zeitschrift für die gesamte Staatswissenschaft*, vol. 16 (1860), pp. 461–716. There he admitted having learned most from Knies. Cf. in this context C. Brinkmann (1937, pp. 19ff.). He was offered his first professorship in Halle having written a paper on the trade census in Württemberg in 1861 which he had directed together with his brother-in-law, G. Ruemelin. This paper thus represented his habilitation thesis. Roscher was, at least at the beginning of Schmoller's career, very much admired by Schmoller, who promoted the young Schmoller. An extensive correspondence between them illustrates this (W. Ed. Biermann, 1922).

38. For more on this, see Coats (1960, p. 556).

39. On H. Schumacher, cf. E. Welter (1952), a student of Schumacher (ibid.), and S. Wendt (1956). Amongst other things, Schumacher was the first Kaiser Wilhelm Professor at Columbia University (in 1906) where he was later given an honorary doctorate (ibid.).

40. For more on F. Oppenheimer cf. B. Schultz (1954).

41. In the interview just quoted (Seuss, 1987), Friedman gave proof of his excellent memory for minor events: 'There [at the foundation meeting in Vevey/Switzerland]

Walter Eucken has, for the first time after the war, eaten an orange' he told the interviewer.

42. Cf. on this, among others, R. L. Reynolds (1985) who relates the Property Rights Approach by Furuboton and Pejovich to the work of Ely.

43. Anyone thinking this way will rather find Schmoller to be a like-minded ancestor. The latter is not totally opposed to cartels, for example, and even has anticipated basic elements of the concept of 'countervailing power' (Schmoller, 1923, pp. 537ff.).

44. For more on J. M. Clark's ideas on planning an economy and those of other Institutionalists cf. A. G. Gruchy (1968, pp. 464f.). Also cf. A. Montaner (1948) for American Institutionalism in general. The connections between the Historical School and American Institutionalism and between Schmoller and Veblen in particular are refered to on pp. 49ff.

45. This difference in approach may partly be responsible for the disappointment of a number of representatives of the New School for Social Research – the 'University in Exile' – about Erhard's economic policy, a policy which, of course, appears utterly conservative in the light of Lowe's 'instrumental analysis' and 'good function order'. Cf. C.-D. Krohn for the New School for Social Research. For more details on A. Lowe's ideas cf. ibid., pp. 171ff.

46. I am not going to discuss German economic policy itself. If one ignores early comments of English socialists, it is generally considered successful. Cf. (in chronological order) Wallich (1955), Stolper-Roskamp (1979), Hutchison (1981), or 'The Right to Smile' (1986).

47. Non-Germans should be reminded that the Federal Republic of Germany only came into being in 1949. Between 1945 and 1949 there were only various degrees of cooperation among the parts of the western zones of occupation. For details on the postwar circumstances, cf. N. Balabkins (1964) and a collection of articles in the journal *Das Parlament* (1987) on the so-called '*Bizone*' preceding the Federal Republic, containing eye-witness reports and further literature.

48. For the beginnings of the social market economy, cf. Ambrosius (1977), 'Müller-Armack (1974) and (1981), Nicholls (1984) and Starbatty (1986).

49. It would be incorrect to contend that the Ordoliberals in the narrow sense were or are opposed to 'social policy measures'. As has been pointed out in the example of agricultural subsidies, they would, however, require such measures to pass the test of Table 3.2 and interpret them as a generally agreed upon insurance.

50. Erhard (1962, p. 8) later expressed the doubt that his radical policy would have been possible in a democracy in normal times.

51. K. Borchardt (1981, p. 47) expressed this opinion; however, he used the broader expression 'theory of institutional change' (*Theorie des institutionellen Wandels*).

52. There are different 'generations' of Ordoliberals to be distinguished: Eucken, Boehm, and their contemporaries form the first generation, the second one consists of their students (such as Lenel and Mestmäcker), and the third one is represented by the students of the students (e.g. Moeschel).

53. For a further development of order policy in that direction cf. the explanations concerning the so called *Koordinationsmängelkonzept* (identification concept for coordination deficiencies) in Borchert/Grossekettler (1985, pp. 170ff.).

54. Cf. Grossekettler (1984) and Kloten (1986).

References

Alsmoeller, H. (1982), *Wettbewerbspolitische Ziele und kooperationstheoretische Hypothesen im Wandel der Zeit. Eine dogmengeschichtliche Untersuchung von Einstellungen zu Verbundsystemen und von Gründen für diese Einstellungen*, Tübingen: Mohr.

Ambrosius, G. (1977), *Die Durchsetzung der sozialen Marktwirtschaft in Westdeutschland 1945–1949*, Stuttgart: Deutsche Verlagsanstalt.

Avery, G. (1987), 'Agriculture policy: European options and American comparisons',

European Affairs, no. 1/87, pp. 62–74.
Balabkins, N. (1964), *Germany Under Direct Controls. Economic Aspects of Industrial Disarmement 1945–1948*, New Brunswick, NJ: Rutgers University Press.
Biermann, W. Ed. (1922), *Briefwechsel zwischen Wilhelm Roscher und Gustav Schmoller-Wilhelm Stieda. Zwei Beiträge zur Literaturgeschichte der Nationalökonomie*, Greifswald.
Blumenberg-Lampe, Chr. (1973), *Das wirtschaftspolitische Programm der 'Freiburger Kreise'. Entwurf einer freiheitlich-sozialen Nachkriegswirtschaft. Nationaloekonomen gegen den Nationalsozialismus*, Berlin: Duncker & Humblot.
Blumenberg-Lampe, Chr. (ed.) (1986), *Der Weg in die Soziale Marktwirtschaft. Referate, Protokolle, Gutachten der Arbeitsgemeinschaft Erwin von Beckerath 1943–1947*, Stuttgart: Klett-Cotta.
Boehm, F. (1933), *Wettbewerb und Monopolkampf. Eine Untersuchung zur Frage des wirtschaftlichen Kampfrechts und zur Frage der rechtlichen Struktur der geltenden Wirtschaftsordnung*, Berlin: Heymanns.
Boehm, F. (1937), *Die Ordnung der Wirtschaft als geschichtliche Aufgabe und rechtsschoepferische Leistung*. Nebst Einleitung der Herausgeber, Stuttgart and Berlin: Kohlhammer.
Boehm, F. (1950), 'Die Idee des ORDO im Denken Walter Euckens. Dem Freunde und Mitherausgeber zum Gedaechtnis', *ORDO*, vol. 3, pp. xv–lxiv.
Boehm, F. (1957), Die Forschungs- und Lehrgemeinschaft zwischen Juristen und Volkswirten an der Universitaet Freiburg in den dreißiger und vierziger Jahren des 20. Jahrhunderts, in: H. J. Wolff (ed.), *Aus der Geschichte der Rechts- und Staatswissenschaften zu Freiburg i. Br.*, Freiburg: E. Albert, pp. 95–113.
Borchardt, K. (1981), Die Konzeption der Sozialen Marktwirtschaft in heutiger Sicht, in O. Issing (ed.), *Zukunftsprobleme der Sozialen Marktwirtschaft*, Berlin: Duncker and Humblot, pp. 33–53.
Borchert M. and Grossekettler, H. (1985), *Preis- und Wettbewerbstheorie. Marktprozesse als analytisches Problem und ordnungspolitische Gestaltungsaufgabe*, Stuttgart etc.: Kohlhammer.
Brinkmann, C. (1937), *Gustav Schmoller und die Volkswirtschaftslehre*, Stuttgart.
Brinkmann, C. (1956), 'Schmoller, Gustav', in E. von Beckerath et al. (eds), *Handwörterbuch der Sozialwissenschaften*, vol. 9, Stuttgart: Fischer, Tuebingen: Mohr, Göttingen: Vandenhoeck & Ruprecht, pp. 135–7.
Buchanan, J. M. (1987), 'The constitution of economic policy', *American Economic Review*, vol. 77, pp. 243–50.
Coats, A. W. (1960), 'The first two decades of the American Economic Association', *American Economic Review*, vol. L., pp. 555–74.
Coats, A. W. (1968), 'Ely, Richard T.', in D. Sills (ed.), *International Encyclopedia of the Social Sciences*, vol. 5, London: Macmillan and New York: Free Press, pp. 33–5.
Commons, J. R. (1934), *Institutional Economics*, Madison: University of Wisconsin Press.
Demsetz, H. (1967), 'Towards a theory of property rights', *American Economic Review*, Papers and Proceedings, vol. 57, pp. 347–359.
Dorfmann, J. (1968), 'Commons, John R.', in D. Sills (ed.), *International Encyclopedia of the Social Sciences*, vol. 3, London: Macmillan and New York: Free Press, pp. 22–4.
Duerr, E.-W. F. (1954), *Ordoliberalismus und Sozialpolitik*, (Diss.) Winterthur: Keller.
Eick, J. (ed., 1985), *So nutzt man den Wirtschaftsteil der Tageszeitung*, Frankfurt: Societas-Verlag.
Erhard, L. (1962), *Deutsche Wirtschaftspolitik. Der Weg der Sozialen Marktwirtschaft*, Düsseldorf Wien: Econ, Frankfurt: Knapp.
Eucken, W. (1923), *Kritische Betrachtungen zum deutschen Geldproblem*, Jena: Fischer.
Eucken, W. (1932), 'Staatliche Strukturwandlung und die Krisis des Kapitalismus', *Weltwirtschaftliches Archiv*, vol. 36, pp. 297–321.
Eucken, W. (1942), 'Wettbewerb als Grundprinzip der Wirtschaftsverfassung', in G. Schmoelders (ed.), *Der Wettbewerb als Mittel volkswirtschaftlicher Leistungssteigerung und Leistungsauslese*, Berlin: Duncker & Humblot, pp. 29–49.

Eucken, W. (1947), *Nationaloekonomie wozu?*, 3rd extended edn, Godesberg: Kuepper.
Eucken, W. (1948), 'On the theory of the centrally administered economy: an analysis of the German experiment', translated by T. W. Hutchison, *Economica*, n.s., vol. 15, pp. 79–100 (Part I), and pp. 173–93 (Part II).
Eucken, W. (1949), 'Die Wettbewerbsordnung und ihre Verwirklichung,' *ORDO*, vol. 2, pp. 1–99.
Eucken, W. (1954), *Kapitaltheoretische Untersuchungen*, 2nd edn, supplemented by three articles with an introduction by F. A. Lutz: Die Entwicklung der Zinstheorie seit Boehm-Bawerk,Tübingen: Mohr, Zürich: Polygraphischer Verlag (first published in 1934).
Eucken, W. (1965), *Die Grundlagen der Nationaloekonomie*, 8th unrevised edn, Berlin-Heidelberg–New York: Springer. (First published in 1940, 6th edn (of last revision) 1950.)
Eucken, W. (1975), *Grundsätze der Wirtschaftspolitik*, posthumously ed. by E. Eucken and K. P. Hensel, 5th edn, Tübingen: Mohr (first published in 1952).
Frankfurter Allgemeine Zeitung (ed.) (1983), *Dokumentation 'Alles über die Zeitung'*, 16th, compl. rev. edn, Frankfurt: FAZ-Verlag.
Gestrich, H. (1936), *Neue Kreditpolitik*, Stuttgart and Berlin: Kohlhammer.
Gideonse, H. D. (1953), 'Die Steuerung der Wirtschaft durch den Wettbewerb als Ziel der amerikanischen Wirtschaftspolitik,' in L. Einaudi et al., *Wirtschaft ohne Wunder*, Erlenbach-Zürich: Rentsch, pp. 158–86.
Gördeler, C. (1944), 'Gedanken eines zum Tode Verurteilten – September 1944 im Gefängnis: über den künftigen inneren Zustand Deutschlands', Anhang 1, pp. 553–60, in G. Ritter (1954), *Carl Goerdeler und die deutsche Widerstandsbewegung*, Stuttgart: Deutsche Verlags-Anstalt.
Grossekettler, H. (1984), 'Verwaltungsstrukturpolitik', in H. -J. Ewers and H. Schuster (eds), *Probleme der Ordnungs- und Strukturpolitik*, Festschrift für H. St. Seidenfus zum 60. Geburtstag, Göttingen: Vandenhoeck & Ruprecht, pp. 16–51.
Gruchy, A. G. (1968), 'Economic thought VII: The Institutional School', in D. L. Sills (ed.), *International Encyclopedia of the Social Sciences*, vol. 4, London: Macmillan and New York: Free Press, pp. 462–7.
Harter, Jr, L. G. (1962), *John R. Commons – His Assault on Laissez-faire*, Corvallis, Oregon: Oregon State University Press.
von Hayek, F. A. (1953), 'Entstehung und Verfall des Rechtsstaatsideals', in L. Einaudi et al., *Wirtschaft ohne Wunder*, Erlenbach-Zürich: Rentsch, pp. 33–65.
von Hayek, F. A. (1967), 'Grundsätze einer liberalen Gesellschaftsordnung', *ORDO*, vol. 18, pp. 11–33.
Heckscher, E. F. (1932), *Der Merkantilismus*, vol. 1, Jena: Fischer.
Helmstaedter, E. (1987), 'Vor fünfzig Jahren: Selbstauflösung des Vereins für Socialpolitik, in *Zeitschrift für Wirtschafts- und Sozialwissenschaften*, vol. 107, pp. 159–61.
Herbst, J. (1965), *The German Historical School in American Scholarship. A Study in the Transfer of Culture*, Ithaca, New York: Cornell University Press.
Herbst, L. (1982), *Der Totale Krieg und die Ordnung der Wirtschaft. Die Kriegswirtschaft im Spannungsfeld von Politik, Ideologie und Propaganda 1939–1945*, Stuttgart: Deutsche Verlags-Anstalt.
Herkner, H. (1924), 'Zur Stellung G. Schmollers in der Geschichte der Nationaloekonomie, in *Schmollers' Jahrbuch für Gesetzgebung, Verwaltung und Volkswirtschaft im Deutschen Reiche*, vol. 47, pp. 3–10.
Homann, K. (1985), 'Legitimation und Verfassungsstaat. Vertragstheoretische Interpretation der Demokratie', in *Jahrbuch für Neue Politische Oekonomie*, vol. 4, pp. 48–72.
Hutchison, T. W. (1981), *The Politics and Philosophy of Economics. Marxians, Keynesians and Austrians*, Oxford: Basil Blackwell.
Hutchison, T. W. (1984), 'Institutionalist economics old and new', *Zeitschrift für die gesamte Staatswissenschaft*, vol. 140, pp. 20–9.
Joehr, W. A. (1950), 'Walter Euckens Lebenswerk', *Kyklos*, vol. 4, pp. 257–78.
Keynes, J. M. (1936), *The General Theory of Employment, Interest and Money*, London:

Macmillan.

Kloten, N. (1986), *Der Staat in der Sozialen Marktwirtschaft*, Tübingen: Mohr.

Krohn, C. D. (1987), *Wissenschaft im Exil. Deutsche Sozial- und Wirtschaftswissenschaftler in den USA und die New School for Social Research*, Frankfurt and New York: Campus.

Lachmann, L. M. (1963), 'Wirtschaftsordnung und wirtschaftliche Institutionen', *ORDO*, vol. 14, pp. 63–77.

Laitenberger, V. (1986), *Ludwig Erhard. Der Nationaloekonom als Politiker*, Göttingen and Zürich: Muster-Schmidt.

Lenel, H. O. (1987a), 'Walter Eucken', in J. Starbatty (ed.), *Klassiker des oekonomischen Denkens*, München: Beck. Forthcoming, references refer to the manuscript.

Lenel, H. O. (1987b), 'The concept of an "economic order" and the social market economy', in *The Political and Economic Thought of German Neoliberalism*, Volume in preparation by the Trade Policy Research Centre, London: Macmillan.

Linder, W., Helbling, H. and Buetler, H. (eds) (1979), *Liberalismus – nach wie vor*, Zürich: NZZ-Verlag.

Lippmann, W. (1937), *An Inquiry into the Principles of the Good Society*, Boston: Little, Brown.

Lutz, F. A. (1936), *Das Grundproblem der Geldverfassung*, Stuttgart and Berlin: Kohlhammer.

Lutz, F. A. (1961), 'Eucken, Walter', in E. von Beckerath et al. (eds), *Handwörterbuch der Sozialwissenschaften*, vol. 3, Stuttgart: Fischer, Tübingen: Mohr, Göttingen: Vandenhoeck & Ruprecht, pp. 353–6.

Mercier de la Riviére, P. F. (1767), *L'Ordre naturel et essential des sociétés politiques*, London: Nourse, Paris: Desaint.

Mestmäcker, E.-J. (1985), 'Ansprache zur Erinnerung an Franz Boehm aus Anlaß des 90. Geburtstages', in *Recht und Gesittung in einer freien Gesellschaft*, Bonn: Ludwig-Erhard-Stifung, pp. 49–52.

Meyer, W. (1983), 'Entwicklung und Bedeutung des Property-Rights-Ansatzes in der Nationaloekonomie', in A. Schueller (ed.), *Property Rights und oekonomische Theorie*, München: Vahlen, pp. 1–44.

Miksch, L. (1937), *Wettbewerb als Aufgabe. Die Grundsätze einer Wettbewerbsordnung*, Stuttgart and Berlin: Kohlhammer.

Miksch, L. (1947), *Wettbewerb als Aufgabe. Grundsätze einer Wettbewerbsordnung*, 2nd extended edn, Godesberg: Kuepper.

Moeller, H. (1939), 'Ordnung der Wirtschaft. Bemerkungen zu der Schriftenreihe "Ordnung der Wirtschaft" ', in *Archiv für mathematische Wirtschafts- und Sozialforschung*, vol. 5, pp. 130–42.

Moeller, H. (1983), *Zur Theorie und Politik der Wirtschaftsordnung*, Tübingen: Mohr.

Moeschel, W. (1985), 'Das Kartellgesetz heute – aus ordoliberaler Sicht', in *Recht und Gesittung in einer freien Gesellschaft*, Bonn: Ludwig-Erhard-Stiftung, pp. 35–48.

Moeschel, W. (1987), 'Wettbewerbspolitik aus ordoliberaler Sicht', in *Festschrift für Gerd Pfeiffer*, Köln–Berlin–Bonn–München: Carl Heymanns.

Montaner, A. (1948), *Der Institutionalismus als Epoche amerikanischer Geistesgeschichte*, Tübingen: Mohr.

Monzel, N. (1967), *Katholische Soziallehre*, vol. 2: *Familie, Staat, Wirtschaft, Kultur*, posthumously ed. by T. Herweg with the assistance of K. H. Grenner, Köln: Bachem.

Müller-Armack, A. (1966), *Wirtschaftsordnung und Wirtschaftspolitik. Studien und Konzepte zur Sozialen Marktwirtschaft und zur Europäischen Integration*, Freiburg i. Br.: Rombach.

Müller-Armack, A. (1974), 'Die Anfänge der Sozialen Marktwirtschaft – Zugleich eine Dokumentation ihrer Entwicklung in den Jahren 1945, 1946, 1947, 1948', in R. Loewenthal and H.-P. Schwarz (eds), *Die zweite Republik. 25 Jahre Bundesrepublik Deutschland – eine Bilanz*, Stuttgart: Seewald, pp. 123–48.

Müller-Armack, A. (1981), *Genealogie der Sozialen Marktwirtschaft. Frühschriften und weiterführende Konzepte*, 2nd extended edn, Bern and Stuttgart: Haupt.

Nawroth, E. E. (1961), *Die Sozial- und Wirtschaftsphilosophie des Neoliberalismus*, Heidelberg: Herle and Loewen: Nauwelaerts.
von Nell-Breuning, S. J. O. (1975),'Können Neoliberalismus und katholische Soziallehre sich verständigen?', in H. Sauermann and E. and J. Mestmaecker (eds), *Wirtschaftsordnung und Staatsverfassung*, Tübingen: Mohr, pp. 459–70.
Nicholls, A. J. (1984), 'Das andere Deutschland – Die "Neoliberalen"', in *Zeitschrift für Wirtschaftspolitik*, vol. 33, pp. 241–59.
North, D. C. (1986), 'The New Institutional Economics', *Journal of Institutional and Theoretical Economics (JITE)*, vol. 142, pp. 230–37.
Oliver Jr, H. M. (1960), 'German neoliberalism,' *Quarterly Journal of Economics* vol. 74, pp. 117–49.
Olson, M. (1982), *The Rise and Decline of Nations. Economic Growth, Stagflation, and Social Rigidities*, New Haven and London: Yale University Press.
Das Parlament (1987), *Vor 40 Jahren: die Bizone*, Supplement to 'Das Parlament', 8 August 1987, vol. 37, no. 32.
Partsch, K. J. (1954), 'Die verfassungsmaeßige Sicherung von Wirtschaftsprinzipien', *ORDO*, vol. 6, pp. 19–38.
Rauscher, A. (1977), 'Soziallehre, kirchliche', in W. Albers et al. (eds), *Handwörterbuch der Wirtschaftswissenschaft*, vol. 7, Stuttgart–New York: Fischer, Tübingen: Mohr, Goettingen: Vandenhoeck & Ruprecht, pp. 41–51.
Recht und Gesittung in ener freien Gesellschaft (1985), Vortragsveranstaltung zur Erinnerung an Franz Boehm aus Anlaß des 90. Geburtstages, Bonn: Ludwig-Erhard-Stiftung.
Reder, M. W. (1982), 'Chicago Economics: permanence and change', *Journal of Economic Literature*, vol. 20, pp. 1–38.
Reynolds, R. L. (1985), 'Institutionally Determined Property Claims', *Journal of Economic Issues*, vol. 19, pp. 941–9.
'The Right to Smile' (1986), A survey of West Germany, *The Economist*, 6–12 December.
Riha, T. (1985), *German Political Economy: The History of an Alternative Economics*, Bradford: MCB University Press (International Journal of Social Economics, vol. 12, no. 3/4/5).
Robinson, J. (1972), 'The second crisis of economic theory', *American Economic Review, Papers and Proceedings*, vol. 62, pp. 1–10.
Röpke, W. (1942), *Die Gesellschaftskrisis der Gegenwart*, Erlenbach–Zürich: Rentsch.
Rothbard, M. N. (1968), Article 'von Mises, Ludwig', in D. L. Sills (ed.), *International Encyclopedia of the Social Sciences*, vol. 16, London: Macmillan and New York: Free Press, pp. 379–82.
Samuels, W. J. (ed.) (1976), *The Chicago School of Political Economy*, East Lansing: Michigan State University.
Sauermann H. and Mestmäcker, E. -J. (eds) (1975), *Wirtschaftsordnung und Staatsverfassung. Festschrift für Franz Boehm zum 80. Geburtstag*, Tübingen: Mohr.
Schmidt, I. and Rittaler, J. B. (1986), *Die Chicago School of Antitrust Analysis. Wettbewerbstheoretische und -politische Analyse eines Credos*, Baden-Baden: Nomos.
Schmoller, G. (1860), 'Zur Geschichte der national-oekonomischen Ansichten in Deutschland während der Reformations-Periode', *Zeitschrift für die gesamte Staatswissenschafts*, vol. 16, pp. 461–716.
Schmoller, G. (1923), *Grundriß der allgemeinen Volkswirtschaftslehre*, reprint of the supplemented and enlarged 2nd edn, München–Leipzig: Duncker & Humblot.
Schultz, B. (1954), 'Franz Oppenheimer als Lehrer und Oekonom', *Zeitschrift für die gesamte Staatswissenschaft*, vol. 110, pp. 472–89.
Seuß, W. (1987), ' "Ich bin durch und durch ein alter Liberaler". Zum 75. Geburtstag von Milton Friedman', in *Frankfurter Allgemeine Zeitung*, no. 172, 29 July 1987, p. 12.
Simons, H. C. (1948), 'A positive program for *laissez-faire*. Some proposals for a liberal economic policy', in H. C. Simons, *Economic Policy for a Free Society*, Chicago: University of Chicago Press, pp. 40–77. [First published in 1934.]
von Stackelberg, H. 1949), 'Möglichkeit und Grenzen der Wirtschaftslenkung',

published posthumously, *ORDO* vol. 2, pp. 193–206.

Starbatty, J. (1986), 'Die Soziale Marktwirtschaft aus historisch-theoretischer Sicht', in H. Pohl (ed.), *Entstehung und Entwicklung der Sozialen Marktwirtschaft,* Beiheft 45 der Zeitschrift für Unternehmensgeschichte, Stuttgart: Steiner, pp. 7–26.

Stigler, G. J. (1965), *Essays in the History of Economics*, Chicago and London: Chicago University Press.

Stigler, G. J. (1968), *The Organization of Industry*, Homewood, Ill.: Irvin and Nobelton: Irvin-Dorsey.

Stolper W. F., and Roskamp, K. W. (1979), 'Planning a free economy: Germany 1945–1960', *Zeitschrift für die gesamte Staatswissenschaft,* vol. 135, pp. 374–404.

Stuetzel, W., Watrin, Chr., Willgerodt, H. and Homann, K. (1981), *Grundtexte zur Sozialen Marktwirtschaft. Zeugnisse aus zweihundert Jahren ordnungspolitischer Diskussion,* Stuttgart and New York: Fischer.

'*In der Stunde Null*' (1979), *Die Denkschrift des Freiburger 'Bonhöffer-Kreises': Politische Gemeinschaftsordnung. Ein Versuch zur Selbstbesinnung des christlichen Gewissens in den politischen Noeten unserer Zeit* introduced by H. Thielicke, with an epilogue by Ph. von Bismarck, Tübingen: Mohr.

Thalheim, K. C. (1955), 'Zum Problem der Einheitlichkeit der Wirtschaftspolitik', in K. Muhs (ed.), *Festgabe für G. Jahn zur Vollendung seines 70. Lebensjahres*, Berlin: Duncker & Humblot, pp. 577–87.

Tuchtfeldt, E. (1957), 'Das Instrumentarium der Wirtschaftspolitik. Ein Beitrag zu seiner Systematik', in *Hamburger Jahrbuch für Wirtschafts- und Gesellschaftspolitik*, vol. 2, Tübingen: Mohr, pp. 52–64.

Uhr, C. G. (1960), *Economic Doctrines of Knut Wicksell*, Berkeley, Los Angeles: University of California Press.

Vanberg, V. (1987), ' "Ordnungstheorie". As Constitutional Economics – The German Conception of a "Social Market Economy"', *ORDO*, vol. 39 (1988), pp. 17–31.

Wagner, A. (1984), *Grundlegung der politischen Oekonomie. Zweiter Teil: Volkswirtschaft und Recht, besonders Vermoegensrecht*, 3rd edn, Leipzig: Winter.

Walker, D. A. (1986), 'Walras's Theory of the Entrepreneur', *De Economist*, vol. 134, pp. 1–24.

Wallich, H. C. (1955), *Mainsprings of the German Revival*, New Haven, Conn: Yale University Press.

Watkins, J. W. N. (1952), 'Walter Eucken, Philosopher – Economist', *Ethics*, vol. 63, pp. 131–6.

Watrin, Chr. (1985), 'Staatsaufgaben – Die oekonomische Sicht,' *Zeitschrift für Wirtschaftspolitik*, vol. 34, pp. 131–59.

Weber, H. (1970), *Theologie – Gesellschaft – Wirtschaft. Die Sozial- und Wirtschaftsethik in der evangelischen Theologie der Gegenwart*, Göttingen: Vandenhoeck & Ruprecht.

Weisenborn, G. (1981), *Der lautlose Aufstand. Bericht über die Widerstandsbewegung des deutschen Volkes 1933–1945*, 3rd cdn (reprint), Frankfurt/Main: Roederberg.

Welter, E. (1952), 'Hermann Schumacher. Bild eines akademischen Lehrers', *Frankfurter Allgemeine Zeitung*, no. 232, 7 October 1957, p. 6.

Welter, E. (1953), 'Die wirtschaftspolitische Bildungsaufgabe', in L. Einaudi et al., *Wirtschaft ohne Wunder*, Erlenbach-Zürich: Rentsch, pp. 340–56.

Wendt, S. (1956), 'Schumacher, Hermann', in E. v. Beckerath et al. (eds), *Handwörterbuch der Sozialwissenschaften*, vol. 9, Stuttgart: Fischer, Tübingen: Mohr and Goettingen: Vandenhoeck & Ruprecht, pp. 150–51.

Wicksell, K. (1896), *Finanztheoretische Untersuchungen nebst Darstellung und Kritik des Steuerwesens Schwedens*, Jena: Fischer.

Wicksell, K. (1913), *Vorlesungen über Nationaloekonomie auf der Grundlage des Marginalprinzipes. Theoretischer Teil*, vol. 1, Jena: Fischer.

Wicksell, K. (1922), *Vorlesungen über Nationaloekonomie auf der Grundlage des Marginalprinzipes,* vol. 2: Geld und Kredit, Jena: Fischer.

Wicksell, K. (1962), 'A new principle of just taxation, translation of an extract of Wicksell', (1896) by J. M. Buchanan, in R. A. Musgrave and A. T. Peacock (eds),

Classics in the Theory of Public Finance, London and New York: Macmillan, pp. 72–118.

Willenborg, K. -H. (1979), 'Markt oder Plan. Der Kampf um die Wirtschaftsordnung', in J. Weber (ed.), *30 Jahre Bundesrepublik Deutschland*, vol. 2: Das Entscheidungsjahr 1948, München: Landeszentrale für politische Bildungsarbeit, pp. 235–58.

Willgerodt, H. (1985), 'Die Sachlogik der Wirtschaft im Spiegel des Rechts', in *Recht und Gesittung in einer freien Gesellschaft*, Bonn: Ludwig-Erhard-Stiftung, pp. 13–34.

Williamson, O. E. (1975), *Markets and Hierarchies: Analysis and Antitrust Implications. A Study in the Economics of Industrial Organization*, New York. The Free Press and London: Macmillan.

Williamson, O. E. (1985), *The Economic Institutions of Capitalism. Firms, Markets, Relational Contracting*, New York: The Free Press and London: Macmillan.

PART II

JOHN
MAYNARD KEYNES

4 The reception of Keynes' *Treatise on Money:* a review of the reviews

Robert W. Dimand

The dramatic impact of Keynes' *General Theory* upon the economics profession has received considerable attention. The reception of his first attempt to revolutionize monetary theory *A Treatise on Money* (1930), is not nearly as well known. The four monumental volumes of *Critical Assessments of John Maynard Keynes*, edited by John Cunningham Wood, reprint all the articles on Keynes and the *General Theory* that appeared in scholarly journals from 1936 onwards, but no reviews of his earlier work. The success of the *General Theory* diverted attention from the *Treatise*. None the less, just as knowledge of the *Treatise* adds to understanding the *General Theory*, so is there much to be learned from the reviews of the *Treatise*. The reception of the *Treatise* as a path-breaking, revolutionary work puts to rest the view that the *Treatise* was simply an elaboration and extension of the familiar quantity theory of money, which Keynes then abandoned in writing the *General Theory*. The reactions of reviewers also reveal a great deal about the state of monetary theory in English-speaking countries on the eve of the 'Keynesian revolution.' Most importantly, critical reaction forced Keynes to recognize flaws and gaps in the theoretical framework of the *Treatise* and thus affected the direction in which he began reworking his theory of money, abandoning the fundamental equations for the value of money and attempting to explain why, in his parable of a thrift campaign in a banana plantation, an increase in saving would lead to the re-establishment of equilibrium at a lower level of income, rather than an unlimited deflation and contraction.

The *General Theory* has so eclipsed the *Treatise* in the consciousness of the economics profession that it is startling to note that when Sir Josiah Stamp proclaimed that 'In many respects I regard Mr. Keynes' work as the most penetrating and epoch-making since Ricardo', and Charles Hardy predicted in the *American Economic Review* that 'the serious work of the next generation on business cycles, central banking, and international finance will be more profoundly modified as the result

of this than of any other book which has been published since the war',
they were referring to the *Treatise*. This reaction was not limited to
English-speaking countries: Achille Loria, in a review which appeared
as the leading article in *La Riforma Sociale*, pronounced the *Treatise* 'a
masterly intellectual obelisk, sculpted, it is true, with hieroglyphs and
arabesques, of which some are bizarre and others hard to decipher, but
adorned in every part with august and magnificent characters and
rearing its dazzling summit into the hyper-space of creative thought.' It
is a striking indication of the attention given to Keynes' work that the
leading article in the next issue of *La Riforma Sociale* (a Turin journal
edited by Luigi Einaudi) was also devoted to Keynes, a critique by A.
Cabiati of Keynes' proposal for a revenue tariff. Joseph Schumpeter
wrote to Keynes on 18 October 1930, just before publication of the
Treatise, 'I do not think that any scientific book has been looked for with
so universal an impatience – in our time at least – as yours is', but the
later history of what he hailed as 'truly a Ricardian *tour de force*' has not
lived up to Schumpeter's prediction to Keynes on 29 November that 'it
will ever stand out as a landmark in its field' (*JMK*, XIII, 176, 201).

Bouquets and Brickbats
Sir Josiah Stamp reviewed the *Treatise* for the *Economics Journal*,
which Keynes edited. Stamp's long service as secretary of the Royal
Statistical Society, editor of its journal, chairman of the governing body
of the London School of Economics, and chairman of a railway
company paralleled Keynes' career as secretary of the Royal Economic
Society, editor of its journal, bursar of King's College, and chairman of
an insurance company and an investment trust. Like Keynes, Stamp had
too many claims on his time to hold a professorial chair or a lectureship.
He was one of the few British economists of his day to hold a PhD in the
subject, and his scholarly prominence was attested by the presidency of
learned societies: the Royal Statistical Society in 1932, and both the
British Association for the Advancement of Science and the Geographi-
cal Association in 1936. A director of the Bank of England, Stamp was
Keynes' colleague on the Economic Advisory Council (1930–39) and on
the Chancellor's Consultative Council in the wartime Treasury, eventually receiving, like Keynes, a peerage for his public services. John
Gunther, suggesting ten possible names for an 'inner ring' of the British
ruling class in *Inside Europe* (1936), included 'the great economist Sir
Josiah Stamp'. If anyone could be regarded as the voice of The
Establishment on economics, it was Stamp.

Stamp's enthusiastic review emphasized the separation of investment
and saving decisions in the *Treatise* and the book's acceptance, following

on from this separation, of 'temporary disequilibrium, adjustable by a changed rate of interest, as a chronic state of affairs in society'. This view of an unstable economy in which monetary policy is effective contrasts with the classical vision of an inherently stable private sector disrupted by unanticipated actions of the monetary authority. Stamp pointed out the affinity between the deflationary effect of saving in the *Treatise* and the underconsumption doctrines of John Hobson, later hailed as a precursor in the *General Theory*, and of Foster and Catchings, heretics outside the mainstream of economics. Stamp noted the important distinction that the cause of deflation in the *Treatise* was saving that was not matched by a decision to invest, while for the underconsumptionists oversaving was synonymous with overinvestment. They shared, however, a concern with investment and saving as crucial influences on the price level and the credit cycle. Stamp provided a concise summary of Keynes' trade cycle theory, noting its implications for government investment (public works) as well as interest rate policy:

> [I]n Mr. Keynes' analysis, the purchasing power withheld from consumption-goods lowers the demand and the price, and produces business losses which, put crudely here, are 'financed' by that very excess of purchasing power transferred to saving. At some subsequent date it may be possible to create an excess of *investment* over savings, and reverse the process, but this is mere equivalence and not an absorption of the original error. Dynamically, *at the moment* when private investment is less than savings, the surplus of the latter might be prevented from financing losses by being absorbed in public investment which creates a demand for the right commodities and prevents a deflation of their price on the supply existing.

While Prof. A. C. Pigou held in *The Nation and Athenaeum* that the *Treatise* simply presented orthodox monetary theory, with the fundamental equations at best a more convenient form of the equation of exchange, Stamp insisted that Keynes was an innovator in theory rather than in policy proposals:

> In the realm of pure theory and analysis, I am convinced that our sense of indebtedness to him will continually grow. It was not only stout Cortez upon a peak in Darien who had a Pacific to stare at! And the days of path-breakers are clearly not yet ended.

Keats' exaltation upon first looking into Chapman's *Homer* was also recalled by Kenneth Boulding, who paired the reference with a line from Wordsworth:

> I shall never forget the excitement, as an undergraduate, of reading Keynes' *Treatise on Money* in 1931. It is a clumsy, hastily written book and much of its

theoretical apparatus has now been discarded. But to its youthful readers it was a peak in Darien, opening up vistas of uncharted seas – 'Great was it that dawn to be alive, and to be young was very heaven!' [Stein, 1969, p. 162].

One of the longest reviews of the *Treatise* was a 41-page leading article in the *Quarterly Journal of Economics* by John H. Williams, Dean of the Graduate School of Public Administration at Harvard and economic adviser to the Federal Reserve Bank of New York. Williams' review was favourable: 'As one who has rather a prejudice against big books I can merely say that I have seldom read two large volumes with as much pleasure.' Like Stamp, he noted that Keynes differed from Foster and Catchings by distinguishing the acts of saving and investing, and praised him for seeing the special significance of savings deposits for portfolio choice and the determination of interest rates: 'So far as I know all theories previous to Keynes' have failed to make use of the statistical division of deposits into demand and time.' Williams caught one crucial theoretical point missed by other reviewers, Keynes' vacillation between profits as realized windfalls and profits as perceived opportunities to earn more than the normal competitive rate of return on new investments. Williams stressed that expectations form the basis of investment and production decisions, and that windfall profits as surprises matter only as one source of new information for entrepreneurs to use in forming expectations about future profitability.

Williams' overall opinion of the *Treatise* was warm enough for Harcourt, Brace and Co. to put it on the jacket of reprints of the book: 'It exhibits a rare combination of penetration in theoretical analysis, grasp of mathematical statistical method, and felicity of expression. I cannot hope to give a just impression of its scope and richness.' However, he expressed scepticism about the effectiveness of the monetary policy advocated in the book on the grounds that expansionary open market operations might bid up factor prices instead of reducing the real rate of interest, and felt that the 'fundamental equations' were not among the book's important contributions on a level with the analysis of the effect of the interest rate on investment and the price level.

The most incisive appraisal of the *Treatise* was by Charles Hardy of the Brookings Institution, who reviewed the first volume, on the pure theory of money, in the *American Economic Review*, and the second volume, on the applied theory, in an article in the *Journal of Political Economy*. After terming the book 'a masterly analysis, comprehensive, penetrating, and extraordinarily free from minor errors' (the last of which is dubious) Hardy explained the intellectual lineage of the *Treatise*:

> In a field which has been perhaps more intensively cultivated during recent years than any other branch of economics, Keynes says much that is new, much more that is new to those who do not read German, still more to those who do not read either German or D.H. Robertson. . . . In analyzing the causes of discrepancies between the rate of saving and the rate of formation of capital, Keynes follows closely in the footsteps of Wicksell, whose work he brings almost for the first time to the attention of readers of English.

This last comment is particularly interesting in light of Keynes' subsequent reputation for taking scant notice of the work of his non-Cambridge contemporaries and being insufficiently aware of his Swedish predecessors. Maurice Dobb, in a short review in the *Cambridge Review*, also stressed the acknowledged dependence of Keynes' analysis of the divergence between investment and saving on Wicksell's distinction between the natural and market rates of interest.

Hardy regretted that the *Treatise* did not recapitulate Keynes' 1922 analysis of 'Inflation as a Method of Taxation', which had been reprinted in Keynes' *Tract on Monetary Reform* (1923). He also corrected a slip in Keynes' handling of Irving Fisher's distinction between real and nominal interest rates, reminding Keynes that anticipated price changes matter, not past ones, except in so far as experience forms the basis for expectations. Hardy noted that the 'fundamental equations' were tautologies, not testable propositions, and that the empirical parts of the book offered historical illustrations rather than a test of Keynes' theories. He felt that 'Professor Keynes' program of monetary reform contains less that is new than does his theoretical analysis', and pointed out the crucial flaw in the *Treatise*, the unconscious shift 'from the stabilization of business activity to the stabilization of prices' as a goal:

> All this analysis Mr. Keynes forgets when he reaches his practical program. The stabilization of the price level emerges either as an end in itself or as a standard so closely tied to the ultimate ojective as to be practically identified with it.

Critiques

In 1932, Alvin Hansen of the University of Minnesota published a three paragraph *AER* note entitled 'A Fundamental Error Keynes's "Treatise on Money"', pointing out that Keynes' first 'fundamental equation' was valid beyond the base year only if technical progress proceeded at the same pace in the capital goods and consumption goods sectors. Keynes accepted this criticism in a brief reply in the same journal, and suggested ways in which the fault could be remedied. Lord Kahn recently revealed in his Mattioli Lectures that he had drawn Keynes' attention to this index number problem before publication, but that Keynes could not then spare the time to fix it. Hansen and Herbert Tout returned to the matter the next year, in the inaugural volume of *Econometrica*. The necessary modifications are not extensive – the 'fundamental error' can claim that name only because it is an error in a 'fundamental equation'. The 'fundamental error' was discussed further in the *AER* by B.P. Adarkar (1933) and K. Rubner-Petersen (1934), as well as in a *JPE* article by A. G. Hart on Keynes' price-level concepts (1933). These discussions are of less interest than they otherwise might be because Keynes' two fundamental equations for the price level of consumption goods and of output as a whole are tautologies, true by definition (apart from slips such as the 'fundamental error'). By concentrating on this tautology, Hansen and the others neglected the macroeconomic theory advanced in the book (on which see Dimand, 1986).

Hansen and Tout argued that the divergence between investment and saving cannot cause windfall profits or losses because, by Keynes' definition, the divergence *is* the windfall. What matters here, however, is the functional dependence of changes in investment on past profits, so that a divergence between I and S in one period would generate a larger profit disequilibrium in the next period by changing I. The causal forces at work are reflected not in the tautological fundamental equations, but in the functional specification of the variables appearing in the equations. Hansen and Tout also made the odd comment that if Keynes' definitions of investment and saving were discarded, 'the equations then fall to the ground', as if it were not possible to invalidate any equation by redefining the variables.

B.R. Shenoy of Nowrosjee Wadia College, Poona, India, wrote two articles using the fundamental equations in the *QJE*. In 'An Equation for the Price-Level of New Investment Goods' (1932), he used Keynes' equations for the price of consumption goods and of output as a whole to derive the corresponding equation for the price of investment goods. The following year, Shenoy wrote on the interdependence of the price levels, deriving the price of output as a whole as a weighted average of the sectoral price levels, and obtained the unsurprising result that the price of output as a whole must rise if both sectoral price levels rise. Shenoy's diligent but fruitless efforts to work with the fundamental equations cast greater doubt on the equations' usefulness than Hansen's criticism had done.

Friedrich von Hayek, the newly appointed Tooke Professor of Economic Science and Statistics at the London School of Economics, reviewed the first volume of the *Treatise* in the August 1931 and February 1932 issues of *Economica*, with a reply by Keynes to the first part of the review and a rejoinder by Hayek in the November 1931 issue. This exchange led to a heated correspondence between Hayek and Keynes from December to February, of which eleven letters survive, including a letter from Hayek to Keynes on Christmas Day with a reply the same day. Hostilities reopened in March with Piero Sraffa's harsh *EJ* review of Hayek's *Prices and Production* (1931), followed in print by a reply by Hayek, a rejoinder by Sraffa and a note by Keynes denying Hayek's claim that Sraffa had misinterpreted the *Treatise*. Hayek objected not to the particular equations Keynes used for his price indices, but rather to the use of price indices at all. Hayek presented the Austrian arguments that individuals base their decisions on prices of individual commodities, not weighted averages, that weights could change over time, and that information was lost in aggregation. He did not accept that the theory of index numbers as presented in Book II of the *Treatise* overcame these objections, and objected to Books III and IV of Volume I, the theoretical heart of the work, being cast in terms of price indices. He regretted that Keynes had built upon the monetary theory in the second volume of Wicksell's *Lectures* but not on the Austrian capital theory of Wicksell's first volume. In view of the capital theory controversy then raging between Frank Knight and the LSE Austrians, which revealed a number of paradoxes and problems involving such Austrian concepts as the average period of production, Hayek's invitation to base a theory of the trade cycle on changes in the period of production was not an appealing one.

While Hayek found much to praise in the second volume of the *Treatise*, on the applied theory of money, his rejection of the index number basis of Volume I prevented any meeting of minds. At the end of the first part of Hayek's review, the most heavily annotated article in the surviving copies of Keynes' journals, Keynes protested that 'Hayek has not read my book with that measure of "goodwill" which an author is entitled to expect of a reader. Until he does so, he will not know what I mean or whether I am right.' But how much goodwill or understanding was displayed in this comment on Hayek's book in Keynes' reply?

> The book, as it stands, seems to me to be one of the most frightful muddles that I have ever read, with scarcely a sound proposition in it beginning with page 45, and yet it remains a book of some interest, which is likely to leave its mark on the mind of the reader. It is an extraordinary example of how, starting with a mistake, a remorseless logician can end up in Bedlam.

Despite the distinction of Keynes, Hayek and Sraffa as economic theorists, and the extent and complexity of their exchange, the only suitable comment on their debate was made by Keynes in a note to

Sraffa and Kahn: 'What is the next move? I feel that the abyss yawns – and so do I. Yet I can't help feeling that there *is* something interesting in it' [*JMK*, XIII, 252, 265].

Dennis Robertson, Reader in Economics at Cambridge, wrote an *EJ* article on the *Treatise*, to which Keynes replied. Robertson seized on two passages which revealed serious flaws in the work. One was the parable of the effect of a thrift campaign in a banana plantation. He failed to note Keynes' implicit assumption that (apart from a throwaway remark about the thrift campaign petering out due to growing poverty) the falling level of income would fail to restore equilibrium by reducing saving before all production came to a halt, but he did argue that since savers can save only by acquiring some asset, someone must be making abnormal profits from the bidding up of 'mechanical banana-cutters' which would balance the losses of the banana growers.

Robertson also criticized Keynes' widow's cruse passage, which held that if entrepreneurs decided to consume out of profits, this would increase profits by as much as entrepreneurs' spending increased. He showed that since Keynes had explicitly ruled out any rise in cost (factor earnings) per unit of output, and tacitly assumed away 'the possibility that output, and thus *aggregate* costs, can be increased', the widow's cruse followed from the truism that all money must be somewhere: 'the money spent on any day by one entrepreneur must be found at nightfall in the bank balance of another.' In a footnote, Robertson thanked James Meade, an Oxford economist spending a year at Cambridge and a member of the 'Cambridge circus', 'for putting me on the right track' about the assumed constancy of output.

Ralph G. Hawtrey, Assistant Secretary in charge of the Financial Enquiries Branch of H.M. Treasury, wrote a brief review of the *Treatise* in the *Journal of the Royal Statistical Society*, and a longer, far more important set of comments on the page proofs of the *Treatise* which he sent to Keynes shortly before the book was published and which was revised as a chapter in Hawtrey's *The Art of Central Banking* (1932). In his comments on the proofs of the *Treatise* in September 1930 [*JMK*, XIII, 150–62], Hawtrey not only drew Keynes' attention to the implicit assumption of constant real output underlying much of the analysis in the *Treatise* but also found the flaw in the parable of the thrift campaign in a banana plantation that Keynes had presented both in the *Treatise* (I, 176–8) and in his evidence to the Macmillan Committee (*JMK*, XX, 78–80). Picking up on the possibility, to which Keynes had given a third of a sentence, of the thrift campaign petering out due to growing poverty, Hawtrey gave a clear numerical example of how changes in the level of income would restore the equality of investment and saving after an initial shock because the volume of saving depended on the level of income. [See *JMK*, XIII, 139–49; and Davis (1980) for Keynes' defensive but impressed reaction.] Hawtrey extended this analysis in a Macmillan Committee working paper, and then included an algebraic model of the multiplier, showing how autonomous spending affected equilibrium income, as an appendix to his 1932 chapter. Keynes wrote to Hawtrey in January 1931 that he had found the Macmillan Committee working paper 'tremendously useful' [*JMK*, XXIX, 10]. In his Harris Foundation Lectures at the University of Chicago in June 1931, Keynes discussed the effect of lower income and employment on saving as a reason why the fall in income caused by a drop in investment would not continue without limit, but did not use either Hawtrey's or Kahn's version of the multiplier to determine how much lower income would be as a result of reduced investment.

Conclusion
Excepting only Pigou, the reviewers of the *Treatise*, whether generally favourable or critical, regarded it as a new and revolutionary contribution to theory, rather than a reformulation of familiar monetary theory disguised by new notation. Contrary to some later views, they found Keynes' policy proposals familiar but the underlying theory new. It is also clear from the reviews that many prominent economists, including several such as Hardy and Williams who were later cool toward the *General Theory*, were open to attempts to construct a new theory of a monetary economy and were dissatisfied with existing monetary theory. Some commentators, notably Hansen, were distracted by the intricacies of the fundamental equations for the price level, but Hardy, Stamp, Williams and others passed these uninteresting tautologics by to examine Keynes' theory of price changes. The reviews highlighted the major weaknesses of the *Treatise*: the confusion between realized and anticipated profits, the need for a theory of output adjustment rather than price adjustment, the effect of income changes on saving as a equilibrating force. Hawtrey's critique was outstanding on these points, because he went beyond pointing out problems to offer a version of the theory of the multiplier. Hawtrey's contribution was thus of far greater importance to the development of the economics of Keynes than such better-known reviews as Hansen's criticism of the index number problem in the fundamental equations or Hayek's rejection of an approach based on price indices. Although the *Treatise* has not borne out E.C. Dyason's prediction in the *Economic Record* that it was 'destined, unless – perhaps even if – an impatient proletariat sweeps away the capitalist system, to influence political and economic thought

as powerfully in our own times as did the *Wealth of Nations* that of an earlier day', it is still worthwhile to examine the reception of the book. The critical reception of the work, and especially Hawtrey's contribution, established the agenda for Keynes' working out of the book that was to have the impact predicted by Dyason.

References

Adarkar, B.P. (1933), 'The "fundamental error" in Keynes' *Treatise*', *American Economic Review* (March).
Cabiati, A. (1931), 'Il neo-protezionismo del Prof. Keynes', *La Riforma Sociale* (May–June), English summary in *Economic Journal* (1931), p. 511.
Davis, Eric G. (1980), 'The correspondence between R.G. Hawtrey and J.M. Keynes on the *Treatise*: The genesis of output adjustment models', *Canadian Journal of Economics* (November).
Dimand, Robert W. (1986), 'The Macroeconomics of the *Treatise on Money*', *Eastern Economic Journal* (December).
Dobb, Maurice (1930), 'Mr Keynes on money', *Cambridge Review* (28 November).
Dyason, E.C. (1931), 'Scourging the money-changers', *Economic Record* (November).
Hansen, Alvin (1932), 'A fundamental error in Keynes' *Treatise on Money*', *American Economic Review* (September), and reply by Keynes (December).
Hansen, Alvin and Herbert Tout (1933), 'Annual survey of business cycle theory: investment and saving in the business cycle', *Econometrica* (April).
Hardy, Charles O. (1931a), Review of *Treatise*. I. *American Economic Review* (March).
Hardy, Charles O. (1931b), 'Savings, investment and the control of business cycles', *Journal of Political Economy* (June).
Hart, A.G. (1933), 'An examination of Mr. Keynes' price-level concepts', *Journal of Political Economy* (October).
Hawtrey, Ralph G. (1932), *The Art of Central Banking*, London.
Hayek, Friedrich A. von (1931–2), 'Some reflections on the pure theory of money of Mr. J.M. Keynes', *Economica* (August 1931, February 1932), with reply by Keynes and rejoinder by Hayek (November 1931).
Kahn R.F. (Lord) (1984), *The Making of Keynes' General Theory*, Cambridge.
Keynes, John Maynard (1971–83), *Collected Writings*, 29 vols. London.
Loria, Archille (1931), 'Keynes sulla moneta', *La Riforma Sociale* (March–April), English summary in *Economic Journal* (1931), 511.
Pigou, A.C. (1931), 'Mr. Keynes on money', *Nation and Athenaeum* (24 January).
Robertson, Dennis, H. (1931), 'Mr. Keynes' theory of money', *Economic Journal* (September), with reply by Keynes and rejoinder by Robertson (December).
Rubner-Petersen, K. (1934), 'The error in the fundamental equations: a new interpretation', *American Economic Review* (December).
Shenoy, B.R. (1932), 'An equation for the price-level of new investment goods', *Quarterly Journal of Economics* (November).
Shenoy, B.R. (1934), 'The interdependence of the price-levels P. P' and π,' *Quarterly Journal of Economics* (January).
Stamp, Sir Josiah (1931), review of *Treatise*, *Economic Journal* (June).
Stein, Herbert (1969), *The Fiscal Revolution in America*, Chicago.
Williams, John H. (1931), 'The monetary doctrines of J.M. Keynes', *Quarterly Journal of Economics* (August).

5 Keynes on speculation

Steven Pressman

There is abundant evidence that the world economy has been on a speculative binge. Over the past decade we have witnessed increased trading in stocks, in futures and in foreign exchange; and there has been greater volatility in stock prices, interest rates and exchange rates. People have become caught up in get-rich-quick schemes, as documented by the insider trading scandal on Wall Street and the popularity of multi-million dollar state lotteries. Capitalist economies, argues Susan Strange, more and more resemble gambling casinos.[1]

Questions naturally arise concerning the economic consequences of these activities. How does speculation influence real economic activity? What is the impact of speculation on the stability of the economy? Finally, what policies can be used to reduce the extent of speculation or prevent a nation from becoming enthralled with speculative activities? This chapter turns to the works of John Maynard Keynes to begin to answer these questions.

Frank Knight argued[2] that speculation is good for an economy because it increases business investment. Speculation, according to Knight, reduces uncertainty by converting it to measured risk. For example, through hedging contracts producers can eliminate the possibility of loss or gain through changes in raw material prices. In this way, the uncertainty of doing business becomes a risk of the professional speculator. With less uncertainty, investment rises and the economy prospers.

Keynes' view was quite different. For Keynes the probability calculus could not in principle be applied to uncertainty – for uncertainty is not measurable.[3] Therefore, from Keynes' viewpoint Frank Knight was talking about shifting risk rather than shifting uncertainty. Shifting risk, however, does not necessarily increase aggregate investment. The uncertainty of economic life remains; and speculation does not have the benefits Knight pointed to. In contrast to Knight, Keynes believed speculation was a *negative* economic force, tending to reduce business investment. As a result, he continually sought policies to mitigate this effect of speculative activity.

Keynes' reasons for believing that speculation reduced investment changed with his changing perceptions of the way economies operated. In the *Treatise on Money* Keynes held that speculation was a problem because of its effect on money demand and thus on the rate of interest. If speculation was a monetary problem, so must its solution be monetary. By the time he wrote the *General Theory*, however, Keynes viewed the problem of speculation in terms of its tendency to reduce the marginal efficiency of capital, and thus restrain business investment and aggregate demand. If speculation was a problem of demand, then the solutions required would have to be policies to increase aggregate demand. Alternatively, policies could be developed to counter the root causes of excessive speculation in the economy.

The *Treatise* view of speculation

The *Treatise on Money*[4] sets forth a monetary theory of speculation. Speculation was a problem, according to Keynes, because of its effect on the rate of interest, and through the interest rate, on other economic variables. He wrote: 'a change in the disposition of the public towards securities other than savings deposits, uncompensated by action on the part of the banking system, will be a most potent factor affecting the rate of investment relatively to savings and a cause of disturbance, therefore, to the purchasing power of money' (V, p. 130).

Keynes began his analysis by distinguishing *industrial circulation*, deposits used for the production of goods and services, from *financial circulation*, deposits used to purchase and hold 'existing titles to wealth (other than exchanges resulting from the specialization of industry), including stock exchange and money market transactions, speculation and the process of conveying current savings and profits into the hands of entrepreneurs' (V, p. 217).

The sum of industrial and financial circulation comprises the total stock of money in the economy. For financial circulation, the required quantity of money equals the volume of trading times the average value of instruments traded (V. p. 222). With the total stock of money controlled by the central bank, industrial circulation becomes a residual. Therefore, the greater the volume of trading in financial assets that takes place and the higher the price of these assets, the more money that is required for financial purposes and the less money that is available for industrial circulation.

Given these preliminaries, Keynes' analysis of the economic effects of speculation is straightforward. The supply of savings deposits available for investment depends on two groups: (1) those people who permanently want savings account balances, and (2) those 'bears' who believe that security prices will fall and thus prefer to hold savings account balances rather than securities in the short run. A rise in bearish sentiment increases the supply of savings deposits for industry and reduces the interest rate. In contrast, a rise in bullish sentiment tends to reduce savings deposits and increase the rate of interest. Speculation, which is one form of financial circulation, tends to exert a downward pressure on investment and the price level. The analysis here is that a greater demand for money for speculation (a rise in bullish sentiment) reduces the supply of money for industry and raises interest rates. In contrast, a rise in bearish sentiment reduces the demand for money for speculation, and frees up more money for business investment.

The *Treatise* also views speculation as a short-run problem. It can cause temporary fluctuations in output and prices, but can do no lasting damage. Investors, Keynes thought, were ignorant of the remote future. They focus on the short run rather than the long run. Consequently, they 'are the prey of hopes and fears easily aroused by transient events' (VI, p. 323). This is true as well of the general public: 'Most people are too timid and too greedy, too impatient and too nervous about their investments, the fluctuations in the paper value of which can so easily obliterate the results of so much honest effort, to take long views' (VI, p. 324).

Because everyone has a short-run focus, overvaluation of stocks results in profit-taking, while undervaluation results in bargain-hunting. This is especially true, Keynes maintained, of the small fringe of professional financiers who primarily determine the value of securities. Any large rise in security prices causes some professionals to adopt bear positions in the market, thus curbing speculative excesses and providing more savings for industrial circulation. 'As soon as the price of securities has risen high enough, relatively [sic] to the short-term rate of interest, to occasion a difference of opinion as to the prospects, a "bear" position will develop, and some people will begin to increase their savings deposits either out of their current savings or out of their current profits or by selling securities previously held' (V. p. 229).

These two aspects of speculation – its short-run focus and its monetary nature – have two important consequences.

First, the short-run focus of speculation creates a danger of speculative bubbles and collapses. A price increase may lead to beliefs of further increases, leading to further price rises, additional beliefs about rising prices, and greater increases in security prices. This is the classic case of a speculative bubble. In contrast, falling prices lead to beliefs of further price declines. Acting on this belief by selling securities results in further price declines. This leads to expectations of additional price drops, more selling, and expectations of prices falling further.

Second, the central bank is faced with a difficult dilemma. They can keep interest rates constant in the face of rising speculation by increasing the volume of bank money. This, however, would encourage the bull market, and lead to even higher asset prices and expectations of future price increases. On the other hand, the central bank can refuse to increase the supply of money. This option would make less money available for investment and increase interest rates, creating a deflationary tendency in the economy (V, p. 227).

Keynes' policy solution in the *Treatise* was to require the central bank to go through the horns of this dilemma. He wanted the central bank to supply exactly the right sum of money. This would be the amount of money that increases interest rates just enough to (i) discourage speculation somewhat, (ii) keep the bullish sentiment from causing overinvestment in the future, and (iii) keep investment from falling (V, p. 227).

Not all Keynes' early work argued that speculation was a short-run and monetary problem. In an article in *The Nation* on 11 August 1923, Keynes first advanced the idea that investment might be inhibited by a speculative collapse. 'A *general expectation* of falling prices may inhibit the productive process altogether. For if prices are expected to fall, not enough people can be found who are willing to carry a speculative "bull" position, and this means that lengthy productive processes involving a money outlay cannot be undertaken' (XIX, p. 114). Full development of this argument and the theoretical analysis behind it, however, did not take place until 1936.

The *General Theory* view of speculation
The major argument of the *General Theory* is that insufficient demand has severe negative effects on an economy. Anything that adversely affects spending will depress a nation's economy – reducing its level of output and increasing its rate of unemployment. In addition, Keynes argued that a depressed economy would not rebound on its own; rather, economic policies were necessary to ensure full employment.

In the *General Theory*, Keynes cites speculation as one factor contributing to insufficient demand. He suggests three reasons for this: (1) speculation may replace enterprise, (2) speculation may misdirect investment, and finally, (3) speculation may worsen the trade cycle. In all three cases speculation reduces investment demand in the economy, thereby lowering output and creating unemployment. In addition, because current yields determine future yields, speculation will exert a negative force on the state of long-term expectations. Keynes' analysis has thus become both real and long-run.

Substitution for enterprise

In the *General Theory* Keynes was careful to distinguish speculation from enterprise. He used the term speculation 'for the activity of forecasting the psychology of the market' (*GT*, p. 158). Speculative activity occurs in investment markets, especially stock exchanges. It is characterized by the short-run search for profits, and arises from the desire to make money quickly (*GT*, p. 157). Speculation is carried out by speculators, whose goal it is to 'beat the gun' and purchase assets just before the general public does. Speculators 'are concerned, not with what an investment is really worth to a man who buys it...but with what the market will value it at, under the influence of mass psychology' (*GT*, p. 154f.).

In contrast, enterprise is 'the act of forecasting the prospective yield of assets over their whole life' (*GT*, p. 158). Enterprise involves producing things in order to make money. This requires a long-run perspective because in real economies production takes time. Contractual commitments are made today to buy labour, machinery and raw materials. Goods are then produced with these inputs and brought to market for sale. Purchase of inputs requires that the capitalist overcome the uncertainty of a long-run future that is impossible to forecast.

A well-functioning economy needs both speculators and entrepreneurs. The former will reduce the risks for the latter; while entrepreneurs make the profits that allow for continued speculation. Problems arise only when speculation dominates enterprise. 'Speculators may do no harm as bubbles on a steady stream of enterprise. But the position is serious when enterprise becomes the bubble on a whirlpool of speculation' (*GT*, p. 159).

A likely reason for this, although Keynes is not explicit here, is that speculation, in contrast to production, creates no output and no employment.[5] Consider a firm that must decide between building a new plant and purchasing a plant by buying the stock of an already existing company. Only in the former case will there be more investment, and through the multiplier, even greater increases in output.

If the firm expects larger gains in the next year from buying the stock than it expects from building the plant, then the stock will be bought rather than the plant. From the short-run perspective, this increases the profits of the firm; but there is no new investment and no new demand. Moreover, it might be more profitable to keep passing around the stock of the existing plant, making financial gains on each round, rather than building any new plants. Here enterprise has become a bubble on a stream of speculation, and the level of demand continually suffers.

This point is an expansion of arguments from the *Treatise*. There Keynes argued that speculation is a problem because it is a demand for assets. In the *General Theory* Keynes recognized that speculation was a demand for assets *rather than a demand for goods*. It is not just a problem of higher interest rates affecting investment demand. Rather, speculative activity reduces spending throughout the economy as we all focus more on financial gains and less on the production of goods and services. Even consumers may reduce their spending for goods and services as they spend more money on stocks, lotteries and other get-rich-quick schemes.

Misdirected investment

Keynes was not totally opposed to speculative activity in the *General Theory*. Speculation had a role to play – that of financing investment. When functioning properly, speculation finances the most efficient or profitable investment undertakings. As Keynes wrote: 'The measure of success attained by Wall Street . . . is to direct new investment into the most profitable channels in terms of future yield' (*GT*, p. 159).

When Wall Street directs investment to the most profitable endeavours, expected profits will increase (assuming, of course, that expected profits are in part a function of current profits) and give rise to additional investment. Wall Street, as such, has the potential of providing a positive economic stimulus.

However, 'when the capital development of a country becomes a by-product of the activities of a casino, the job is likely to be ill-done' (*GT*, p. 159). Here, speculation directs investment into areas that provide short-term gains at the expense of intermediate and long-run profitability. In this case, the result will be reduced profits, lower expected profits, and hence less investment in plants and equipment. Effective demand thus suffers in the long run due to speculative excesses now.

Not discussed by Keynes, but also worth considering, is how speculation affects *human* capital investment. Because speculative activity is highly rewarded when the economy becomes more and more like a casino, it attracts the nation's best minds and provides employment for its most creative and original thinkers. And training more people to speculate creates a greater likelihood of speculation in the future. In addition, as Robert Reich notes, 'Today's corporate executives spend an increasing portion of their days fending off takeovers, finding companies to acquire, conferring with their financial and accounting specialists, and responding to discovery in lawsuits, instead of attending to their products.'[6] Managers and business executives learn more and more about how to show profits on the quarterly balance sheet, but not how to produce goods and services efficiently. They are also forced, as a defence against hostile takeovers and shareholders dissatisfaction, to focus on short-run profitability at the expense of the long-run.

Worsens the trade cycle
Finally, Keynes noted that movements in the stock market intensified the trade cycle (*GT*, p. 320). In boom times, market gains increase wealth. This increases consumption at the same time that greater expected profits cause an investment boom. In addition, greater wealth will tend to increase the propensity of an economy to consume, and hence the multiplier, giving a further push to economic expansion. By way of contrast, in times of rapidly declining stock prices consumption would fall at the same time that investment was being cut back. Thus, speculative activity expands effective demand when demand needs to be contracted, while it reduces effective demand just when demand needs expanding.

In addition, speculative excesses lead to greater volatility in the stock market. Speculative bubbles are created which eventually will burst. This collapse, Keynes felt, would have serious economic consequences, as evidenced by the stockmarket crashes of the late 1920s and the resulting world depression. The market crash, according to Keynes, dampened animal spirits and made businesses reluctant to invest regardless of the rate of interest. Real economic activity is thus reduced in the long run as a result of speculative binges now.

Some policy solutions
In the *Treatise*, Keynes looked to monetary authorities to control interest rates, and thereby investment and economic activity. By raising interest rates to just the right level they would dampen speculative sentiment, but not reduce the level of business investment.

Keynes, however, was sceptical that central bankers could set the rate of interest at the precisely required figure. 'To diagnose the position precisely at every stage and to achieve this exact balance may sometimes be, however, beyond the wits of man' (V, p. 227).

Keynes also had little faith in the *Treatise* that the central bank could limit the degree of speculation in the economy through open market operations (VI, pp. 333ff.). First, there was a limit to its ability to buy and sell government securities – that limit being the existing stock of those securities. Second, Keynes argued that the rate of interest would not respond to changes in the supply of money caused by the central bank (VI, p. 334). This is Keynes' famous liquidity trap argument. Finally, Keynes worried about the international complications of domestic money management. If one country's central bank operated contrary to the actions of the central bank throughout the rest of the world, international financial flows would counteract the desires of those lone central bankers. Higher interest rates to reduce speculation, for example, might attract capital from abroad, which in turn would fuel the speculative fires.

Despite these problems, in the *Treatise* Keynes still advocated monetary management to control speculation. He did so because he had no other policies at hand to deal with the problem. Also, because speculation was perceived as a monetary and a short-run problem, more drastic or more active policy measures were deemed unnecessary.

By the writing of the *General Theory*, however, Keynes' theoretical analysis had developed to the point where other policy solutions were both possible and necessary. Fiscal policies and the socialization of investment replaced the reliance on monetary policy that was prevalent in the *Treatise*.

The solution to inadequate and fluctuating investment in the *General Theory* is for government to assume the responsibility of maintaining and stabilizing investment. This is Keynes' famous proposal for a socialization of investment.[7] However, government socialization of investment does not solve speculative problems relating to business investment; rather it contributes to the speculative frenzy. When investment is financed by the government going into debt and issuing negotiable securities, the supply of securities on which to speculate rises.

As a result of this, Keynes needed an alternative solution. The policy he advanced followed a pattern Keynes followed throughout his life – attacking economic problems directly by treating causes rather than symptoms. If the problem was an economy run as a casino, the solution is to prevent those casino-like activities from occurring through government policies. This could be done either directly through government restrictions on speculative activities, or indirectly through creating economic disincentives for speculative activities. Essentially, these 'casinos should, in the public interest, be made inaccessible and expensive' (*GT*, p. 159).

For this reason, Keynes looked favourably upon the high brokerage fees and transfer taxes in Britain, and advocated similar measures for the United States. 'The introduction of a substantial Government transfer tax on all transactions might prove the most serviceable reform available, with a view to mitigating the predominance of speculation over enterprise in the United States' (*GT*, p. 160). Transfer taxes have an added advantage from the viewpoint of Keynesian economics – they are countercyclical economic stabilizers. In boom times, as trading increases government tax receipts rise and disposable income falls.

In a similar vein, though not mentioned explicitly by Keynes, one could imagine Keynes approving high taxes on capital gains as a means to provide a disincentive to speculation. This too would discourage speculation relative to production, while also acting as a built-in stabilizer.

Keynes also considered, but dismissed, making all investment purchases permanent – that is, making securities non-negotiable (*GT*, p. 160). This would directly prevent speculation by making it impossible. But Keynes dismissed this proposal because he was concerned that this would negatively affect investment, and so this cure he considered to be worse than the disease.

Finally, Keynes mentioned – but then proceeded to drop – one of the more intriguing ideas of the *General Theory*. One of Keynes' major contentions was that investment markets encouraged speculation, and that as these markets became more organized and developed, speculation came to dominate enterprise. We can see this today in the rise of futures markets for all sorts of goods, in the rise of options trading (which all experts agree is the most speculative sort of investment), and in the new financial indices and instruments that are being devised to stimulate speculative trading. While Keynes would bemoan these financial innovations, he never discussed how they could be controlled. However, all that is needed to stop the development of certain markets is to prohibit trading of a given sort. Here the role of the central bank and other government regulators of the securities industry becomes important in preventing speculation.

Something akin to this is what Keynes actually proposed as part of the post-World War II international financial arrangements. Keynes then was adamant about fixing exchange rates. He wrote that the 'game of blind man's buff with exchange speculators serves no useful purpose and is extremely undignified. It upsets confidence, hinders business decisions, occupies the public attention in a measure far exceeding its real importance' (XXI, p. 295).

Keynes' solution to this problem was simply to prohibit speculation through keeping exchange rates fixed. If exchange rates are fixed by governments or central banks there is nothing to speculate about.

Prohibiting certain sorts of domestic speculation would certainly be consistent with this, and is something that Keynes might have advanced even though he did not actually do so.

An evaluation of Keynes on speculation

There are two ways to go about evaluating Keynes' views on speculation. From an historical point of view one can ask about the influence of Keynes on subsequent economists. From an empirical perspective, one can ask whether or not history supports Keynes.

The latter question is the more difficult one because of problems with measuring the degree of speculative activity in an economy. Difficulty, however, does not mean impossibility; and difficulty should not discourage creative attempts to measure economic variables.

One creative search has been carried out by Robert Shiller,[8] who has focused on variations in stockmarket prices as a measure of speculation. Efficient market theories of the stock market exchange[9] hold that stock prices accurately reflect all information about the future profitability of firms. According to Shiller, highly volatile stockmarkets, stock prices which move counter to stock dividends and which fluctuate more than dividend fluctuations all indicate that something is wrong with efficient market theories. Anomalies, like the fact that returns on stocks are higher on some days of the week and in certain months of the year, cast further doubt on efficient market theories. As Shiller notes, this indirectly supports Keynes' position that speculation plays a major role in stockmarkets.

Following Shiller's lead, empirical evidence can be brought to bear on Keynes' theory of speculation. We can then ask whether or not Keynes' three theses on speculation hold. Does speculation lower economic growth? Does it misdirect investment, thereby reducing productivity? Does it worsen the trade cycle?

Table 5.1 attempts to answer these questions using two different measures of speculation. The first, following Shiller directly, is the daily percentage change in stock prices. The second relates stock price changes to investment activity. Remember, Keynes maintained speculation was a problem only when it became a 'bubble on enterprise'. Thus, as daily stock prices change more and more relative to the degree of investment taking place in the economy, Keynes would predict worse economic performance.

Table 5.1. provides some support for Keynes' theses. Greater speculation seems to be associated with lower levels of economic growth and with greater variance in the economic growth rate. Thus it seems to worsen both economic performance and the trade cycle. Evidence of the

Table 5.1

	Daily percentage change in stock prices	*Stock price changes* Ratio of investment to GNP	Real economic growth	Variance of real economic growth	Productivity growth
1961–1965	0.45%	2.75	4.63%	1.3	3.7%
1966–1970	0.57%	3.41	2.99%	4.0	1.8%
1971–1975	0.78%	4.58	2.24%	7.3	1.7%
1976–1980	0.64%	3.63	3.43%	4.2	0.8%
1981–1985	0.68%	4.17	2.35%	8.6	1.2%

Source: Economic Report of the President (1986).

effect of speculation on productivity is less persuasive. Part of the problem may be our inability to measure productivity accurately.[10] Or it may be that factors besides speculation are also important determinants of productivity growth. None the less, while the data do not strongly support Keynes here some correlation appears to be present in the data; and Keynes' insight on the relationship between speculation and productivity probably warrants further research and analysis.

Finally, Keynes' theory of speculation has had an impact on several economists. Besides Shiller, mentioned above, the contemporary economist most influenced by Keynes' views on speculation is certainly Hyman Minsky.[11] In fact, Minsky himself has claimed that his financial instability hypothesis arose 'out of an attempt to understand Keynes',[12] and he has subtitled an article on the financial instability theory 'An Interpretation of Keynes'.

Keynes and Minsky both are worried about the real consequences of speculative activity, and both believe that speculation worsens the trade cycle. Minsky's financial instability hypothesis contends that speculative finance has been responsible for and contributed to economic booms and then to economic crisis when the boom cannot be sustained. These ideas are certainly consistent with Keynes' views on speculation and the trade cycle.

Minsky and Keynes differ, however, in their views on how speculation affects current economic activity. Keynes, as we have seen, mainly views speculation as an alternative to enterprise, production and investment. When speculation increases, investment falls because of reduced investment demand. In contrast, for Minsky, speculation increases investment and economic activity in the short run. During an investment boom long-run expectations improve, thus giving rise to a greater investment demand. As time goes on, however, investment projects become increasingly risky and lenders become increasingly speculative. At some point, 'Ponzi finance' takes over, and new money is merely used to pay off interest on old debts. It is only here that speculation fails to contribute to economic growth. The general rule though for Minsky, in contrast to Keynes, is that speculation increases economic growth. The data from Table 5.1, however, seems to support Keynes over Minsky on this point.

Summary and conclusion

This chapter has argued that Keynes' perception of speculation changed over the course of his life. In the *Treatise on Money*, he viewed speculation as a short-run and a monetary problem. In the *General*

Theory Keynes came to view speculation as a real and a long-term problem.

As a consequence of these different views of speculation Keynes proposed different policies to deal with the problem. The *Treatise* advocated monetary policies to keep the rate of interest, the level of investment, and the price level from fluctuating as a result of speculation. The *General Theory* advocated tax policies to discourage speculation and government regulation to prohibit speculative activity.

Empirical evidence seems to confirm Keynes' view that speculation negatively affects economic growth and worsens the business cycle. Keynes' thesis that speculation misdirects investment and retards productivity growth is suggestive, but needs further development.

As we worry about the consequences of an abrupt end to our current speculative frenzy, the dangers which Keynes warned us about in the *General Theory* seem ever close. Perhaps it is time to heed the warnings of Keynes and consider seriously the policy proposals he advanced in an earlier era of speculative excess and crash.[13]

Notes

1. Susan Strange (1986), *Casino Capitalism*, Oxford: Basil Blackwell.
2. Frank H. Knight (1964), *Risk, Uncertainty and Profit*, New York: Augustus M. Kelley, p. 255ff. The views of Keynes in the *Tract* are similar in a number of respects to the views of Knight. There Keynes saw speculation as a way to reduce price fluctuations, and argued that stable prices induce business investment. He also saw speculation as reducing risk for the businessman by passing it on to the professional speculator. See *The Collected Writings of John Maynard Keynes*, ed. Donald Moggeridge (1971), Volume IV, *A Tract on Monetary Reform*, London: Macmillan, pp. 90, 92, 102, and 112f.
3. John Maynard Keynes (1964), *The General Theory of Employment, Interest, and Money*, New York: Harcourt, Brace & World, 162f. All future references to this work will be made parenthetically in the text. Also note the following remark in Keynes's February 1937 *Quarterly Journal of Economics* article 'The General Theory of Employment': 'The sense in which I am using the term is that in which the prospect of a European war is uncertain, or the price of copper and the rate of interest twenty years hence, or the obsolescence of a new invention, or the position of private wealth owners in the social system in 1970. About these matters there is no scientific basis on which to form any calculable probability whatever' (pp. 213–14). For a more detailed description of Keynes's views of uncertainty and the probability calculus see C. Alan Garner (1982) 'Uncertainty, human judgment, and economic decisions', *Journal of Post-Keynesian Economics*, Vol. IV, No. 3 (Spring), 413–24.
4. John Maynard Keynes, *The Collected Writings of John Maynard Keynes* (London: Macmillan, various years) ed. Donald Moggeridge. Volume V, p. 30. All future references to the *Collected Writings* will be made parenthetically in the text with volume and page numbers.
5. George P. Brockway (1983), 'On Speculation: a footnote to Keynes'. *Journal of Post Keynesian Economics*, Vol. V, No. 4 (Summer), 515f.
6. Robert Reich (1983), *The Next American Frontier*, New York: Times Books, p. 159.
7. John Maynard Keynes (1964), *The General Theory of Employment, Interest, and Money*, New York: Harcourt, Brace & World, p. 378. Also see 'The end of *Laissez-faire*', reprinted in John Maynard Keynes (1963) *Essays in Persuasion*, New

York: Norton, pp. 312–22.

8.   Robert J. Shiller (1986), 'Financial markets and macroeconomic fluctuations', *Keynes' Economic Legacy*, ed. James L. Butkiewicz, Kenneth J. Koford and Jeffrey B. Miller, New York: Praeger.

9.   For a good summary of efficient market theory and some of the anaomalies of the theory see Douglas K. Pearce (1987), 'Challenges to the concept of stock market efficiency', *Economic Review*, Federal Reserve Bank of Kansas City, Vol. 72, (Sept/Oct.), pp. 18–33.

10.   On this issue see Sar A. Levitan and Diane Werneke (1984) *Productivity: Problems, Prospects, and Policies* Baltimore: Johns Hopkins University Press. Michael R. Darby (1984), 'The U.S. productivity slowdown: a case of statistical myopia', *American Economic Review*, Vol. 74 (June), pp. 301–22; and Jerome A. Mark, (1986), 'Problems Encountered in Measuring Single- and Multifactor Productivity', *Monthly Labor Review*, Vol. 109 (December), pp. 3–11.

11.   See the essays in Hyman P. Minsky (1982) *Can 'It' Happen Again*? Armonk: M.E. Sharpe.

12.   Hyman P. Minsky, 'The financial instability hypothesis: an interpretation of Keynes and an alternative to "standard" theory', in Minsky, *op. cit.*, p. 60.

13.   The author thanks Donald Walker and Nancy Wulwick for their helpful comments and suggestions, and Jeanne Applegate for her invaluable research assistance.

6 From the 'banana parable' to the principle of effective demand: some reflections on the origin, development and structure of Keynes' *General Theory*

Ingo Barens[1]

. . . industrial output will toboggan down an icy hill towards total inactivity. What then stops this ruinous process?

E. A. G. Robinson[2]

Looking back, I think it was more difficult to see what the problems were than to solve them . . .

Charles Darwin[3]

1

On the basis of a careful reconstruction of Keynes' transition from the *Treatise on Money* to the *General Theory*,[4] this chapter tries to show that Keynes' *General Theory* can be regarded as the consequence of solving the problem of unstable equilibria.[5] In order to substantiate this claim, we shall analyse why Keynes came to reject the traditional ideas of an economy gravitating towards a full-employment long-period position, with discrepancies between the 'natural' rate of interest, determined by 'real' factors (productivity and thrift), and the market rate of interest, determined by 'monetary' factors, being eliminated by changes in the general level of prices. It will be shown how he came to adopt the 'revolutionary' idea of an economy gravitating towards an underemployment, long-period position, with savings and investment being equilibrated through changes in output and employment while the marginal efficiency of capital adjusts to the 'monetary' rate of interest through changes in capital stock.[6]

The chapter is organized as follows. After a short description of the *Treatise*, we demonstrate how its central weakness – the instability of the full-employment, long-period equilibrium position – came to the surface in the 'banana parable' (section 2). In section 3, how Keynes

111

solved the problem of instability and how his solution in turn led him to the notion of the consumption function and the Principle of Effective Demand (i.e. the notion of underemployment equilibrium) are analysed; and we show how a rearrangement of already existing theoretical building-blocks (theory of investment and theory of the rate of interest, respectively), made necessary by the Principle of Effective Demand, brought the new monetary theory of output, employment and interest to completion (section 4). Finally, we show that Keynes had to defend his 'revolutionary' vision against the self-adjusting potential of changes in money wages and the rate of interest (section 5). The concluding section offers some reflections on the origin, development and structure of Keynes' *General Theory* in the light of the results presented in the chapter, together with some remarks on its relation to the *Treatise*. The Epilogue discusses alternative interpretations of two decisive stages of Keynes' transition towards the *General Theory*.

2

The *Treatise on Money* was well rooted in the orthodox marginalist tradition:[7] the purpose of monetary theory is to study the determinants of the equilibrium position of the price level and to analyse the causes of oscillations around this equilibrium position. Although monetary factors are of the utmost importance to the disequilibrium behaviour of prices *and* quantities, eventually 'it all comes out in the wash' (VI, p. 366). In the long run money is neutral, playing no part in the determination of the real variables of the long-period position of the economy. Accordingly, in a very Wicksellian fashion, the process of gravitation of the market rate of interest towards the 'natural' rate takes the centre of the stage. In short, in the *Treatise*, the actual behaviour of the economy is analysed, quite traditionally, in terms of short-period deviations from a full-employment long-period position. All these similarities notwithstanding, there was one new twist to the *Treatise*, and as the consequence of this innovative element, Keynes stressed the menacing possibility that the 'length' of the short period might be socially and politically intolerable, thus confronting economic policy with severe problems.

This innovative element of the *Treatise* consists in a new analytical technique – the price level together with its oscillations (i.e. the credit cycle) are no longer analysed in terms of the quantity of money, but instead in terms of savings and investment. This new technique soon raised doubts about the validity of the traditional wisdom, according to which 'savings always find their way into investment'.[9] In contrast to this view, Keynes thinks it possible for savings to occur without any corresponding investment, because saving decisions and investment decisions are made by quite different individuals (V, pp. 250–1). Thus it is 'saving which does not lead to a correspondingly large volume of investment . . . which is at the root of the trouble' (V. p. 161) of protracted depression and persistent unemployment. Savings as such do not necessarily have a positive effect on the welfare of the community.

As an illustration of his heretical view on the effects of saving, Keynes invented a little parable about an economy consisting entirely of banana plantations (V, pp. 158–60; XX, pp. 76–81). In this economy bananas are the only commodity produced and consumed, and initially an equilibrium exists between savings and investment with the factors of production fully employed.

Now, suppose that '[i]nto this Eden there enters a thrift campaign, urging the members of the public to abate their improvident practices of devoting nearly all their current incomes to buying bananas for daily food' (V, p. 158). What will be the consequences of this increase in the propensity to save? As the same quantity of bananas is brought to the market, while consumption expenditure has been curtailed, the price of bananas must fall. In his exposition, Keynes assumes that investment stays constant for a variety of reasons.[10] Because bananas cannot be stored, the price decline will be in exact proportion to the increase in savings.[11] During this first stage, increased savings have yielded, so it seems, only positive effects. Although having become wealthier, the consumers are still able to consume the same quantity of bananas as before.

But what has happened to the plantation owners? If initially wages, or more generally, costs of production[12] have not changed, entrepreneurs will suffer windfall losses. According to Keynes, it becomes clear that the additional savings have not increased the wealth of the community in the aggregate, they only have caused its redistribution from the pockets of the entrepreneurs to the pockets of the general public. 'The savings of the consumers will be required, either directly or through the intermediary of the banking system, to make good the losses of the entrepreneurs' (V, p. 159). As long as entrepreneurs stick to the full-employment level of output they have to make good their windfall losses by borrowing. Thus the rate of interest stays at its initial level because, according to Keynes, the additional supply of savings calls forth an additional demand for savings in exactly the same amount (XIII, p. 331, 334; XX, p. 77; XXIX, p. 14).

So far, Keynes has shown that savings as such do not increase aggregate wealth. But 'the full horror of the situation' (XX, p. 77) is yet to come. Eventually, entrepreneurs will seek to protect themselves against the windfall losses by reducing their costs of production. Two alternatives are open to them: they can reduce the money wages of their workers, i.e. reduce nominal income with real income constant; or they can cut their workforce, i.e. reduce real income with money wages constant. 'But even this will not improve their position, since the spending power of the public will be reduced by just as much as the aggregate costs of production' (V, pp. 159–60). The decline of output and employment, set into motion by a reduction in consumption expenditure, will not stop until 'all production ceases and the entire population starves to death' (V, p. 160).[13] This, then, is the paradox of saving: savings, if not accompanied by investment, not only do not increase aggregate wealth, in fact, they tend to diminish it! When Keynes presented this heresy before the Committee on Finance and Industry, its chairman Lord Macmillan was urged to comment: 'That is a strange doctrine to a Scotsman!' (XX, p. 80).

Of course, Keynes' reasoning is full of glaring deficiencies. But if these are put aside for a moment and the conclusions of the 'banana parable' accepted as correct for the sake of the argument, the situation gets even worse. Because then a far more dramatic consequence shows up: the full employment equilibrium in the *Treatise*, the point of reference for all its analytical conclusions, turns out to be an unstable equilibrium! As theoretical results based on the analysis of unstable equilibrium are meaningless, the author of the *Treatise* is confronted with a dilemma. He must repudiate either his new analytical technique or the theoretical results of the *Treatise*. Both alternatives boil down to the same outcome: everything that is new and original in the *Treatise* runs the danger of becoming meaningless and therefore obsolete.

The only other alternative would be to show how the instability implied by the new technique can be avoided. Here, a closer look at the deficiencies in Keynes' reasoning can yield some instructive clues. In the 'banana parable', by simply speaking of changes in aggregate costs of production, Keynes obviously has failed to distinguish between the effects of changes in money wages (nominal income) on the one hand, and changes in real income on the other hand. In addition, as soon as real income starts to decline, entrepreneurs no longer need to make good their windfall losses at the same rate as before.[14] But in this case, the reason for the rate of interest to stay constant in spite of an increase in savings no longer exists and Keynes must take into consideration the behaviour of the rate of interest and its impact on the instability of the equilibrium position.

Keynes must have been well aware of the threat an unstable equilibrium posed to his analysis, because in what seem to be the earliest extant draft chapters of the *General Theory* (XIII, pp. 381–96), he takes up the argument of the 'banana parable' again. He restates it systematically and analyses it rigorously to find 'what emergency exits there may be . . . from so devastating a result' (XIII, p. 385). He starts by giving a simplified version of the 'Fundamental Equations' (XIII, p. 381). Under the heading 'The *Instability* of a Profit-Seeking Organization of Production' (emphasis added) he then probes deeper into the mechanism of the downturn (XIII, pp. 382–5), analyses the effects of changes in real income on windfall losses (XIII, pp. 385–9) and then proceeds to a discussion of the effects of changes in the rate of money earnings (XIII, p. 390–4) as well as in the rate of interest (XIII, pp. 394–6).

This early analysis shows a very distinctive feature, one that, as will be shown below, is characteristic of his later analysis as well. It is in the part dealing with the effects of changes in real income that Keynes almost immediately arrives at his startling new conclusions concerning the possibility of underemployment equilibrium. But he considers this result as preliminary as long as the effects of changes in money wages and the rate of interest are left unaccounted for. The indirect effects of changes in money wages on the rate of interest threatened to undermine the validity of the results derived from the analysis of quantity adjustments.

3

It is convenient to start the reconstruction of Keynes' analysis with his own modification of the 'Fundamental Equations', focusing on windfall losses (or profits) as the relevant magnitude. As in the *Treatise*, windfall losses (or profits) (Q) are defined as the difference between investment (I) and savings (S):

(1) $Q = I - S$

Keynes takes this one step further by explicitly expressing (Q) in terms of aggregate demand (D) (or 'disbursement', as he calls it) and income or earnings (E) (in the *Treatise* sense). The connecting link is savings, defined as the excess of income over consumption expenditure (F):

(2) $Q = I - (E - F) = I + F - E = D - E$

In the earliest draft manuscripts Keynes works with a still different version, reformulating expressions (1) and (2) in terms of *changes* in windfall losses (XIII, p. 381):

(3) $\Delta Q = \Delta I - \Delta S = \Delta I + \Delta F - \Delta E = \Delta D - \Delta E$

Although this reformulation does not give any new information, it nevertheless yields a clear insight into the logic of the 'banana parable'. Its central argument was that a spontaneous increase in savings will lead to windfall losses, i.e. $Q < O$, while the resulting contraction of output and employment will have no effect whatsoever on these windfall losses, i.e. $\Delta Q = O$. This argument now turns out to hinge on the assumption

(4) $\Delta D = \Delta E$

i.e. on the assumption that 'the amount of disbursement declines by . . . the same amount as the decline in earnings' (XIII, p. 384). In order to simplify the exposition the same assumption about the behaviour of investment as in the 'banana parable' will be made in what follows. It will be assumed that investment remains constant during the downturn of activity.[15] With $\Delta I = O$, expression (4) becomes

(5) $\Delta F = \Delta E$.

This at once sheds light on the implicit assumption of the 'banana parable': the windfall losses remain constant because consumption expenditure falls by the same amount as income. Getting somewhat ahead of the story, this of course is equivalent to the propensity to consume (or spend) (Patinkin, 1976, pp. 67–8). By way of clarifying the 'condition of *in*stability' implied by Keynes' argument, expression (5) at the same time points towards the solution of the 'banana parable', because now the 'condition of instability' can easily be transformed into a 'condition of stability'. In order for the windfall losses to vanish during the contraction of output and employment, the *changes* in(Q) must be positive; and expression (5) shows that

(6) $\Delta Q > 0$, if $\Delta F > \Delta E$ (with $\Delta F, \Delta E < O$),

'a falling off in F at a slower rate than the reduction in E' (XIII, p. 385).

   In the opposite case of windfall profits the 'condition of stability' would be:

(7) $\Delta Q < 0$, if $\Delta F < \Delta E$ (with $\Delta F, \Delta E > O$).

Starting from this hint, it takes Keynes three consecutive steps to arrive at a solution. The first step is to consider the consequences of a subsistence level of consumption. In this case, 'the pressure of increasing poverty' (XIII, p. 386) will sooner or later cause savings to fall off and windfall losses, in turn, will eventually vanish. Thus the devastating result of the 'banana parable' can be avoided. An increase in savings will not result in the total collapse of productive activity, but only in a decline down to the level of output consistent with the subsistence level of consumption demand and the given level of investment demand. Keynes feels sure about this first and most important conclusion: 'Indeed the mere law of survival must tend in this direction. For communities, if any, the inborn character of which was such that they obeyed remorselessly the dictates of thrift . . . [would] have long ago starved to death and left no descendants!' (XIII, p. 386).

The second step consists in applying an analogous argument to the opposite case of increases in real income, starting from the low equilibrium level of output the economy has settled at after the initial full employment position had been disturbed. In this case, once 'spending . . . ceases to increase as rapidly as earnings' (XIII, p. 388), an equilibrium of savings and investment may be attained before the full employment level of output has been reached.[16] If such spending behaviour is probable – and Keynes thinks it is (ibid.) – something like a 'range of instability' does exist.[17] On the one side it is limited by a stable equilibrium position at the subsistence level and on the other side by a stable equilibrium position somewhere below the full employment level.[18]

The third step consists in narrowing down this 'range of instability' to only one stable equilibrium position below full employment output. The 'range of instability' would reduce to an unique equilibrium position if the condition of stability would be effective not just beyond two specified levels of output, but instead at every level. In Keynes' own words:

> . . . provided that spending always increases less than earnings increase and decreases less than earnings decrease, i.e. provided ΔS and ΔE have the same sign, and that investment does not change, any level of output is a position of stable equilibrium. For any increase of output will bring in a retarding factor, since ΔS will be positive and consequently I being assumed constant ΔQ will be negative; whilst equally any decrease of output will bring in a stimulating factor since ΔS will be negative and consequently ΔQ positive. (VIII, p. 387)

In this passage Keynes, for the very first time,[19] gives a clear description of the Principle of Effective Demand.[20]

If expressions (6) and (7) are written in a slightly different manner, it immediately becomes clear that the condition of stability does imply the notion of a (marginal) propensity to consume of less than 1:[21]

$$(8) \quad \frac{\Delta F}{\Delta E} < 1$$

Indeed, it can be shown that Keynes' 'fundamental psychological law' represents nothing but the result of his attempt to lend *economic* plausibility to the condition of stability derived from a *logical* analysis. In order to see this, it is necessary to take stock of Keynes' analytical results so far.

In three steps, Keynes has derived the condition necessary for the existence of stable and unique equilibrium. But up to now, he still only knows that the dynamic process will be an *adjustment* process, i.e. will equilibrate savings and investment, *if* this condition is fulfilled. But is it economically plausible to make such an assumption? Keynes approaches this problem along two different paths. On the one hand, he tries to justify this assumption by referring to the actual behaviour of individuals (on the average); on the other hand, he tries to justify it by referring to the actual stability of the real-world economy. Thus at first he argues, still rather tentatively,[22] that it is reasonable in general to assume the condition of stability to be fulfilled, even though the opposite is not inconceivable (XXIX, p. 39).[23] This attitude changes very soon. In 1933 Keynes thinks this assumption to be 'in accordance with what our knowledge of popular psychology leads us to expect' (XXIX, p. 103).[24] In addition, he now relies on 'the fact that a point of equilibrium is reached in experience when incomes fall is confirmation of the validity of this expectation' (ibid.). Just one year later, he coins the term 'fundamental psychological law' (XIII, p. 445). In the remaining years, Keynes' reasoning undergoes no further material changes.[25] In the *General Theory* he again makes use of both lines of argument (for instance, compare VII, p. 97 with VII, pp. 251–2). Eventually, every different argument put forth in the draft manuscripts re-emerges – even the 'range of instability'.[26]

Even though with the help of the consumption function – the result of an economic interpretation of the condition of stability – Keynes can solve the problem of the 'banana parable', the analysis of the Treatise has to be abandoned. The new stable equilibrium established by the working of the Principle of Effective Demand will,[27] as he immediately realizes, not be a full-employment position again; instead it will imply involuntary unemployment: 'The reader will notice that . . . there is no presumption whatever that the equilibrium output will be anywhere near the optimum output' (XIII, p. 387).

This result undermines the essential feature of the *Treatise* – its notion of a full-employment long-period position (or centre of gravitation). It is replaced by the truly 'revolutionary' notion of an underemployment centre of gravity. This notion marks Keynes' radical departure from orthodox theory. An underemployment centre of gravity makes it possible to view the problem of unemployment from a drastically different perspective: it no longer is, as it had been in the *Treatise*, a concomitant of a departure from the long-period position, i.e. a phenomenon of the short period (of intolerable 'length', perhaps). By contrast, unemployment now is a feature of the centre of gravitation itself![29]

From his analysis of the stability of equilibrium Keynes is able to draw some further conclusions with a distinctive 'Keynesian' flavour. Even though, at this stage, he does not have a precise quantitative relationship at hand to determine the level of output the economy will settle at, he is able to specify the fundamental factors determining this equilibrium position: 'the actual level of output depends, given the policies of the community in respect of saving, on their habits and policies in respect of investment' (XIII, p. 388). This, in turn, implies that 'the level of output, which will be a stable level, entirely depends on the policy of the authorities as affecting the amount of investment' (ibid.). With investment the decisive factor, 'it might be truer to say that the amount of saving . . . depends on the amount of investment, than the other way round' (ibid.).[30] Under these circumstances, economic policy is of crucial importance for the attainment and maintenance of full employment: 'An active policy of stimulating investment renders a greater volume of saving consistent with a greater volume of output' (ibid.).[31] Compared to these early insights, the multiplier, later adopted by Keynes, really represents not much more than an extremely condensed account of the determinants of equilibrium output and employment. The only progress beyond the results of the first draft manuscript lies in the fact that the multiplier gives a definite and precise quantitative relation between investment and income (or between primary and total employment).[32]

4

Up to now, Keynes' analysis has produced two results: (1) stable equilibrium is established by changes in real incomes that act on savings in a systematic manner: and (2) the equilibrium thus established need not be a full-employment position. At this stage, Keynes is confronted with two questions. On the one hand, he has to show how this equilibrium level of output can be determined. As has been shown above, he already possesses some firm clues. With given savings behaviour, the equilibrium level of output depends on the 'habits and policies in respect of investment' (XIII, p. 388). Accordingly, Keynes has to provide a theory of investment. On the other hand, his analysis of saving and investment leaves the rate of interest 'hanging in the air'

(XIV, p. 212). Thus he has to provide a new theory of the rate of interest,[33] but in contrast to the development of the Principle of Effective Demand, Keynes can now fall back on pieces of analysis that were already present in his *Treatise*. Basically, what he does is to adopt, with some modification and refinements, both his theory of investment and his theory of the market rate of interest.[34] Although he can make use of already existing building-blocks, introducing the theory of the market rate of interest into the new theoretical scheme calls for a rearrangement that in turn brings about a drastic change compared to the orthodox theory of the *Treatise*. In the *Treatise*, the market rate of interest, determined by monetary factors, oscillates around the 'natural' rate (its centre of gravity), determined by real factors, adjusting to the latter via movements in the price level.   Keynes can no longer accept this view of the causal relationship between the rate of interest on money and the marginal productivity (or efficiency) of capital. If equilibrium is possible at any level of output, as his analysis suggests, a unique 'natural' rate of interest no longer exists.[35] Clinging, in spite of this, to an explanation in terms of real factors (i.e. marginal productivity of capital), must, according to Keynes, end up in circular reasoning.[36] The only way to avoid this circularity is to consider the rate of interest as a strictly monetary phenomenon, as 'a thing in itself, dependent on liquidity preference and the quantity of money' (XIII, pp. 399–400). Because the theory of the market rate can no longer be linked to any 'real' theory of the rate of interest, it is turned into a 'monetary' theory of *the* rate of interest: 'instead of the marginal efficiency of capital determining the rate of interest, it is truer . . . to say that it is the rate of interest which determines the marginal efficiency of capital' (XIV, p. 123). Thus, in contrast to orthodox teaching, it is the marginal efficiency of capital that oscillates around the rate of interest of money, adjusting to the latter via changes in the stock of real capital (VII, pp. 217–18, 356). The centre of gravity is determined by the rate of interest on money (XXIX, p. 57).

At this point it becomes clear that Keynes' monetary theory of the rate of interest represents nothing but a reversal of the orthodox causal link between the 'natural' and the market rate of interest, a reversal made necessary by the implications of the Principle of Effective Demand.[37] That is why Keynes, at one time in the course of drafting the *General Theory*, could write that 'this book . . . turns mainly on developing a new theory of relationship between the marginal efficiency of capital and the rate of interest' (XIV, p. 362).[38] After having completed his new monetary theory of output and employment, Keynes has to recognize that eventually the decisive question concerning the existence of underemployment has changed. It has turned into the question why the rate of interest 'does not automatically fall to the appropriate level' (VII, p. 31).

5

This brings us back to the 'banana parable'. As will be recalled, at the time of the *Treatise*, Keynes' exposition of the 'banana parable' considered neither the potential effects of a decline in real or nominal income on the rate of interest nor the effect of changes in the rate of interest on investment. After arriving at his new and 'revolutionary' results in the first draft manuscript, he concedes that these results will be only preliminary as long as the effects of changes in money wages and the rate of interest have not been accounted for (XIII, p. 389). In this section, Keynes' approach to this problem will be reconstructed, focusing on the indirect effects of reductions in money wages via the rate of interest and the role of the Liquidity Trap.[39]

Although, elsewhere in the *Treatise*, Keynes had already hinted at the possibility that money wage reductions might exert an indirect effect via changes in the rate of interest (V, p. 144),[40] in the 'banana parable' he does not follow up this trace. In the first draft manuscript he introduces this indirect effect of reductions in money wages explicitly: 'the reduced demand for money, consequent on a fall in wages, may be one of the forces relied upon to produce the reduction in the rate of interest' (XIII, p. 389). He even seems to consider this indirect link as part of the traditional doctrine (XIII, p. 395). After restating the fact that, 'as output, and consequently the community's real income, declines, the proportion of earnings which is saved will also decline'. Keynes outlines the way the rate of interest will work as an 'automatic' force, 'upon which it has been customary to rely in the long run' (XIII, p. 395). With prices and output declining

> . . . the proportion of the stock of money to income will . . . tend to increase. This growing relative abundance of money will, unless the general desire for liquidity relatively to income is capable of increasing without limit, lead in due course to a decline in the rate of interest. (ibid.)

Two things are to be noted in this passage. On the one hand, Keynes only speaks of declining output and prices, not of a reduction in money wages. Nevertheless, as he had announced to deal with the indirect effects of reductions in money wages while analysing the rate of interest (VIII, p. 389), one seems to be entitled to assume that declining money wages are part of his argument. On the other hand, although Keynes already hints at the possibility of a liquidity trap ('the general desire for liquidity . . . increasing without limit'), he does not rest his argument on this possibility. Keynes continues:

> although the decline in the rate of interest may be prevented for a time by various 'bearish' factors from exercising a favourable influence on investment, sooner or later it will do so. Thus we may expect to reach a point at which, with saving declining and investment increasing, the turn of the tide comes, whereupon the recovery will feed on itself...until we are back again at optimum output.' (XIII, pp. 395–6)

In this passage, Keynes mentions a second obstacle that might introduce a retarding element into the adjustment process – pessimistic expectations of entrepreneurs. Again, he does not make use of it in the further course of analysis. Instead, the reason for rejecting this description as incorrect is that 'there is no safeguard against savings increasing faster than they can be absorbed by investment' (XIII, p. 396). The idea behind his rather confused remark seems to be that during the recovery of output somehow savings and investment will again be equalized before the economy has returned to the full employment level of output.[41] In this case a monetary policy 'deliberately aimed at making a rate of interest sufficiently stimulating to investment', as it is characterized by Keynes, will be necessary for the restoration of full employment, but 'under an "automatic" system there is no certainty, or even possibility, of this' (XIII, p. 396).

Even if the apparent confusion about the behaviour of savings during downturn and recovery is neglected, this attempt to criticize the traditional doctrine of self-adjustment stands on shaky ground. If money wages decline in the presence of unemployment and if potential obstacles (like the liquidity trap and pessimistic expectations of entrepreneurs) are excluded, then, even if savings and investment should again be equalized, the rate of interest will tend to fall as long as output is below the full-employment level. Thus, Keynes' analysis of the implications of the 'banana parable' is, at best, still incomplete. It does not answer the question whether the underemployment result can be maintained in spite of the effects of flexibility on money wages and the rate of interest.   Keynes returned to this problem once more during his transition from the *Treatise* to the *General Theory*. In a fragment (XXIX, pp. 54–7), on which he seems to have based his lecture of 14 November 1932, he first expounds the drastic conclusion to be drawn from the Principle of Effective Demand:

> there is no unique long-period position of equilibrium equally valid regardless of the character of the policy of the monetary authority. On the contrary there are a number of such positions corresponding to different policies. Moreover there is no reason to suppose that positions of long-period

equilibrium have an inherent tendency or likelihood to be position of optimum output. (XXIX, p. 55)[42]

In order to substantiate this claim, he once again takes up the problem of the 'banana parable', the depressing influence of a diminished propensity to spend.[43] As before, if savings are in excess of investment, 'prices will fall, rates of earnings will fall, and output will fall, (XXIX, p. 56). Now the ambiguity in the discussion of savings that marred the earlier analysis is gone and Keynes is able to give a clear account of the adjustment process (again without relying on obstacles like Liquidity Trap or entrepreneurial pessimism):

> the demand for money in the active circulation will fall, which in turn will affect the state of liquidity preference so that there will be a lowering *cet.par.* of the rate of interest corresponding to the given quantity of money. As a result of this, therefore, we can reckon on a fall in the rate of interest which will retard saving . . . and stimulate investment until they are once again restored to their former equality. (XXIX, p. 56)

This might give rise to the impression that the depressing effect of an increase in the propensity to save will be restricted to the short period only, while as far as the long-period position is concerned, 'automatic' forces are set in motion 'which will eventually restore equality between saving and investment with . . . the factors of production again fully employed' (ibid.). But, according to Keynes, such an impression would be erroneous. While he agrees that the adjustment process indeed will bring about a new equilibrium of savings and investment, he insists that 'this is quite a different thing from concluding that the long-period position of equilibrium corresponding to the new situation is the same as the original position, both being positions of optimum output' (XXIX, pp. 56–7). Because of its retarding effect on savings, the decline of output below the full employment level will be necessary for the maintenance of the new equilibrium position.

Again, Keynes' analysis falls short of answering the crucial question: and like before, the same argument applies. With money wages flexible, the rate of interest must fall to a level compatible with full employment. When the influence of monetary policy on the real variables of the long-period position is taken up again in the *General Theory* the picture has changed (VII, p. 191). At last the self-regulatory potential of flexible money wages via the rate of interest is fully allowed for. Because of this Keynes now has to admit that the 'number of positions of long-period equilibrium' is drastically reduced. With money wages falling as long as there is unemployment 'there will, it is true, be only two possible long-period positions – full employment and the level of employment corresponding to the rate of interest at which liquidity-preference becomes absolute (in the event of this being less than full employment)' (VII, p. 191).[44]

Thus, as this reconstruction of the development of Keynes' analysis suggests, in the end, the introduction of the Liquidity Trap seems to have been the only way to prevent a full-employment equilibrium in spite of the working of the Principle of Effective Demand. The passage just quoted is no isolated case; in many other places, Keynes explicitly or implicitly refers to the downward inflexibility of the rate of interest as the ultimate cause of unemployment.[45]

6

The results of this reconstruction of Keynes' transition from the *Treatise of Money* to the *General Theory* suggest that the *origin* of 'Keynes' economics' was the problem of unstable equilibrium thrown up by the new analytical technique of the *Treatise*, the savings-investment approach. Furthermore, these results suggest that the *development* of Keynes' thought after the publication of the *Treatise*, culminating in the *General Theory*, may best be understood as a process of spelling out the implications of the solution to the 'banana parable', i.e. the notion that savings (being a function of real income) and investment are equilibrated by changes in real income.[46] This may help to keep a potentially misleading remark made by Keynes in proper perspective. In the Preface to the *General Theory* he characterizes its relation to the earlier *Treatise* as 'a natural evolution in a line of thought which I have been pursuing for several years' although this 'may sometimes strike the reader as a confusing change of view' (VII, p. xxii). This might be understood as describing the transition towards the *General Theory* as a gradual development without any new theoretical insights. In particular. it might be understood as implying that the Principle of Effective Demand was already present in the *Treatise*. The findings presented in this chapter suggest a different interpretation of this 'natural evolution'. Keynes did arrive at his new and decisive analytical conclusion about the equilibrating role of changes in real income only *after* the publication of the *Treatise*. This analytical advance was linked to the *Treatise*. It evolved quite naturally out of the solution to the 'banana parable'. All the essential features of the *General Theory* in turn evolved quite naturally out of the Principle of Effective Demand by way of rearranging theoretical building-blocks already present in the earlier book.

Finally, concerning the *structure* of Keynes' thought, the results suggest a somewhat schizophrenic division. From the very beginning of his transition towards the *General Theory*, Keynes worked within the framework of the Principle of Effective Demand while at the same time trying to cope with the self-regulative potential of changes in money wages and the rate of interest within the marginalist framework. Thus, ironically, the formation of his basically non-marginalist theory of output and employment, with its main implication being the existence of underemployment equilibrium, was, almost step-by-step, accompanied by the unfolding of the marginalist riposte against precisely this implication. While getting a clearer understanding of the working of the Principle of Effective Demand, at the same time Keynes had to realize ever more clearly that his 'revolutionary' results could not be maintained in the presence of a systematic relationship between the level of aggregate demand and the rate of interest. Even if the latter does not equilibrate savings and investment, it nevertheless still proves capable of *adjusting* investment to savings out of full employment income. Keynes' attack on orthodox theory boiled down to the attempt to show that the rate of interest will not fall to a level compatible with full employment.[47] Thus it was his adoption of the marginalist theory of investment into his non-marginalist theory of output that created insurmountable difficulties.[48] The rise to prominence of the liquidity trap seems to be but the sad reflection of this schizophrenia.

Epilogue

This epilogue is devoted to a critical discussion of two recent interpretations of Keynes' work. Don Patinkin's (1980; 1984) and Murray Milgate's (1983), that, while using the same material as this paper, arrive at conclusions contrary to the ones presented here. On the basis of the material in *JMK* (XIII, p. 381–96) Patinkin comes to the conclusion that in these pages Keynes

> had not yet fully recognized what he was later to designate as the 'conclusion of vast importance to [his] own thinking' about the 'psychological law that when income increases, the gap between income and consumption will increase' – at all levels of income. (Patinkin, 1984, p. 20)

Pointing out that these draft chapters do not contain any explicit reference either to an aggregate demand function or its component consumption and investment functions (on this see below), Patinkin denies the possibility that

> this simply reflects a failure to state explicitly and formally what was implicitly understood. For Keynes' contention . . . that 'once we have reached the point at which spending decreases less than earnings . . . *any* level of output is a position of stable equilibrium' shows that he had not yet achieved a full understanding of the basic C + I = Y equilibrium condition that was to constitute his theory of effective demand. (ibid., pp. 20–1)

According to Patinkin, Keynes seems to argue that stable equilibria can be attained at *any* level of output, as soon as savings start to decrease at *some* level of output. Such a notion indeed would reveal little understanding of the 'condition of stability'.But when quoted in full, both sentences referred to by Patinkin convey a very different meaning:

1. 'Indeed once we have reached the point at which spending decreases less than earnings decrease with investment stable, the attainment of equilibrium presents no problem.'
2. 'For provided that spending always increases less than earnings increase and decreases less than earnings decrease, i.e. provided that ΔS and ΔE have the same sign, and that investment does not change, *any* level of output is a position of stable equilibrium.'

The first thing to be noticed is the fact that, contrary to the impression produced by Patinkin's citation, Keynes does *not* use the fact that eventually spending will decrease less than earnings as an argument in favour of the notion that the attainment of stable equilibrium will be possible at any level of output, the actual equilibrium level depending on consumption and investment demand. This contention is raised only in the second sentence, and the argument put forth in its favour in fact is nothing but the 'condition of stability'. If the first sentence is related to Keynes' analysis based on the notion of a subsistence level of consumption, the 'first step' referred to in the text above, it immediately becomes clear that the ideas expressed in both sentences are very different. The first sentence simply expresses the idea that the downturn of activity will not end in total inactivity if spending starts to decrease less than earnings at some level of output, such as the level of subsistence. The second sentence expresses the far more advanced idea that, with the 'condition of stability' being fulfilled, after a disturbance equilibrating forces will spring up at once and irrespective of whether the disturbance is in the downward or upward direction. To put these two ideas on the same footing, as Patinkin's citation suggests, proves to be highly misleading, to say the least. Some remarks should be made concerning Patinkin's view that no explicit reference either to the aggregate demand function or its component parts can be found in the draft chapters under discussion and his inference that this does not reflect 'a failure to state explicitly . . . what was implicitly understood' (Patinkin, 1984, p. 20). Three arguments may be raised against this interpretation. First, it should be kept in mind that, as argued in the paper, Keynes was able to arrive at a solution to the problem of unstable full employment equilibrium precisely because he reduced the complexity of the problem by keeping investment stable (i.e. considering it as exogeneously given) without trying to probe deeper into its determinants. Thus, the logic of his approach, at this decisive stage, did not demand, and thus did not direct his attention to, the derivation of an investment function. To be more precise, it was not directed to the incorporation of the theory of investment already outlined in the *Treatise*. In addition, it should be noted that to consider savings as a function of real income and investment as stable at an exogenously given level, as Keynes' solution implies, betrays the logical structure of the simple multiplier. Second, attention should be drawn to the fact that in these pages Keynes indeed *does* speak, even if in a somewhat unusual manner, about the component parts of aggregate demand, when he states that 'the actual level of output depends, given the habits and policies of the community in respect of saving, on their habits and policies in respect of investment' (XIII, p. 388; see also p. 395).

Finally, it might be pointed out that the fact that not every possible implication (propensity/inducement to invest, liquidity preference etc.) of a certain conclusion (savings and investment being equalized via changes in the real income) is explicitly stated can not be considered as unambiguous evidence that this conclusion has not been drawn.[49]

Milgate (1983), in an attempt to assess Keynes' analytical development in the period 1931–34 comes to the conclusion 'that during the 1932 lectures Keynes was still following the orthodox marginalist train of thought' (1983, p. 195). Specifically, he argues that when Keynes, in his lecture of 14 November 1932 (XXIX, pp. 54–7), asserts that contrary to orthodox thought long-period positions need not be positions of full employment, 'the argument Keynes produces to sustain this conclusion is not entirely consistent, and illustrates the fact that he had not yet fully broken away from the orthodox theory' (ibid., pp. 193–4). According to Milgate, in this lecture Keynes discusses the effects of an increase in the market rate of interest, the 'natural' rate being unchanged. From this perspective, Keynes' argument indeed must seem to be strewn with inconsistencies. In fact, Keynes discusses quite a different problem, namely a decrease in the 'natural' rate of interest (due to a diminished propensity to spend; XXX, p. 56), the market rate initially being unchanged. Looked at from *this* perspective, all the inconsistencies detected by Milgate disappear. This reappraisal of the 'banana parable' in the light of Keynes' new findings indeed is consistent and leaves only one problem unsolved: the effects of flexible money wages on the equilibrium level of employment via the rate of interest (as has been shown in the text above).[50]

The arguments put forth seem sufficient to establish that Patinkin's and Milgate's alternative interpretations of the development of Keynes' thought do not invalidate the conclusions presented in this chapter.

Notes
1. I want to thank H. Baisch, R.W. Clower, A. Leijonhufvud and P. Trescott for their constructive comments and D.A. Walker for his support. Of course the usual disclaimer applies.
2. E.A.G. Robinson (1936, p. 471).
3. Letter to C. Lyell (30 September 1859); in Darwin (1887, p. 170).
4. The present chapter is based on the results of the author's doctoral dissertation: see Barens (1987).
5. This aspect has not been taken into account sufficiently in the existing literature on the development of Keynes' thought between the *Treatise* and the *General Theory*: see, for instance, the writings of Moggridge and Patinkin in the bibliography and, in addition, Davis (1977; 1980), Dimand (1983), Kahn (1983), Lambert (1969) and Mehta (1978).
6. At present, it is still highly controversial whether the idea of an underemployment *long-period* position really represents Keynes' critical intentions; on this see Barens (1987, Part 2), Eatwell and Milgate (1983), Harcourt (1981; 1985), J. Robinson (1936), Milgate (1982) and Schumpeter (1952, pp. 282–3).
7. For different views on the *Treatise* and its relation to marginalist theory as well as the *General Theory*, see, for instance, Patinkin (1976) and Milgate (1982).
8. Here Myrdal's (1939, p. 8) remark – made with reference to Wicksell's similar approach in *Geldzins und Güterpreise* (see Wicksell 1898) – about Keynes' 'unnecessary originality' should be kept in mind. Keynes himself analysed the credit cycle in terms of disequilibrium of savings and investment as early as 1913 (XIII, p. 2ff.).
9. See for instance (XIII, p. 249).
10. See (V, pp. 158–9) and (XX, p. 76).
11. This is the reason why Keynes restricted his analysis to non-storable commodities; in addition, see (XX, p. 77).
12. Keynes uses the term 'wages in a very wide sense, to cover what economists call "renumeration of the factors of production"' (XX, p. 45).
13. In addition, Keynes lists as possible causes that might prevent output from declining to total inactivity: stimulating investment, a decline in savings because of growing impoverishment, a petering out of the thrift campaign and a cartel of producers aiming at keeping up the prices of bananas, see (V, p. 160; XX, p. 78).
14. Here Hawtrey's comments on the *Treatise* most likely have been a decisive influence on Keynes' thinking: 'The greater the contraction of output, the less is the windfall loss' (XIII, p. 152). Kaldor made the same point after the publication of the Treatise (XIII, p. 239). On Hawtrey's role during Keynes' transition from *Treatise* to *General Theory*, see Davis (1977; 1980) and Dimand (1983).
15. See (XIII, pp. 385–6, 393–4) for Keynes' analysis of the effects of changes in real income and money wages on investment.
16. Of course, this argument is far less plausible than the one resting on subsistence consumption.
17. But Keynes does not hesitate to point out that this instability is not his main concern (XIII, p. 395).
18. To be precise, these two equilibrium positions only are 'semi'-stable, i.e. the lower equilibrium position is stable from above (for contractions of output and employment), while the upper position is stable from below (for expansions of output and employment); see Gandolfo (1987).
19. In a letter to Kahn of 20 September 1931 (XIII, pp. 373–5), Keynes may have given an even earlier description.
20. Patinkin's (1984, pp. 20–1) interpretation of this passage stands in contrast to the one presented here; on this see the Epilogue.
21. See Milgate (1983, pp. 192–3) for the same observation in a different context.
22. After deriving the 'condition of stability' and its implications in the first draft

chapters, Keynes does not yet examine the problem of its validity.
23. See as well (XIII, pp. 401–2).
24. In addition, see the lecture notes taken by Tarshis and quoted in Patinkin (1984, p. 22).
25. For instance, see (XIV, p. 447 and VII, pp. 97–8); for a similar statement from the time after the publication of the *General Theory*, see (XIV, pp. 273–7).
26. See (VII, p. 252).
27. On the basis of this interpretation, it comes as no surprise that the consumption function and the theory of effective demand are especially concerned with the stability of the equilibrium solution, as Fender (1981, p. 55) and Patinkin (1984, p. 10) have pointed out. In particular, against this background the multiplier must be understood as the reflection of stability analysis and not – as in Leijonhufvud (1968) – as an expression of the destabilizing consequences of quantity adjustments.
28. Of course, the idea of savings changing with real income did not come as a complete surprise to Keynes. Even at the time of the *Treatise*, he hints at the possibility that declining real income sooner or later will effect savings; see (XIII, pp. 143–4) 184; XX, p. 127). At the same time he either considers this 'an alleviation which is not to be relied upon' (VI, p. 131) or he thinks that unemployment will disappear again as soon as an equilibrium of savings and investment is again established (XX, p. 127).
29. This was clearly understood by Robertson; see (XIII, pp. 500, 506). Under these circumstances, the traditional approach to the unemployment problem, i.e. the attempt to stabilize employment, must prove to be completely inapt, because it will only succeed to stabilize *un*employment; see (VII, pp. 326–7) and J. Robinson (1937, p. 120).
30. In addition see (XIII, pp. 276, 407; XXIX, pp. 106–9). This passage is a half-way house between the *Treatise's* tentative conjecture that 'the increase and decrease of capital depends on . . . investment and not on . . . saving' (V, p. 156) and the outright statement in the *General Theory* that 'saving . . . is a mere residual' (VII, p. 64).
31. Another consequence of Keynes' analysis is the rejection of Say's Law. If understood as implying the 'condition of *in*stability', i.e. $\Delta D = \Delta E$, the impossibility of a coexistence of Say's Law and the Principle of Effective Demand at once is obvious; see (XIV, p. 370) and (XXIX, pp. 80–81).
32. See Patinkin (1984, pp. 29–30). Before integrating the multiplier, Keynes' results were restricted to stating that 'whilst we cannot deduce from changes in investment the exact *amount* of the changes in other factors, we can infer with a degree of probability approaching to certainty the *direction* of these changes' (XXIX, p. 41).
33. For the following, see Keynes' own account (XIV, pp. 84–5, 212–13).
34. For Keynes' theory of investment in the *Treatise*, see (V, pp. 138–9, 180–81) and Fender (1981, pp. 224–5), Hicks (1967, pp. 196–8), Mehta (1978, pp. 128–33) and Leijonhufvud (1968, pp. 162–3). For the theory of the rate of interest, see (V, pp. 127–32, 225–5) and Shackle (1974, p. 54).
35. In addition, the notion of 'normal profits' loses all meaning and Keynes has to address the problem of explicitly taking into account profit maximization by entrepreneurs. This turned out to be one of the most thorny problems he had to tackle on the way to the *General Theory* and might have been the reason why he eventually chose to expound an inherently long-period vision with the help of a short period model, as Schumpeter (1952, pp. 282–3) once observed. For some of the first steps towards an incorporation of a supply curve, see (XXIX, pp. 12, 72).
36. See (VII, p. 137; XIII, p. 452; XIV, pp. 103–4, 212, 477–8; XXIX, pp. 115, 119) and Garegnani (1978/83, pp. 51–2).
37. Keynes leaves no doubt about this fact; see (VII, pp. 242–3). Eshag (1963, pp. 62, 66–7) and Fender (1981, pp. 121–1) have reached similar conclusions.
38. According to Hawtrey (1951, p. 195), it is this reversal of the causal link that marks the crucial difference between 'classical' theory and Keynes' analysis.
39. For Keynes' analysis of the direct effects of reductions in money wages via making

business more profitable, see (XIII, pp. 390–4). There Keynes comes to the conclusion 'that there is no presumption that an *all-round* reduction...will prove favourable to the volume of employment' (XIII, 394).

40. In the course of examining Pigou's evidence before the Committee on Finance and Industry on 28 May 1930, Keynes had elaborated on this possibility. See Committee (1931; Questions nos. 6134–51). See (XIII, p. 317) as well.

41. Keynes seems to assume that savings will respond to a change of real incomes differently, depending on the *direction* of the change.

42. Compare this passage – and a similar one (XXIX, p. 57) – with Keynes' remark about the full-employment position only being 'a limiting point of the possible positions of equilibrium' in the first chapter of the *General Theory* (VII, p. 3).

43. According to Milgate (1983), in this fragment Keynes analyses quite a different problem, i.e. the departure of the market rate from an unchanged 'natural' rate of interest; on this see the Epilogue.

44. For the changes this passage has undergone from the first proof to the final manuscript of the *General Theory*, compare (XIII, p. 642 and XIV, p. 485).

45. See (VII, pp. 18, 232–3, 252–3, 266–7, 304, 308–9). For a discussion of the role of the Liquidity Trap in the literature on Keynes, see Barens (1987, Part 6).

46. Another possibility to reconstruct the development of Keynes' economics would consist in reconstructing, on the basis of Marshall's writings, a Marshallian short-period model and to study the modifications necessary to arrive at Keynes' results; see Caspari (1986) and Caspari (forthcoming) for some first results.

47. On the basis of the reconstruction presented in this chapter, one could study the different roles money had to play in different phases of the transition from *Treatise* to *General Theory*; see Barens (1988).

48. On this see Garegnani (1978/83, pp. 57–61).

49. There is some further evidence in favour of the view that Keynes arrived at the notion of stable *and unique* equilibrium in the earliest draft chapters. The original manuscripts in Keynes' own writing that have been reproduced as (XIII, pp. 381–96) are in the Keynes Papers deposited at the Marshall Library at Cambridge. These originals contain a paragraph that was not included in the *Collected Writings*. It is located between the sentence ending with 'to reduce output again below the critical figure' and the one starting with 'Thus the actual level of output depends . . .' (XIII, p. 388). In this paragraph, which is crossed out, Keynes argues that this 'critical' level of output (designated with the letter A) will be a stable equilibrium. The last sentence in the paragraph makes it clear beyond any doubt that Keynes regards this stable position as an unique equilibrium as well; it reads (with O for output): 'Hence O = A is a position of stable equilibrium.' Keynes continues with a remark about the determinants of this stable and unique equilibrium (this passage does not belong to the crossed-out portion of the manuscript) 'The actual position of A depends, of course, on the habits and policies of the community, in respect of investment as well as in respect of saving . . .' I am indebted to Prof. D. Moggridge for his kind permission to make use of this material.

50. See Barens (1985) for a thorough discussion of Milgate (1983).

References

Barens, I. (1985), 'Milgate on the 'new' Keynes Papers: a comment', unpublished manuscript.

Barens, I. (1987), *Geld und Unterbeschäftigung. John Maynard Keynes Kritik der Selbstregulierungsvorstellung*, Berlin: Duncker & Humblot.

Barens, I. (1988), 'Die (doppelte) Rolle des Geldes bei Keynes', in H. Hagemann and O. Steiger (eds), *Keynes' General Theory nach fünfzig Jahren*, Berlin: Duncker & Humblot.

Caspari, V. (1986), *The Marshallian Foundations of Keynes' 'General Theory'*, unpublished manuscript.

Caspari, V. (forthcoming), *Walras, Marshall, Keynes. Zum Verhältnis von Mikro- und Makroökonomie* Berlin: Duncker & Humblot.
Committee On Finance And Industry (1931), *Minutes of Evidence*, London: HMSO.
Darwin, F. (ed.) (1887), *The Life and Letters of Charles Darwin*, vol. II, London: John Murray.
Davis, E.G. (1977), 'The role of R.G. Hawtrey in Keynesian economics and the economics of Keynes', discussion paper no. 77–12, Carleton University.
Davis, E.G. (1980), 'The correspondence between R.G. Hawtrey and J.M. Keynes on the *Treatise*: the genesis of output adjustment models', *Canadian Journal of Economics*, XIII, no. 4, pp. 716–24.
Dimand, R.W. (1983), *From the 'Treatise' to the 'General Theory': the Formulation of Keynes' Theory of Employment and Output*, Ph.D. dissertation, Yale University.
Eatwell, J., and Milgate, M. (eds) (1983), *Keynes' Economics and the Theory of Value and Distribution*, London: Gerald Duckworth.
Eshag, E. (1963), *From Marshall to Keynes. An Essay on the Monetary Theory of the Cambridge School*, Oxford: Basil Blackwell.
Fender, J. (1981), *Understanding Keynes. An Analysis of 'The General Theory*, Brighton: Wheatsheaf.
Gandolfo, G. (1987), 'Stability', in J. Eatwell, M. Milgate and P. Newman (eds), *The New Palgrave. A Dictionary of Economics*, London: Macmillan, vol. 4, pp. 461–4.
Garegnani, P. (1978/83), 'Notes on consumption, investment and effective demand', *Cambridge Journal of Economics*, vols 2 and 3, cited as reprinted in: Eatwell and Milgate (1983, pp. 21–69).
Harcourt, G.C. (1981), 'Marshall, Sraffa and Keynes: incompatible bedfellows?', *Eastern Economic Journal*, 7, pp. 39–50.
Harcourt, G.C. (ed.) (1985), *Keynes and his Contemporaries*, London: Macmillan.
Hawtrey, R.G. (1952), *Capital and Employment*, 2nd edn, London: Longman.
Hicks, J. (1967), 'A note on the *Treatise* in *Critical Essays in Monetary Theory*, Oxford: Clarendon Press, pp. 189–202.
Kahn, R. (1983), *The Making of Keynes' 'General Theory'*, Raffaele Mattiolo Lectures, Cambridge: Cambridge University Press.
Keynes, J.M. (1973), *The Collected Writings of John Maynard Keynes*, London: Macmillan. (All references are to the appropriate volume and page number of this edition.)
Lambert, P. (1969), 'The evolution of Keynes' thought from the *Treatise on Money* to the *General Theory*', *Annals of Public and Co-operative Economy*, 40, pp. 243–63.
Leijonhufvud, A. (1968), *On Keynesian Economics and the Economics of Keynes. A Study in Monetary Theory*, London–Toronto: Cambridge University Press.
Mehta, G. (1978), *The Structure of the Keynesian Revolution*, New York: St. Martin's Press.
Milgate, M. (1982), *Capital and Employment. A Study of Keynes' Economics*, London: Academic Press.
Milgate, M. (1983), 'The new Keynes papers', in Eatwell and Milgate (1983, pp. 187–99).
Moggridge, D.E. (1973), 'From the *Treatise* to the *General Theory*: an exercise in chronology', *History of Political Economy*, 5, pp. 72–88.
Moggridge, D.E. (1977), 'Cambridge discussion and criticism surrounding the writing of the *General Theory*: a chronicler's view', in Patinkin and Leith (1977, pp. 64–71).
Moggridge, D.E. (1980), *Keynes*, 2nd edn, London: Macmillan.
Myrdal, G. (1939), *Monetary Equilibrium*, London: W. Hodge.
Patinkin, D. (1975), 'The collected writings of John Maynard Keynes: from the *Tract* to the *General Theory*', *Economic Journal*, 85, pp. 249–71.
Patinkin, D. (1976), *Keynes' Monetary Thought. A Study of its Development*, Durham: Duke University Press.
Patinkin, D. (1977), 'The process of writing the *General Theory*', in Patinkin and Leith (1977, pp. 3–24).
Patinkin, D. (1980), 'New material on the development of Keynes' monetary thought',

History of Political Economy, 12, pp. 1–28.
Patinkin, D. (1984), *Anticipations of the General Theory and other Essays on Keynes*, 2nd printing, Chicago: Chicago University Press.
Patinkin, D., and Leith, J.C. (eds) (1977), *Keynes, Cambridge and the General Theory: the Process of Criticism and Discussion Connected with the Development of the General Theory*, London: Macmillan.
Robinson, E.A.G. (1936), 'Mr. Keynes on money', *The Economist*, 29, pp. 471–2.
Robinson, J. (1936), 'The long-period theory of employment', *Zeitschrift für Nationalökonomie*, VII, pp. 74–93.
Robinson, J. (1937), *Introduction to the Theory of Employment*, London: Macmillan.
Schumpeter, J.A. (1952), *Ten Great Economists. From Marx to Keynes*, London: Allen and Unwin.
Shackle, G.L.S. *Keynesian Kaleidics*, Edinburgh: Edinburgh University Press.
Wicksell, K. (1898), *Geldzins und Guterpreise. Eine Studie über die den Tauschwert des Geldes bestimmenden Ursachen*, Jena: Gustav Eischer.

7 Keynes' *General Theory:* the Marshall connection

Robert W. Clower[1]

Some dozen years ago, in a paper entitled 'The Keynesian Perplex', I remarked in passing that Keynes' intention in writing the *General Theory* was 'to offer the world an analytically manageable aggregative version of the kind of general process analysis that Marshall himself might have formulated had he ever felt a need explicitly to model the working of the economic system as a whole'.[2] My object in that paper was to argue that Keynesian economics had been shunted onto the wrong track by the Neo-Walrasian resurgence, so I somehow never thought to ask: What kind of aggregative model *would* Marshall have constructed had he ever felt the need for one? It is another question whether such a counterfactual analysis is worth pursuing. Were contemporary macroeconomics in less of a muddle I might have some doubts; but as matters stand, some doctrine-history 'backtracking'[3] would seem to be in order.

1. Preliminaries

It will be helpful to start with Marshall's earliest graphic account of short-period equilibrium of 'normal' demand and supply for a particular commodity.[4] Referring to a diagram like that shown in Figure 7.1, Marshall first describes the 'supply' curve S as showing, for 'any particular amount of a commodity [that] is to be brought to a certain market at a certain time . . . the price at which it can so be brought.' This price is called the *supply price* and may be denoted by p^s.[5] Similarly, the 'demand' curve D is described as showing, for any particular amount of a commodity that is 'to be sold in the market during [a] given time, [the] price at which it can be so sold.' This price is called the *demand price* and may be denoted by p^d.[6] As for the determination of market equilibrium, it seems best to let Marshall speak for himself (p. 132):[7]

> At a point at which the curves cut one another there will be equilibrium, that is the amount bought will be such that the price at which it can just be

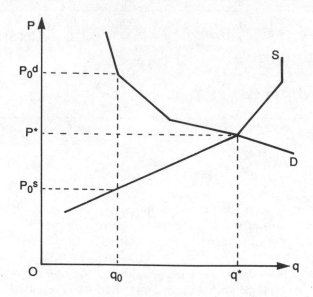

Figure 7.1.

brought into the market will be equal to the price at which that amount can be just got rid of . . . For let the amount supplied at any time be [q_0 in Figure 7.1] . . . If [p^s_0], the cost of supply, be less than [p^d_0], the price at which it can be sold, the trade will be a profitable one, production will be stimulated and [q] will move to the right. So if [p^s_0] be greater than [p^d_0], the trade will be an unprofitable one, production will be checked and [q] will move to the left.

A continuation of the same line of argument quickly establishes the familiar Marshallian 'stability' condition,[8] namely, that 'to the *left* of the point of intersection the supply curve lies *below* . . . the demand curve.' In contrast to the more common Walrasian stability criterion of modern textbooks, the Marshallian condition is independent of the absolute slopes of the S and D curves; as Marshall observes ('Essay on Value', Whitaker, I, p. 132), 'It has reference simply to the relative positions of the curves in the neighbourhood of the point of intersection.'

This account might seem to suggest that Marshall's short-period analysis – like that of Walras – was intended to model the working of a highly organized competitive auction market. In fact, Marshall seems to have had in mind a much more loosely organized, though still highly competitive market in which

the forces of demand and supply have free play; . . . there is no close combination among dealers on either side, but each acts for himself, and there is much free competition; that is, buyers generally compete freely with buyers, and sellers compete freely with sellers. But though everyone acts for himself, his knowledge of what others are doing is supposed to be generally sufficient to prevent him from taking a lower or paying a higher price than others are doing. This is assumed provisionally to be true both of finished goods and of their factors of production, of the hire of labor and of the hiring of capital. (*Principles*, 8th edn., p. 341)[9]

As Whitaker has observed (Whitaker I, p. 125): 'Marshall's conception of competition was from the first a qualified one akin to monopolistic competition.'

Starting from this conception of competition, it would have been but a short step for Marshall to develop an explicitly dynamic treatment of variations over time in the asking and sale prices of, and the quantities offered for sale and sold by individual producers within a particular market, proceeding along lines suggested by the phase-diagram method for handling a system of differential equations that he used in his 'Essay on International Trade' (*c.* 1873; cf. Whitaker, I, pp. 264–5; 11, p. 115). But Marshall lacked the intellectual audacity for such an undertaking. As he remarked in a related context (Whitaker, I, p. 162, fn. 4): 'the mathematical functions introduced into the original differential equation could not . . . be chosen so as to represent even approximately the economic forces that actually operate in the world. And by integrating them we should move further away from, instead of approaching nearer to the actual facts of life.'

So much for Marshall's short-period partial equilibrium analysis for a particular market. The preceding sketch does scant justice to the subtlety and wisdom of Marshall's thought. It was not without reason that, after Marshall's death in 1924, Keynes wrote of him: 'As a scientist he was, within his own field, the greatest in the world for a hundred years' (*JMK*, X, p. 173). It might be added that, as an analyst, Marshall had no peer in the art of 'recognizing hard problems and then hiding them in plain sight'[10].

2.   A Marshallian macro-model

It is a straightforward exercise to extend Marshall's short-period analysis of a particular market to the case of output as a whole, though we must deal with one or two complications along the way.

As in the preceding section, it is convenient to start with a supply and demand diagram (Figure 7.2). Suppose that short-period output for the economy as a whole – here assumed to be a meaningful notion – is initially at the level $q = q_o$ so that the demand price p^d_o, as given by the *ceteris paribus* demand curve $D(Z_o)$, is greater than the supply price p^s_o,

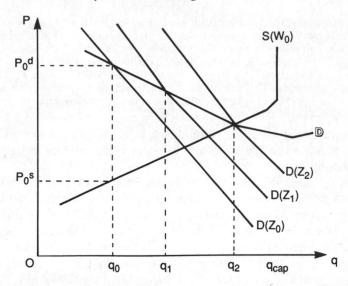

Figure 7.2.

as given by the *ceteris paribus* supply curve $S(w_o)$. If we assume that the current market price of output as a whole lies generally in the neighbourhood of the demand price,[11] then with aggregate output at q_o producers will have an incentive to hire additional factors in order to increase output. Here we run into our first complication.

Unless unemployed workers are available at the going wage rate, actual output cannot be increased except by bidding up the prevailing wage rate, in which case the supply curve will shift upward by an amount depending on the responsiveness of the wage rate to changes in output. To avoid this problem, let us assume provisionally that, at the wage rate w_o, unemployed workers are available for hire at all values of output less then q_{cap}. But then a second complication emerges. In general the demand price for output will depend on the prevailing level of 'aggregate producer outlay', $Z = p^s q$;[12] hence changes in output will produce shifts in the demand curve by amounts that will depend on the responsiveness of aggregate producer outlay to changes in output. This complication can be avoided by defining a *mutatis mutandis* demand curve D as illustrated in Figure 7.2, which shows demand price as a function of aggregate output, i.e. $p^d = D\{q, p^s(q,w_o)\cdot q\}$, due allowance being made for the effect of changes in q on aggregate producer outlay and for the resultant effect of changes in aggregate producer outlay on demand price.[13]

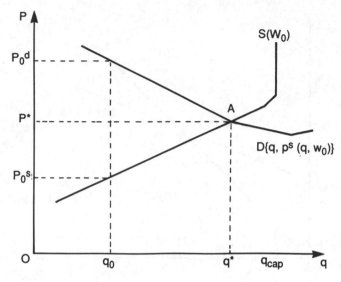

Figure 7.3.

Working now in terms of the *mutatis mutandis* demand curve D and the supply curve S, we obtain short-period equilibrium of aggregate output and price at the point A in Figure 7.3, where $q = q^*$, $p^s = p^d = p^*$, and aggregate expenditure, $E = p^d q = p^* q^* = E^*$ is equal to aggregate producer outlay, $Z = p^s q = p^* q^* = Z^*$ (i.e. where $Z-E = q(p^d - p^s) = 0$).[14] Applying the usual Marshallian stability condition, we may then describe the equilibrium as 'stable' if the supply curve S lies below the demand curve D to the left of the equilibrium point A.

This stability condition can be given a more interesting interpretation if we translate the relations shown in Figure 7.3 into a 'Marshallian Cross' diagram (Figure 7.4). Here, distances along the horizontal axis measure alternative levels of aggregate producer outlay, Z, as determined by the S curve in Figure 7.3 (i.e. distances along 0Y in Figure 7.4 correspond to areas such as $p^s_o q_o$ in Figure 7.3). Similarly, distances along the vertical axis in Figure 7.4 measure alternative levels of aggregate consumer outlay, E, as determined by the D curve in Figure 7.3 (i.e. distances along OE correspond to areas such as $p^d_o q_o$ in Figure 7.3). Then we may define the *aggregate spending function*, $E = f\{Z(q)\}$ parametrically in terms of the variable q, and define the equilibrium level of aggregate producer outlay, Z^*, by the requirement $E = Z$ (i.e., $q(p^d - p^s) = 0$), at which point the spending function must intersect the

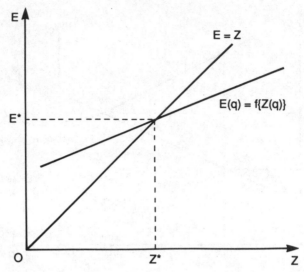

Figure 7.4.

45°-line. On this interpretation, the stability condition is that, in the neighbourhood of the intersection point, the slope of the spending function, which we shall call the *marginal propensity to spend*, must be less than one. But it can be shown that the marginal propensity to spend is less than, equal to, or greater than one according as the quantity elasticity of the demand curve D is less than, equal to, or greater than the quantity elasticity of the supply curve S.[15] Thus the Marshallian Cross 'stability'[16] condition, though it appears outwardly to depend only on the spending proclivities of consumers, depends also on the outlay proclivities of producers.[17]

The case where the marginal propensity to spend is equal to one is of particular interest in the light of post-Marshallian writings. In that case the D and S curves in Figure 7.3 – and therefore the E(q) and E=Z curves in Figure 7.4 – coincide throughout a range of values of q in the neighbourhood of the equilibrium point and we have what Marshall described as *neutral* equilibrium (see Whitaker, I, pp. 153–4). This corresponds to what Keynes (*JMK*, VII, pp. 25–6) later described as 'Say's Law'. Needless to say, this 'Law' forms no part of Marshall's thinking about either particular markets or product markets considered as a whole (cf. Marshall's remarks in a similar connection at p. 201 of Whitaker, II).

Let me conclude this section with a few remarks on some problems that arise if one attempts to generalize the Marshallian model of short-period output equilibrium to deal with broader questions of comparative statics or dynamics. Anyone who is familiar with Marshall's early writings, with his 1898 *Economic Journal* reply to criticisms by Hadley and Irving Fisher (reprinted in Guillebaud, II, pp. 62–75; see especially the long footnote on the theory of market interest rates at p. 74), with his testimony before select committees of Parliament (included in the Pigou volume of Marshall's *Official Papers*), and with early as well as late editions of the *Principles*, will have no difficulty recognizing that these materials provide an ample basis for constructing a 'closed' Marshallian macro-model closely analogous to that set out in Keynes' *General Theory*. In such a generalized model, the *mutatis mutandis* demand function D and the *ceteris paribus* supply function S would include as arguments variables representing such things as the quantity of (outside) money, the money rate of interest, the money wage rate, accumulated real wealth, etc., as well as a variety of shift parameters representing such things as consumer and business 'confidence', expectations of inflation, the state of technology, and so on. It would then be a simple matter to perform various comparative statics ('multiplier') exercises with the model. The question is whether such exercises, if performed at all, might best be carried out with the reduced form spending function that appears in the Marshallian Cross diagram, or with the aggregate demand and supply curves in terms of which the spending function is defined. Views may differ as to the proper answer to this question; but it seems to me that to work with the Marshallian Cross rather than the underlying aggregate demand and supply curves is to court a serious risk of misunderstanding and confusion.

As concerns dynamical extensions of the Marshallian macro-model, I would merely recall my earlier remarks concerning the complexity of the implicit micro-foundations of Marshall's analysis (see the penultimate paragraph of section 1, above). How one might best model a Marshallian macro-system would depend crucially on how one chose to model a competitive economy in which individual producers make their own markets, administer their own asking prices, and adapt their price and output policies in the light of prevailing excess demand conditions in their own 'particular' markets. If this is so, then clearly there is no short or easy path from Marshallian macro-models of short-period equilibrium to intectually satisfying macromodels of real-time dynamics.[18]

3. Was Keynes a Marshallian?
It is commonly argued that the major analytical contribution of the

General Theory lies in the 'theory of effective demand' set out in chapter 3 of Keynes' book.[19] Unfortunately, Keynes' argument in that chapter is occasionally ambiguous or confused, so to this day there is considerable doubt as to how his theory should be interpreted. In the pages that remain, I shall argue that only a Marshallian interpretation is consistent with the letter as well as the spirit of Keynes' argument. What this finding might portend for future research in macroeconomic theory will be the subject of a later paper.[20]

Let me proceed by first restating Keynes' central argument in terms of aggregate demand and supply functions in which output rather than employment is treated as the independent variable.[21] On this assumption, the Keynesian aggregate supply function shown as $Z(q)$ in Figure 7.5a indicates, for any given amount of output, 'the expectation of proceeds which will just make it worth the while of . . . entrepreneurs to produce [that output]' (*JMK*, VII, p. 24). Similarly, the Keynesian aggregate demand function shown as $E\{Z(q)\}$ in Figure 7.5a indicates, for any given amount of output, 'the proceeds which entrepreneurs expect to receive from [that output]' (*JMK*, VII, pp. 25).[22] With appropriate editorial insertions, Keynes' own statement of the theory of effective demand would then read as follows:

> [I]f for a given value of [q] the expected proceeds are greater than the aggregate supply price, i.e. if [E] is greater than Z, there will be an incentive to entrepreneurs to increase [output] and, if necessary, to raise costs by competing with one another for the factors of production, up to the value of [q] for which Z has become equal to [E]. Thus the volume of [output] is given by the point of intersection between the aggregate demand function and the aggregate supply function; for it is at this point that the entrepreneurs' expectation of profits will be maximized. The value of [E], where it is intersected by the aggregate supply function, will be called *the effective demand*. [This] is the substance of the General Theory of Employment, which it will be our object to expound [in] succeeding chapters.[23]

Keynes' argument can be easily translated into a form that makes it indistinguishable from the Marshallian model set out in section 2 above. We have only to interpret Keynes' 'aggregate supply price' as $Z = p^s(q) \cdot q$ and Keynes' 'aggregate demand price' as $E = p^d q = D\{q,Z\} \cdot q$. Then for any chosen value of q, say q_o, the corresponding supply price, p^s_o, is given by the *slope* of the secant OA in Figure 7.5a, while the corresponding demand price, p^d_o, is given by the slope of the secant OB. Equilibrium occurs when the level of output is such that the supply price and demand price secants coincide (so both secants pass through the intersection of Z with E in Figure 7.5a); only at this point are entrepreneurial profits maximized.[24]

But Keynes' theory of effective demand may also be assigned a

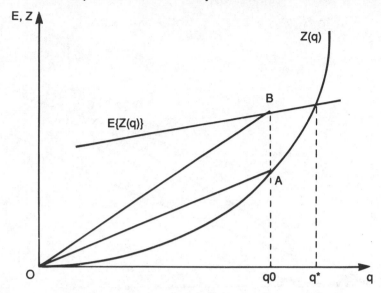

Figure 7.5a.

Walrasian interpretation. This is accomplished by defining 'aggregate supply' as $Z = p \cdot q^s(p)$ and defining 'aggregate demand' as $E = p \cdot q^d = p \cdot \mathbf{D}\{Z(p),p\}$, where p denotes 'market price' and $\mathbf{D}$ is the Walrasian counterpart of the Marshallian *mutatis mutandis* demand function $\mathbf{D}$.[25] Then for any given value of p, say p_o, we can identify the corresponding profit-maximizing level of aggregate output, q_o, with the abscissa of the point of intersection of the aggregate supply curve, Z, with a secant through the origin of slope p_o (point A in Figure 7.5b). Aggregate quantity demanded at the same price can be identified as the abscissa of the point of intersection of the secant OB in Figure 7.5b with a horizontal line representing the value of aggregate expenditure corresponding to q_o, i.e. $E_o = p_o q_o$. On this interpretation, equilibrium occurs if and only if market price attains a value corresponding to the slope of the secant OC in Figure 7.5b so that $E - Z = p(q^d - q^s) = 0$.

We obtain yet another interpretation of Keynes' theory if we adopt a Hicksian 'fix-price' point of view. Specifically, define Z as qp^*, where p^* is some given value of the 'asking price' of producers, and define E as $p^* \mathbf{D}\{p^*, Z(p^*)\}$. These definitions yield a model in which entrepreneurs would like to produce and sell the profit-maximizing level of output $q(p^*)$, defined in Figure 7.5c by the abscissa of the intersection of Z with Z' (Z' is simply the product of output with marginal cost; thus

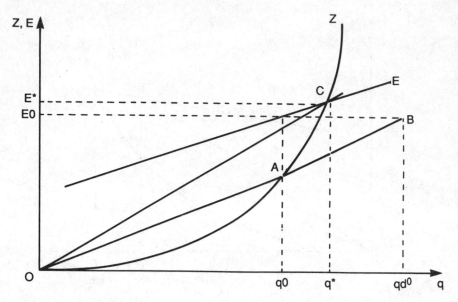

Figure 7.5b.

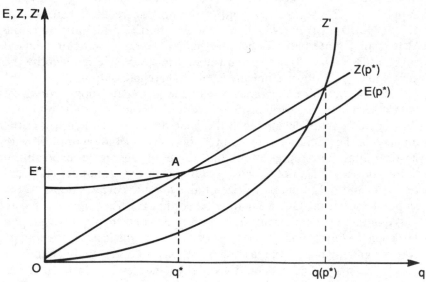

Figure 7.5c.

Table 7.1

Interpretation	Agg. Supply (Z)	Agg. Demand (E)	Equilibrium
Marshallian	$p^s(q) \cdot q$	$p^d(q) \cdot q$	$p^s(q) = p^d(q)$
Walrasian	$p \cdot q^s(p)$	$p \cdot q^d(p)$	$q^s(p) = q^d(p)$
Hicksian Fix-P	$p^* \cdot q$	$p^* \cdot q^d(p^*, q)$	$q = q^d(p^*, q)$

where Z and Z' intersect, asking price equals marginal cost). But short-period sales are limited by aggregate demand, so producers are assumed to aim not at an output that maximizes short-period profit but rather at an output that is saleable under prevailing conditions of aggregate demand. Thus equilibrium occurs in this model if and only if inventory accumulation (virtual or actual) is zero–defined in Figure 7.5c by the point A at which Z intersects E.

For convenient reference, the central characteristics of the three alternative interpretations of Keynes' 'theory of effective demand' are summarized in Table 7.1. The independent variable in the Marshallian case is q; $p^s(q)$ then corresponds to what would nowadays be called marginal (production plus marketing) cost, while $p^d(q)$ represents the highest (uniform) unit price that buyers would be willing to pay for any given (constantly maintained) flow of output q. The independent variable in the Walrasian case is p; $q^s(p)$ is then the profit-maximizing level of output at price p, while $q^d(p)$ is the utility-maximizing level of quantity demanded at p. Finally, in the Hicksian Fix-Price case, quantity produced (q) is again treated as the independent variable (just as in the Marshallian case) while quantity demanded is treated as a function of the fixed price p^* and of current output q (thus combining elements of the Walrasian and Marshallian cases). In this case, unlike the two preceding cases, equilibrium of output as a whole does not entail (expected) profit-maximization; in general, equilibrium output is simply determined by the prevailing state of aggregate demand.

Now, how do each of these interpretations square with Keynes' own statement of the theory of effective demand? As may be quickly confirmed by re-reading Keynes' account of his 'theory' (as cited earlier), the Hicksian Fix-Price interpretation runs directly counter to the letter and spirit of Keynes' argument; yet it is this interpretation – introduced tacitly into the literature through Samuelson's influential textbook presentation of the 'Keynesian Cross' – that has dominated classroom and editorial-page macroeconomics for the past forty years.

Whatever one's view might be about this interpretation as a rendition of Keynes' central message, therefore, there can be no doubt that this interpretation has been marvellously useful for teaching 'Keynesian' economics to bankers and undergraduates; the beauty of the interpretation is that it requires no previous knowledge of economics! It may well turn out that, in some yet-to-be-determined sense, the Hicksian Fix-Price interpretation of Keynes ultimately will be viewed as 'the only way to go' in macroeconomics; be that as it may, it would be grossly disingenuous to claim that this approach owes anything except its initial inspiration to Keynes. The 'theory' in *The General Theory* is decidedly not of the Hicksian fix-price variety.

The Walrasian interpretation fails to conform with Keynes' argument mainly because it presumes that output adjustments are driven by market-determined prices rather than by the competitive jostling of independent profit-seeking, market-making firms. Of course, this is of little consequence unless one is concerned with micro-foundations and related questions involving the dynamics of macroeconomic adjustment. It would surely be unfair to Keynes, however, to hitch his wagon of effective demand to the horse of neo-Walrasian general equilibrium analysis–though, admittedly, that is precisely what was done in early formalizations of the *General Theory* by Hicks, Harrod, Meade, Lange, Modigliani and Klein.

The Marshallian interpretation remains as the only one that faithfully mirrors both the letter and spirit of Keynes' argument. Ironically, it is also the only interpretation among those identified here that has been consistently overlooked or ignored in the post-Keynesian literature. It is not far-fetched to conjecture that the contemporary muddle in Keynesian macroeconomics is due in part to past professional neglect of the Marshall connection. Indeed, I have no doubt that just such a case could be made; but an affirmative argument to that effect must be left for another occasion.

Notes
1. Hugh C. Lane Professor of Economic Theory, University of South Carolina. I owe much to Axel Leijonhufvud of UCLA for numerous conversations about the topics discussed in this chapter. I am grateful also to Daniel Friedman of UC, Santa Cruz, for supplying mathematical notes on the model that underlies the first two sections of the present chapter.
2. Clower (1975, p. 187). For a similar view, see Ohlin (1981, p. 223).
3. 'Backtracking' is part of an oral tradition at UCLA. The term is defined in an unpublished essay by Axel Leijonhufvud on 'The Uses of the Past': 'when the workable vein [of an accepted research programme] runs out, [one] way to go is to backtrack. Back there, in the past, there were forks in the road and it is possible . . . that some roads were more passable than the one that looked most promising at the time' (Leijonhufvud, 1978, pp. 8–9).

4. I refer to his 'Essay on Value' (*c.* 1871), reprinted in Whitaker, 1975, vol.1, pp. 129–32. For the dating of Marshall's essay, see Whitaker's comments, ibid., p. 120.
5. Marshall's definition of (short period) supply price becomes increasingly detailed, though never entirely unambiguous, in later writings. His clearest statement is in the 8th edn of *Principles* (p. 373): 'The general drift of the term normal supply price is always the same whether the period to which it refers is short or long . . . In every case reference is made to a certain given rate of aggregate production . . . In every case the price is that the expectation of which is sufficient and only just sufficient to make it worth while for people to set themselves to produce that aggregate amount; in every case the cost of production is marginal; that is, it is the cost of production of those goods which are on the margin of not being produced at all, and which would not be produced if the price to be got for them were expected to be lower.'
6. Demand price is described in the 8th edn as the 'price at which each particular amount of [a] commodity can find purchasers in a day or week or year.' This concept is no doubt less slippery than the notion of supply price; but whereas Marshall was fairly clear about the factors upon which supply price does or might depend in various circumstances, he was never precise about the 'micro-foundations' of the demand price function.
7. The corresponding passage from the 8th edn of the *Principles* is longer and more explicit but conveys exactly the same message:

> When . . . the amount produced [in a unit of time] is such that the demand price is greater than the supply price, then sellers receive more than is sufficient to make it worth their while to bring goods to market to that amount; and there is at work an active force tending to increase the amount brought forward for sale. On the other hand, when the amount produced is such that the demand price is less than the supply price, sellers receive less than is sufficient to make it worth their while to bring goods to market on that scale; so that those who were just on the margin of doubt as to whether to go on producing are decided not to do so, and there is an active force at work tending to diminish the amount brought forward for sale. When the demand price is equal to the supply price, the amount produced has no tendency either to be increased or to be diminished; it is in equilibrium.

8. I put quotation marks around the word 'stability' because the stability at issue here is purely virtual. Marshall's analysis, like all exercises of its kind, is concerned with *tendencies* that are assumed to be operative in alternative initial situations; it does not refer to real-time adjustment processes (cf. Samuelson, 1947, p. 269ff.)
9. In the 1871 'Essay', Marshall remarks: 'We assume in our theoretical work that competition acts freely: but in so far as it does not the results obtained from the theory will require to be corrected . . . before they can be applied to any particular case.' He then goes on to discuss cases in which competition acts freely but prices *over very short periods* tend to be rigid. This remark might well provide the germ of an alternative treatment of what is now called the theory of monopolistic competition.
10. This is a paraphrase of a remark made originally by Joan Robinson.
11. This seems a sensible supposition in the present context; for if we start with Marshall's conception of competition, then 'impersonal market forces' drive individual asking prices towards equality at the highest price bid by any buyer (cf. Marshall, 1920, pp. 324–5).
12. Defined by Marshall in the 1st edn of the *Principles* (p. 420, fn. 2) as 'the aggregate outlay required for producing any given amount of a commodity'. The magnitude in question corresponds to what Keynes later called 'Aggregate Supply Price', so I follow Keynes' notation and denote it by Z.
13. The graphical derivation of the D curve is straightforward. It is the locus of intersections of alternative *ceteris paribus* demand curves, $D(Z_o)$, $D(Z_1)$, $D(Z_2)$,

etc., with perpendiculars erected from alternative values of aggregate output, q_o, q_1, q_2, etc., which enter into the determination of the corresponding values of aggregate producer outlays Z_o, Z_1, Z_2, etc. Cf. Parranello (1980, p. 72); Kregel, (1985, pp. 544–5).

14. Assuming that demand price is the same for all producers and that supply price may be identified with marginal cost, equilibrium for output as a whole can occur if and only if each producer is maximizing profit. Patinkin's contrary assertion (Patinkin, 1982, p. 127) is simply mistaken.

15. By definition:
$$dE/dZ = (dE/dq)/(dZ/dq) = [d(qp^d)/dq]/[d(qp^s)/dq]$$
$$= [1 + (q/p^d)(dp^d/dq)]/[1 + (q/p^s)(dp^s/dq)].$$
The elasticity result stated in the text then follows.

16. Again it should be emphasized that 'stability' here refers to virtual tendencies, not to real-time adjustment processes. Marshall's writings provide valuable materials for constructing models of real-time adjustment, but few of his actual models can be so construed.

17. Cf. Ambrosi (1981), p. 508.

18. For an apparently different view of this problem, see Patinkin, (1982), pp. 30–1.

19. Compare Patinkin (1982) pp. 8,9. 123; Tarshis (1979), pp. 361–2.

20. Some hint of my present thoughts on this subject may be gleaned from Clower (1988), pp. 85–6.

21. Keynes' failure to adopt the same procedure seems to have been related to his doubts about the theoretical meaningfulness of the concept of 'output as a whole' (cf. *JMK*, VII, p. 38). I don't question the validity of these doubts, but since the meaningfulness of the concept of 'employment as a whole' is equally suspect, I see no reason – other than considerations of analytical convenience – to prefer one concept to the other. For present purposes, aggregate output happens to be a more convenient variable than aggregate employment. For a similar view, see Tarshis (1979), p. 366.

22. Later on p. 25, Keynes changes his language and refers to 'the proceeds which entrepreneurs expect to receive' as 'expected proceeds', yet later (p. 29) as 'the amount which the community is expected to spend', and yet later (p.30) as 'the amount entrepreneurs can expect to get back'. A pedant might regard these different phrases as evidencing serious confusion of thought on Keynes' part, but I believe they reflect nothing more than a prose master's concern that his writing be moderately graceful as well as tolerably precise.

23. It is instructive to compare this paragraph from the *General Theory* with Marshall's analogous account of output equilibrium in a single market (see n. 7, above).

24. Cf. Tarshis (1979), pp. 366–8.

25. For a graphical derivation of **D**, see Kregel (1985), pp. 544–5.

References

Ambrosi, G. M. (1981), 'Keynes and the 45° cross', *Journal of Post-Keynesian Economics*, 3, Summer, pp. 503–9.

Clower, Robert W. (1975) 'Reflections on the Keynesian perplex', as reprinted in Donald Walker (ed.) (1984), *Money and Markets*, Cambridge: Cambridge University Press.

Clower, Robert W. (1987), 'Keynes and the classics revisited', in *Keynes and Public Policy After Fifty Years*, 2 vols, O. Hamouda and J. Smithin (eds), Upleaden: Edward Elgar, 1988, pp. 81–91.

Guillebaud, C. W. (1961), *Marshall's Principles of Economics*, 2 vols, New York: Macmillan.

Keynes, John Maynard (1930), *The General Theory of Employment Interest and Money*, *JMK*, Vol. VII.

Keynes, John Maynard (1933), *Essays in Biography*, *JMK*, Vol. X.

Kregel, Jan (1985), 'Sidney Weintraub's macrofoundations of microeconomics and the theory of distribution', *Journal of Post Keynesian Economics*, 7, Summer, pp. 540–58.

Leijonhufvud, Axel (1987), 'The uses of the past', paper prepared for the 14th Annual meeting of the History of Economics Society, Boston, 19 June–22 June 1987.

Marshall, Alfred (1920), *Principles of Economics*, 8th edn, London: Macmillan.

Myrdal, Gunnar (1972), *Against the Stream: Critical Essays in Economics*, New York: Pantheon.

Ohlin, Bertil (1981), 'Stockholm and Cambridge: Four papers on the monetary and employment theory of the 1930s', *History of Political Economy*, 13, Summer, pp. 189–238.

Patinkin, Don (1982), *Anticipations of the General Theory?* Chicago: University of Chicago Press.

Parrinello, Sergio (1980), 'The price level implicit in Keynes' effective demand'. *Journal of Post-Keynesian Economics*, 3, Autumn, pp. 63–78.

Pigou, A. C. (1926), *Official Papers of Alfred Marshall*, London: Macmillan.

Samuelson, Paul A. (1947), *Foundations of Economic Analysis*. Cambridge, Mass.: Harvard Univeristy Press.

Tarshis, Lorie (1979), 'The aggregate supply function in Keynes' *General Theory*', in *Essays in Honor of Tibor Scitovsky*, ed. M. J. Boskin, New York: Academic Press, pp. 361–92.

Walker, Donald A. (ed.) (1984), *Money and Markets: Essays by Robert W. Clower*. New York: Cambridge University Press.

Whitaker, J. K. (1975), *The Early Economic Writings of Alfred Marshall. 1867–1890*, 2 vols, New York: Free Press.

8 The quantity theory of money of J. M. Keynes: from *Indian Currency* to the *General Theory*

Christopher Marmé and Karl A. McDermott

Introduction

The question addressed in this chapter involves the relationship between the Quantity Theory of Money and J. M. Keynes' *General Theory*. Specifically, is the *General Theory* a work in the tradition of the Quantity Theory? Or is it, as some economists claim, a break with that tradition? To answer this question we shall examine the evolution of Keynes' conception of the Quantity Theory placing significant emphasis upon his *Treatise on Money* recognizing this work as a highly original and effective critique of earlier quantity theories, including his own. Our objective is to argue that the macroeconomics of the *General Theory* grew out of the evolution of Keynes' efforts to understand the nature of the modern market economy, in order to design effective policies that would minimize social waste: in particular unemployment. The nature of Keynes' work is paradoxical, Keynes had to break with the apparent quantity theory tradition in order to give life to the quantity theory. Breaking with the apparent quantity tradition, which focused upon the long-run proportionality of money and prices in and of itself was neither new nor profound; what was profound was the way in which Keynes transformed a tautology into a theory of money. Keynes' break occurred in two stages; the first occurs in the *Treatise* where he rejected the 'monetary aspects' of the quantity equations and the second in the *General Theory* where he broke with 'real aspects' of the classical monetary theory while working out the behavioural relationships which vitalize the quantity equations first developed in the *Treatise*.

In the following pages we propose to argue that:

1. The *Treatise* played a pivotal role in the development of Keynes' thought and the neglect that this work has received has resulted in interpretations of the *General Theory* that are one-dimensional in

nature and often misleading.

2. Given the continuity between the *Treatise* and the *General Theory* Keynes' has provided a consistent critique of the earlier monetary theories in the language of the Quantity Theory providing a clear perspective of his own views as to the break occurring on the 'real side' of the classical quantity theory.

3. Starting with the *Indian Currency and Finance* Keynes begins to develop a conception of the modern monetary economy which blossoms after the *Tract* into a full critique of the assumptions and conclusions of the classical monetary theory.

4. It became apparent to Keynes upon closer scrutiny of the classical theory that it was based upon a model whose structure and incentive properties were very different from the structure and incentives of the real world.

5. The model presented in the *General Theory* and the *Treatise* constitute a framework upon which practical policies could be evaluated in order to identify courses of action that within a modern monetary market economy could achieve greater employment of resources and growth than possible under the classical approach.

The evolution of Keynes' rejection of the traditional Quantity Theory
The first sign of Keynes' disaffection with the traditional approach to the Quantity Theory can be seen in his 1911 review of Irving Fisher's *The Purchasing Power of Money* for the *Economic Journal*. As Keynes notes (1983, p. 376):

> The most serious defect in Professor Fisher's doctrine is to be found in his account of the mode by which through transitional stages an influx of new money affects prices . . . Professor Fisher never explains clearly *how* new gold raises prices *in the first instance*, and is content with showing by the quantity theory that new gold *must* raise them somehow.

Besides this critique of the lack of a developed monetary process by which prices rise, Keynes also questions Fisher's use of weights in developing the index numbers used in his 'fundamental equations of exchange' (1983, p. 379) claiming that 'An index number, weighted in this fashion, seems obviously useless for any purpose except those of monetary theory.' Calculations based on methods not related to the realities of exchange could not be useful in policy development.

The second stage of disaffection can be seen in his presentation to the Political Economy Club meeting of 3 December 1913. In this presentation Keynes takes Fisher's work as a starting point for a critique of how bankers influence the business cycle. It is the beginning of Keynes' attempt to provide detail to the monetary process of inflation and deflation through the analysis of behavioural relationships affecting economic agents' actions. Here Keynes identifies three uses of funds by individuals (1973, pp. 4–5):

> Of the resources of the community earned or available within a given year, a certain part is saved, a certain part spent, and a certain part is held, so far as the individual is concerned, in suspense – it is kept as free resources to be spent or saved according as future circumstances may determine. The portion thus kept in suspense . . . is left by individuals at their bankers.

Here we certainly see the development of the rudimentary theory of precautionary balances held by individuals but placed within the control of bankers. It is this control that bankers exercise which can create a boom. The banker has (1973, pp. 5–6)

> . . . two sources from which goods . . . are available for capital works. That part . . . which is deliberately set aside by individuals for investment, and . . . which individuals hold in suspense. . . . One of the characteristics of a boom period . . . as distinguished from a period of depression is, I suggest, that in the former period investment exceeds savings while in the latter period investment falls short of saving. And it is the machinery of banking which makes this possible.

The possible is only created through the use of the free resources held in suspense by the public. Thus the behaviour of individuals and bankers are linked together in a framework that foreshadows that of the *Treatise*. Furthermore, Keynes identifies the fact that the private incentives of the bankers is to not discourage borrowing because it constitutes the possible loss of good business. These actions yield a tendency towards over-investment. The implicit suggestion is that profit motives in a market economy may not always lead to actions consistent with public welfare.

The third step in Keynes' work is revealed in the same year with the publication of *Indian Currency and Finance*. In this work Keynes reveals his understanding of the complexity as well as the fragility of a monetary system. Moreover he identifies the fact that differences exist in the stage of monetary developments across countries requiring that policy-makers understand these differences in order to avoid the mistake of applying a policy to one economy based upon the monetary and market structure of another. Finally there was the emphasis that Keynes placed upon the role of cheques as a medium of exchange in the British monetary system. The use of cheques and the possibility of overdrafts will play a special role in the *Treatise* when Keynes grapples with the definitions of money which must be controlled to maintain an effective monetary policy.

Between the *Indian Currency* and the *Tract on Monetary Reform*

Keynes was primarily involved in work related to the war and its financing and afterwards the ramifications of the Treaty of Versailles. In what is perhaps the most cogently argued and artistic political work of its time Keynes' *The Consequence of the Peace* reveals a further understanding of the complexities of the modern economic system at both the international and social level. Keynes argues that a beggar-thy-neighbour strategy in dealing with Germany would only succeed in creating economic chaos in Europe. Germany played a key role within the interdependent economic relationship of manufacturing, resource supply and consumption of basic goods. In destroying Germany's economy the Treaty of Versailles was breaking down the linkage sustaining much of Eastern Europe. There is also represented in this work a vision of the social order and role of distribution which is required to maintain a healthy social order. Here Keynes' views link distribution, production and growth together to form the basis of a coherent socioeconomic theory that will continue to reoccur and be expanded in the *Tract* and the *Treatise*.

After the *Consequence of the Peace* Keynes devoted much of his time to the economic ramifications of the Treaty of Versailles. In the area of monetary policy one important instance does arise, however, where Keynes was consulted by Austen Chamberlain in early 1920 on the proper monetary policy to follow. Keynes' response was that a high bank rate and dear money would check inflation. The importance of the advice for our purpose is the mechanism through which this policy would have its effects. Keynes suggested that business expectations of higher profits and prices would be altered lowering their demand for investment and given the high present level of this demand it would not necessarily create unemployment. In Chamberlain's own words (1977, p. 181): 'K. would go for a financial crisis (doesn't believe it would lead to unemployment). Would go to whatever [bank] rate is necessary – perhaps 10% – and keep it at that for three years.' Again some foreshadowing exists in the emphasis upon expectations which become most important in the *General Theory* and the profit mechanism of investment expenditure which becomes predominant in the *Treatise*. Both of these effects resulted from a monetary policy with the ultimate aim of reducing inflation while preserving employment.

During this same period in 1920 Keynes started to work on a book concerned with ancient currency. What is perhaps most important in this work is the development of his thoughts concerning the characteristics of money which have their greatest influence upon the behaviour of economic agents in a monetary economy. Keynes identifies two characteristics at this time; money-of-account and actual money or medium of exchange. It was the money-of-account which was most important (1982, p. 253):

> Now for most important social and economic purposes what matters is the *money-of-account*: for it is the money of account which is the subject of contract and of customary obligation. The currency reforms which matter are those which change the money of account.

This aspect of money is constantly used by Keynes in future works because of the importance which contracts play in the modern monetary market economy. The money of account and contracts imply that debts are incurred and risks born by individuals and in particular these debts and risks will be associated with durable goods which will play a key role in the nature of the economic problems which must be solved in a monetary economy.

At this point in the evolution of Keynes' thought we see a return to the consideration of policy problems and the Quantity Theory of Money. The concern of this work is the effects of inflation and deflation on the purchasing power of money and the effects upon society which these trends will create. Stability of the price level is the chief policy goal, but unlike the traditional quantity theory approach this is not necessarily achieved through maintaining a constant supply of money. The problem of stability had been made abundantly apparent with the dramatic inflation occurring in the Weimar Republic during the 1921–3 period. Keynes' close observation and deep interest in Germany led him to reconsider both the economic and social ramifications of severe price instability in his *Tract on Monetary Reform*. This work was important for a number of reasons in both the scope and nature of its theoretical and policy contributions to economic thought.

To begin this work Keynes chose to emphasize the separation of economic decision-making and the organization of a modern monetary market society (1923, p. v):

> We leave saving to the private investor, and we encourage him to place his savings mainly in titles to money. We leave responsibility for setting Production in motion to the business man, who is mainly influenced by the profits which he expects to accrue to himself in terms of money. Those who are not in favor of drastic changes in the existing organization of society believe that these arrangements, being in accord with human nature, have great advantages. But they cannot work properly if the money, which they assume as a stable measuring-rod, is undependable. Unemployment, the precarious life of the worker, the disappointment of expectations, the sudden loss of savings, the excessive windfalls to individuals, the speculator, the profiteer – all proceed, in large measure, from the instability of the standard of value.

Here most of the major seeds of Keynes' future work are present concerning the modern monetary economy – profit motives, expectations, the problem of coordination of decisions and the threat to our modern society that an unstable value of money represents.

Keynes' analysis proceeded along the lines of investigating the motivations and incentives facing three classes in society: the investing class, the business class and the Earner. The development of this 'investment system' aided the business class by providing savings beyond which they could themselves provide to operate their businesses. If the contracts involved are denominated in money which does not provide for changes in the purchasing power of money, the investor is put at considerable risk. The entrepreneur, on the other hand, must calculate the expected profits of employing his earnings in various lines of business. Rising prices benefit the businessman since he can pay back loans in a depreciated currency. Rising prices also represent the potential for increased profit and Keynes noted that (1923, p.38): 'This is simply to say that the intensity of production is largely governed in existing conditions by the anticipated real profit of the *entrepreneur*.

The major problem with production in the modern economy arises from the speculation of production and the need for durable goods to sustain efficient production over long periods of time. The volatility of prices over the ensuing periods creates a risk (1923, p. 39) which the entrepreneur must bear. If expectations arise which lead to diminished operations of equipment unemployment occurs. Thus (1923, p. 41): 'Whether it likes it or not, the technique of production under a regime of money-contract forces the business world always to carry a big speculative position; and if it is reluctant to carry this position, the productive process must be slackened.' The expectation of falling prices and profits may therefore produce actions on the part of the entrepreneur which sets in motion the reduction of output and employment. Keynes notes the cumulative nature of the price expectation process (1923, p. 42) showing his implicit understanding of the multiplier process. It is in fact Keynes' policy goals to (1923, p. 43):

> urge that the best way to cure this mortal disease of individualism is to provide that there shall never exist any confident expectation either that prices generally are going to fall or that they are going to rise; and also that there shall be no serious risk that a movement, if it does occur, will be a big one.

The means by which we can control 'the individualistic capitalism of today' (1923, p. 45) would be through the judicious use of monetary policy to stabilize the price level of the economy. It is at this point where Keynes breaks somewhat with the conventional quantity theorist approach in that he advocates altering the money supply in response to changes in the individuals' behaviour within the economy, in order to offset price changes that arise from these changes, rather than hold the supply of money constant, based on the classical assumptions that velocities of circulation and levels of output are fairly constant.

In chapter 3 of the *Tract* Keynes employs the Quantity Theory to evaluate the ways in which individual behaviour can influence the price level. Changes can result in the amount of cash a person is willing to hold (k) and that held in banks (k') available for cheques drawn on their accounts, either of which result in a change in prices. More to the point Keynes questioned the assumptions upon which the classical Quantity Theory was often based: that a change in the quantity of money was independent of the amounts held in cash or the banks by individuals and the amount held by banks (r) as a reserve against potential liabilities (k') (1923, p. 87). As Keynes points out, however (1923, p.88): 'In actual experience, a change of n is liable to have a reaction both on k and k' and on r.' What this implies is that changes in the quantity of money can be employed to influence other behavioural factors determining prices and more importantly to offset exogenous changes in these behavioural variables. Thus there was a role for monetary policy in the short run.

While certainly more memorable and less prosaic than Fisher's *Purchasing Power of Money*, there is, however, often little difference between many of Keynes' main points in the *Tract* and the arguments in Fisher's works concerning the Quantity Theory. Keynes still employs the long-run assumptions with his major break being one of a philosophical and policy nature, that the short run is the key to controlling our future, resulting in his most often quoted phrase that 'in the long run we are all dead'. Further reflection upon the problems inherent in the elements of the quantity equation, with special regard to the meaning of the price level, the nature of money and its measurement and control, and the incorporation of the incentives natural to a monetary economy which influence production would preoccupy Keynes in the *Treatise*.

Before the *Treatise* was started, however, Keynes revealed his views on monetary policy but this time emphasizing the importance of the modern banking system left out of the *Tract*. In a response to an Edwin Cannan article published in the *Economic Journal* in March 1924 Keynes developed his differences with the traditional quantity theory further. Employing his *Tract* version of the quantity theory

(1.1) $n = p (k + rk')$

where n = number of units of 'cash' (notes in circulation plus private deposits at the Bank of England), p = price index of each 'consumption unit', k = number of consumption units held in 'cash', k' = number of units held in the bank available against checks, and r = cash reserves as proportion of liabilities (k') held by banks. From this Keynes proceeded to state his views (1983, p. 416):

> Now, the old-fashioned doctrine used to be that if n could be kept reasonably steady, all would be well. My objection was to point out that if k and k' were capable of violent fluctuation, steadiness of n might be positively harmful and must be reflected in extreme unsteadiness of p . . .

Clearly Keynes is attempting to force quantity theorists into considering a role for monetary policy which deviated from tradition. One of his reasons for this deviation is his understanding of the banking system as it had evolved up to that time in England. As Keynes noted (1983, p. 417):

> . . . in a modern community with a developed banking system, an expansion in the circulation of legal tender money is generally the *last* phase of a lengthy process. A tendency towards inflation can operate for a long time before it eventuates in a demand for more money in circulation.

As yet many economists and practical bankers did not understand the role of money creation and deposit multipliers nor did they completely comprehend the role of cheques as a substitute for currency which in many ways increased the efficiency of a given stock of currency. These issues Keynes would take up in the *Treatise*.

The *Treatise* was Keynes' first full-fledged attempt to develop his theoretical model of the monetary economy in order to discuss the proper course of monetary policy. The theory developed was quantity theoretic in nature but not struck in the traditional mould of the equations of exchange. This difference would lead many to believe that Keynes had rejected the Quantity Theory approach but as we shall see in Keynes' own words this was not the case. The *Treatise* was explicitly divided into two volumes, theory and policy. In volume I Keynes endeavoured to bring into focus the nature and types of money, the differences in uses and types of circulation of money, the difficulties of measuring the purchasing power of money and the nature of the dynamics of prices in a monetary economy where specialization in consumption and production decisions, financial markets and bankers actions all influenced price movements.

In volume I Keynes selected as his vehicle of expressing the complex interaction of consumers, entrepreneurs, investors and bankers the set of two equations known as his 'fundamental equations'. The confusion that arose over whether or not these equations represented a quantity theoretic analysis arises, in part, through the fact that the traditional symbol for money does not appear in the equations. His choice of the form of the fundamental equations was designed to reflect the actual process of money flows and the effect which the decisions of entrepreneurs and consumers have on the price of goods.

That Keynes meant these equations to remain consistent with the traditional quantity theory is revealed in an exchange of letters with A. C. Pigou (1973, p. 217), on 15 May 1931:

> My dear Pigou,
> The misunderstanding has been due, I think, to your supposing that I held my equations to be in some way inconsistent with the 'Cambridge equation'. That I certainly do not. . . . What is different is my analysis of the underlying forces determining the two [prices].

His reasons for this selection were again pointed out in correspondence with D. H. Robertson on 3 May 1933 (1979, p. 18):

> In my present state of mind, however, I doubt that either version of the Cambridge equation is of any serious utility, . . . All versions of the quantity theory, which make no distinction between swaps and intermediate transactions and genuine production-consumption transactions, seem to me to tell one nothing.

Here we see a consistency in Keynes' critique dating back to his comment on Fisher's work that the Quantity Theory of money based upon the simplistic equations of exchange could not serve as a basis for policy discussions.

What Keynes recognized in the fundamental equations was the fact that different classes of economic agents are influenced by different sets of incentives and could place money into circulation for either real goods transactions directly (industrial circulation) or into financial transactions which may eventually return into industrial circulation but only through circuitous channels. The fundamental equations embodied not only money flows as components but also they reflected the behavioural elements of economic agents regarding liquidity and profits. Within this general framework, Keynes could analyse the effects of changes in liquidity preference, levels of savings, and the expected profits from production on prices reflected in their effects upon the flow of income to labour and the creation of windfall profits for entrepreneurs.

By taking this approach Keynes was attempting to bring the Quantity Theory of Money to life by analysing the motivations which underlie the meaningful actions of economic agents and identify the true causal processes in operation. Through this approach the factors which lead to either greater or lesser coordination of aggregate economic activity could be identified and policies prescribed to enhance the operation of the economy. The fundamental equations marked the true beginning of the development of a micro-foundation of macroeconomic activity leading to the identification of the paradoxes that exist when making the transition from microeconomic incentives to macroeconomic results. Keynes' effort in the *Treatise* to develop the Quantity Theory to a level that would recognize the distinction between 'swaps' and real 'production-consumption transactions' is a point too often neglected by historians of Keynes' thought.

Within the *Treatise* there is a vast number of topics considered and to single out any subset for special consideration is perhaps unjust; space limitations, however, are binding and force us to narrow our considerations. Central to the *Treatise*'s analysis are four concerns. First, there is the idea of constructing the notion of a set of equilibrium conditions. This need is perhaps a hold-over from the classical approach which links the equilibrium together with the 'long-run' tendencies of the system–an idea Keynes will move away from in the future. Second, the analysis of disequilibrium and the dynamics of growth and cycles feature predominantly in the verbal analysis and also justify the development of the equilibrium conditions. The fundamental equations were designed to show the conditions of equilibrium and disequilibrium in order to identify the causal factors responsible for particular types of adjustments of the system. This point is brought out clearly in a reply to Ralph Hawtrey's comments on the *Treatise* shortly after its publication in a letter on 30 November 1930 (1973, p. 141):

> My point is that to regard [price] as the sum of H2 and H3 is not so helpful as to regard it as the sum of E and I-S. For it does not tell one whether the rise in prices is due to a rise in the cost of production or to a rise in profits. Yet it is essential to know this. For a rise of prices associated with a corresponding rise in the cost of production represents a position of equilibrium; whereas a rise of prices associated with a rise in profits does not. Moreover, it does not bring out the relationship of profits for producers as a whole to the difference between the value of the increment of capital goods and the volume of saving.

Changes in the flows of money which manifest themselves as income changes affecting the costs of production yield new equilibrium prices. Changes in money flows which result in profits result in a series of adjustments to employment and investment the consequence of which require a considerable time-lag to produce a new equilibrium.

The third factor employed in the *Treatise* is the emphasis on money profits and their relationship to savings and investment. Profits are the penultimate signalling device which entrepreneurs employ to guide their decisions regarding production decisions. Moreover, it is the expectation of profits that is important (1930, p. 143):

> . . . in so far as entrepreneurs are able . . . to forecast the relationship

between savings and investment in its effects on the demand for their product
. . . it is obviously the anticipated profit or loss . . . rather than actual profit
. . . on business just concluded, which influences . . . the scale . . . and the
offers . . . to the factors of production . . . strictly: therefore, we should say
that it is the *anticipated* profit or loss which is the mainspring of change. . . .
[emphasis in original]

The role played by expectations, first discussed in the *Tract* and made
the centrepiece in the *General Theory* has its greatest affect in the
Treatise on the entrepreneur.

Keynes gave perhaps his most succinct description of the dynamics of
booms and slumps with reference to the fundamental equations in his
second lecture to the Harris foundation in June of 1931 (1973, pp.
353–4):

Now for my equation, a very simple one, which gives, to my thinking, the
clue to the whole business. The costs of production of the entrepreneurs are
equal to the incomes of the public. Now the incomes of the public are,
obviously, equal to the sum of what they spend and of what they save. On the
other hand, the sale proceeds of the entrepreneurs are equal to the sum of
what the public spend on current consumption and what the financial
machine is causing to be spent on current investment . . .

It follows, if you have been able to catch what I am saying, that when the
value of current investment is greater than the savings of the public, the
receipts of the entrepreneurs are greater than their costs, so that they make a
profit; and when, on the other hand, the value of current investment is less
than the savings of the public, the receipts of the entrepreneurs will be less
than their costs, so that they make a loss.

That is my secret, the clue to the scientific explanation of booms and
slumps (and of much else, as I should claim) which I offer you. For you will
perceive that when the rate of current investment increases (without a
corresponding change in the rate of savings) business profits increase.
Moreover, the affair is cumulative. For when business profits are high, the
financial machine facilitates increased orders for and purchases of capital
goods, that is, it stimulates investment still further; which means that
business profits are still greater; and so on. In short, a boom is in full
progress. And contrariwise when investment falls off.

Here we have Keynes' theory of the business cycle clearly delineated:
the question that remains is how the quantity theory plays a role in this
process? The answer to this is provided by the fourth aspect of the
Treatise, namely the role of bankers. Bankers through the disposition of
loans are in the position to influence the expectations of entrepreneurs
regarding the level of profits and through profits the level of remune-
ration to the factors of production and finally prices. The monetary
mechanism employed in the *Treatise* still greatly relies on interest rates
and their effects on the prospective income realizable from investments:
alternative routes (or transmission mechanisms) by which the quantity

of money could influence production would have to wait until the *General Theory*.

In many respects the *Treatise* fell stillborn from the printing press. Despite the large number of reviews and a wide reading there was a general lack of understanding and acceptance of this work. This greatly disappointed Keynes and forced him to begin to reconstruct his arguments. Before these came to fruition in the form of the *General Theory* Keynes took a number of opportunities to make the points of the *Treatise* more explicit and to clear up misunderstandings. As we have already seen in his letters to Pigou and Robertson, he took great pains to associate the *Treatise* with the Quantity Theory tradition. In a series of responses to the reviews of the *Treatise* Keynes attempted to explicate the position taken in the *Treatise*. Perhaps the most important points expressed in these writings concerned Keynes' dissatisfaction with the traditional monetary theory in its failure explicitly to recognize that money could be directed not only to the purchase of currently produced output or hoards but also to titles to the existing stock of capital. The most important implication of these thoughts were that the aggregate profits of the economy could rise or fall and would not remain constant as critics such as D. H. Robertson and Hayek suggested. This in turn led to the finding that Say's Law would no longer hold, freeing production and employment to become variables whose movement must be explained.

In his first reply to D. H. Robertson, appearing in September 1931 in the *Economic Journal*, he dealt with the question of aggregate profits and the determinants of consumption and investment goods prices (1973, p. 220):

> This central difference of opinion is as follows. Mr. Robertson quotes me, correctly (p. 400) [in the *Economic Journal*, September 1931], as holding the view that if P, the price level of consumption goods, declines owing to an excess of saving over the cost of new investment, then there *need* be no counterbalancing rise in P', the price level of investment goods, 'even though there is no increase in the disposition to hoard money unspent'. Mr. Robertson holds that this result cannot come about 'except as the result of an act of hoarding'. This difference of opinion is evidently a special case of a more general difference as to the character of the forces which determine the price level of investment goods. Mr. Robertson is quite right that it is absolutely fundamental to my analysis to distinguish *two* factors at work, which I have christened the 'excess-savings factor' and the 'excess-bearish factor'. This is the vital matter which I have failed so far to make clear to him.

Robertson believed (1973, p. 227) that

> . . . *unless* an excess of saving is associated with an increase in hoarding, it will mean that an increased flow of purchasing power equal to the excess

saving will be directed to the purchase of investment goods. He thinks that this will involve an *equal* increase in the receipts of the producers of the current output of investment goods, so that the losses of the producers of consumption goods due to the excess saving will be balanced by profits of an *equal* amount accruing to the producers of investment goods.

The point Keynes was making was that money need not be spent on new investment goods and therefore the prices of consumption and investment goods would not rise and fall 'like buckets in a well' and maintain aggregate profits constant. If savings are spent on the titles to old capital goods the profits of both consumption and investment good suppliers may fall and eventually output and employment fall.

The problem Keynes felt lay in the old quantity equations which not only were unrelated to the actual causal relationships influencing prices and output but in fact masked the true relationships. This view was put forward most forcefully by Keynes (1973, pp. 230–1):

> I do not, by the way, understand the relevance of the quantity equation with which Mr. Robertson concludes his 5. We are discussing the relation between the prices of consumption goods and of investment goods – whether, assuming no change in the propensity to hoard, the one must go down when the other goes up, like buckets in a well – which he affirms and I deny. But neither of these price levels occurs in his equations, which are concerned with the price level of output as a whole and the price level of transactions.
>
> I now turn, as briefly as I can, to Mr. Robertson's other comments, beginning with his 2, where I assume that, in speaking of 'the old quantity equations', he has primarily in mind the Fisher equations. I cannot imagine why Mr. Robertson should suppose that the passage he quotes from my p. 147 [*JMK*, Vol. V, p. 133] is inconsistent with the Fisher equations, which are concerned with the volume of *transactions* and the price level of *transactions*, as I have repeatedly explained. I was trying to illustrate the point that the old quantity notions are incapable of leading up to the price level of output, by pointing out that all or any of the variables occurring in the quantity equation might be unchanged and yet the price level of output might be changed. In other words, not only does the price level of output not occur explicitly in the old quantity equation, but it is not even a function of those variables which do occur in it.

There is also the connection made in this rejoinder between government spending, the profits of entrepreneurs in the fundamental equations and the quantity of money; revealing some of the first steps towards the message of the *General Theory* (1973, pp. 232–3):

> There is no difficulty in dealing with government expenditure. . . . So far from the equation being ill-adapted to show the short-period effect of these things, it brings out clearly what nearly everyone overlooks – namely, that the short-period effect, on business profits, of the dole, if financed by borrowing, or indeed of a government deficit arising in any other way, is exactly the same (ignoring secondary repercussions) as the effect of increased investment;

whilst, on the other hand, the balancing of a budget, previously unbalanced, has as disastrous a direct effect on business profits.

In Keynes' reply to Friedrich von Hayek's review of the *Treatise* published in November 1931 in *Economia* many of the same points were reiterated, however, the role of the banking system and the lack of a coordinating mechanism is brought to the fore in the discussion. Once again we see Keynes return to the emphasis of factors other than the quantity of money as playing the key role in economic change (1973, p. 248):

> The point, put very briefly, is, firstly, that money may be advanced to entrepreneurs either to meet losses or to provide for new investment, . . . and, secondly (to indicate a general principle by means of an illustration), that, if, desiring to be more liquid I sell Consols to my bank in exchange for a bank deposit and my bank does not choose to offset this transaction but allows its deposits to be correspondingly increased, the quantity of money is changed without anything having happened either to saving or to investment.

Perhaps more to the point Keynes expressed this idea as the fundamental root of his difference with Hayek over policy matters. Hayek favoured what has been known as a 'neutral' money supply policy allowing prices to fluctuate based on real changes which naturally occur (e.g. crop cycles, people's choice to save, etc.). Keynes, on the other hand, realized that savings and investment would not always be equated challenging the classical economists' reliance on Say's Law and the interest rate mechanism maintaining the equality between saving and investment. As Keynes noted (1973, p. 251):

> *My* analysis is quite different from this; as it necessarily must be, since, in my view, saving and investment (as I define them) can get out of gear without any change on the part of the banking system from 'neutrality' as defined by Dr. Hayek, merely as a result of the public changing their rate of saving or the entrepreneurs changing their rate of investment, there being no automatic mechanism in the economic system (as Dr. Hayek's view would imply there must be) to keep the two rates equal, provided that the effective quantity of money is unchanged.
>
> As I conceive it, a changing price level – due to a change in the relation between saving and investment, costs of production being unchanged – merely *redistributes* purchasing power between those who are buying at the changed price level and those who are selling at it, as compared with what would have happened if there had not been a change in the relation between saving and investment. I am not sure that Dr. Hayek sees clearly the *two* sides of the account. Has he, moreover, apprehended the significance of my equation $S + Q = I$, namely that savings *plus* profits are always exactly equal to the value of new investment?

The discussion over terminology was not an idle one, for in point of fact how one measures income, saving, profit and investment were crucial to the understanding of the economics operation. Keynes' insight was that the entrepreneur in a monetary-market economy was driven by the expectations of a money profit. These conclusions would lead him eventually to his exposition of his monetary theory of production. This point was reiterated time and again by Keynes. In a draft of a letter to D. H. Robertson dated 6 October 1931, Keynes wrote of the evolution of his ideas saying (1973, pp. 272–3):

> In other words I contend that savings and the value of investment can get out of gear without a departure of the banking system from neutrality in Hayek's sense. . . . I think I am on the right track because your view is quite consistent with the view you always used to hold, and which I myself held up to a moderately late date. When you were writing your *Banking Policy and the Price Level*, and we were discussing it, we both believed that inequalities between saving and investment – using those terms with the degree of vagueness with which we used them at that date – only arose as a result of what one might call an act of inflation or deflation on the part of the banking system. I worked on this basis for quite a time, but in the end I came to the conclusion that it would not do. As a result of getting what were, in my opinion, more clear definitions of saving and investment, I found that the salient phenomena could come about without any overt act on the part of the banking system. My theory as I have ultimately expressed it is the result of this change of view, and I am sure that the differences between me and you are due to the fact that you in substance still hold the old view. But I only reached my new view as the result of an attempt to handle the old view with complete thoroughness.

One of the supposed major weaknesses of the *Treatise* was the holding of output constant in the analysis of the fundamental equations. This criticism was unwarranted. In elaborating on the monetary theory of production in the *Treatise*'s verbal analysis, Keynes constantly uses examples of money and/or behavioural changes influencing the level of profits and hence output and employment. Keynes was sensitive to this criticism as indicated in a letter to Joan Robinson of April 1932, saying (1973, p. 270):

> I think you are a little hard on me as regards the assumption of constant output . . . in my *Treatise* itself, I have long discussions with [?of] the effects of changes in output; it is only at a particular point in the preliminary theoretical argument that I assume constant output, and I am at pains to make this absolutely clear.

Keynes' concern with output fluctuation was clearly expressed in his Harris Lectures presented in Chicago in June 1931. Here we see the possibility of an unemployment equilibrium arising through the failure of the banking system to equilibrate savings and investment. Keynes re-emphasized the profit mechanism as the source of output fluctuation in the monetary economy (1973, pp. 355–6):

In the past it has been usual to believe that there was some preordained harmony by which saving and investment were necessarily equal. If we intrusted our savings to a bank, it used to be said, the bank will of course make use of them, and they will duly find their way into industry and investment. But unfortunately this is not so. I venture to say with certainty that it is not so. And it is out of the disequilibriums of savings and investment, and out of nothing else, that the fluctuations of profits, of output, and of employment are generated . . .

These quotations help to substantiate the view expressed by James Meade that by the autumn of 1931 he could take back to Oxford the essential ingredients of the *General Theory*.

Between 1932 and the publication of the *General Theory* Keynes continued to define the elements of his theory and reiterate its points in rebutting his critics. In a note to Robertson (dated 22 March 1932) on the definition of saving, Keynes attempts to force Robertson to see his points on the importance of the link between savings and output fluctuations (1973, p. 279):

> The two matters of primary importance to the community are the aggregate of real output and the increment of real capital. Therefore it is of great significance to show that a decreased expenditure on consumption does not necessarily lead to an increment of real capital even if aggregate real output is unchanged; whilst in practice a decreased expenditure on consumption may lead to a decreased real output (as a result of its effect on Q) and *vice versa*. Indeed it is easy to conceive circumstances in which decreased expenditure on consumption leads to a decrease both of real output and of real investment.

At the same time, in 'Symposium on Saving and Usury' in the *Economic Journal*, Keynes continues to drive home the distinction between hoards and purchases of debts (1979, pp. 13–16):

> The answer to the question whether there is an increment of wealth corresponding to the savings of an individual seldom depends . . . on what he does with the money. . . . In particular, the answer does *not* depend . . . on whether he 'hoards' the money by increasing his cash or uses it to buy a security or some other capital asset. He may use his savings to buy a bond, and yet there may be no increment of capital wealth coming into existence as a result of his saving. I have argued in my *Treatise* that the causes which determine the increment of capital wealth are only contingently and indirectly connected with those which determine the increment of individual savings. If an increment of saving by an individual is *not* accompanied by an increment of new investment – and, in the absence of deliberate management by the central bank or the government, it will be nothing but a lucky accident if it is – then it necessarily causes diminished receipts, disappointment and losses to some other party, and the outlet for the savings of A will be found in financing the losses of B.
>
> Thus when an individual saves, his savings *must* be balanced by the creation either of an asset or of a debt (or a loss paid for by an asset changing

hands). But, as a rule, it lies entirely outside the power of the individual saver to determine which it is to be, and whether the result, or rather the accompaniment, of his saving is to be an asset or a debt. What he has done is to make possible the creation of an asset without a rise in the price level. But failing a simultaneous increment of new investment, either by good management or by a lucky accident, then his act of saving will *cause* an equal loss to someone else; a debt will be created or an asset will change hands, but there will be no increment of wealth.

Slowly but surely Keynes was developing the notion that the key difficulty in the classical model was deeper than just the fact that the banking system could not match savings and investment, that the problem was fundamental to the entrepreneurial economy where money wages were paid to workers and where monetary profits dominated the entrepreneurs incentives. As Keynes described it in his lectures of 11 November 1933:

(a)   They [the producers] don't know what you will want in the future;
(b)   [you] don't give data;
(c)   [you] can't give promise you ever will consume.

In the modern monetary economy the payment of money to the factors of production creates an element of uncertainty that did not exist in the classical real wage, commodity wage or cooperative economy, as Keynes termed it in his 1932–3 drafts of the *General Theory*, and his contribution to the Festschrift for Arthur Spiethoff in 1933.

In summary then, the period between the *Treatise* and the *General Theory* witnessed Keynes' advocacy and defence of the following points:

1.   That the fundamental equations did not constitute a break with the Quantity Theory of Money *per se* but rather with the use of the equations of exchange.
2.   The reason for this was to explicate the importance of profits, financial transactions, liquidity preference and other motivations which could influence prices without there ever being a change in the quantity of money.
3.   That the ability to purchase financial assets, or for that matter, second-hand goods or equipment, broke both the kink between savings and output (e.g. Say's Law) and the connection between the price of consumer and investment goods.
4.   This last point leads to profits and output, in aggregate, becoming variables in part determined by the quantity of money and in part by the actions of individuals and entrepreneurs.
5.   And finally that these aspects of the economy were due in the main to the use of money as the means of payment to factors of production, the reward for production (e.g. profit) and as a measure of wealth and store of value.

Leading into the *General Theory* Keynes had laid the foundations for understanding a monetary-market economy both in terms of its operational characteristics and its weaknesses. Above all these findings led him towards a monetary theory of production where the theory of money and price were no longer separate spheres. Money was no longer the 'veil' of actions but the motivator of actions.

The *General Theory* was Keynes' penultimate work on the monetary theory of production, the capstone of this monumental work would come in the form of his eloquent defence of the *General Theory* in his 1937 article in the *Quarterly Journal of Economics*. The connections between the *Treatise* and the *General Theory* are outlined quite clearly in the preface (1936, pp. vi–vii):

> The relation between this book and my *Treatise on Money*, which I published five years ago, is probably clearer to myself than it will be to others; and what in my own mind is a natural evolution in a line of thought which I have been pursuing for several years, may sometimes strike the reader as a confusing change of view. This difficulty is not made less by certain changes in terminology which I have felt compelled to make. . . . When I began to write my *Treatise on Money* I was still moving along the traditional lines of regarding the influence of money as something so to speak separate from the general theory of supply and demand. When I finished it, I had made some progress towards pushing monetary theory back to becoming a theory of output as a whole. But my lack of emancipation from preconceived ideas showed itself in what now seems to me to be the outstanding fault of the theoretical parts of that work (namely, Books III and IV), that I failed to deal thoroughly with the effects of *changes* in the level of output. My so-called 'fundamental equations' were an instantaneous picture taken on the assumption of a given output. They attempted to show how, assuming the given output, forces could develop which involved a profit-disequilibrium, and thus required a change in the level of output . . .

We can see in these passages some retreat before his critics for reasons that are not entirely clear from his stance that the *Treatise* was dynamic. A second factor which bears identifying is that the role of profits are relegated to a subtler position in the discussion. This could be due to the fact that Keynes felt he had made the point explicitly so many times in the literature after the *Treatise* that his readers would understand their importance. Profits, in the *General Theory*, are embedded in the aggregate supply schedule, that is, the supply schedule includes the normal profit of entrepreneurs. If for a given present level of output the aggregate demand is greater than the supply an excess or windfall profit exists corresponding to that of the *Treatise*; it is this windfall which provides the stimulus to entrepreneurs to expand output or if losses occur, to contract output.

The level of aggregate demand (effective demand) is determined by the quantity of money, in part, with Keynes using the equation MV = D (1936, p. 304) as its representation. Clearly, Keynes is drawing the readers' attention to the relationship between the traditional quantity theory and the concepts employed in the *General Theory*. The relationship, however, is clearly a conditional one as he states (1936, p. 246):

> Thus we can sometimes regard our ultimate independent variables as consisting of (1) the three fundamental psychological factors, namely, the psychological propensity to consume . . . attitudes to liquidity and . . . expectations of future yields from capital assets, (2) the wage-unit as determined by the bargains reached between employers and employed, and (3) the quantity of money as determined by the action of the central bank.

The same factors which Keynes had discussed earlier, with the exception being the propensity to consume, are represented. The relationship between these elements is most clearly delineated in the following passage (1936, p. 173):

> We have now introduced money into our causal nexus for the first time, and we are able to catch a first glimpse of the way in which changes in the quantity of money work their way into the economic system. If, however, we are tempted to assert that money is the drink which stimulates the system to activity, we must remind ourselves that there may be several slips between the cup and the lip. For whilst an increase in the quantity of money may be expected, *cet. par.,* to reduce the rate of interest, this will not happen if the liquidity preferences of the public are increasing more than the quantity of money; and whilst a decline in the rate of interest may be expected, *cet. par.,* to increase the volume of investment, this will not happen if the schedule of marginal efficiency of capital is falling more rapidly than the rate of interest; and whilst an increase in the volume of investment may be expected, *cet. par.,* to increase employment, this may not happen if the propensity to consume is falling off. Finally, if employment increases, prices will rise in a degree partly governed by the shapes of the physical supply function, and partly by the liability of the wage-unit to rise in terms of money. And when output has increased and prices have risen, the effect of this on liquidity-preference will be to increase the quantity of money necessary to maintain a given rate of interest.

Here we see the contingencies outlined and the interrelationships of the major motivational factors elucidated.

Many authors claim that Keynes broke with his quantity theoretic approach of the *Treatise* in the *General Theory* but Keynes, however, makes these links explicit. It is the increase of investment over savings which represents the profits of the *Treatise* which corresponds to the increase of effective demand in the *General Theory* (1936, p. 78):

> The significance of both my present and my former arguments lies in their attempt to show that the volume of employment is determined by the estimates of effective demand made by the entrepreneurs, an expected

increase of investment relatively to saving as defined by my *Treatise on Money* being the criterion of an increase in effective demand.

Thus employment can be increased or decreased as profits rise or fall through the increase or decrease of the effective demand which in turn is linked to the increase or decrease of money adjusted for behavioural responses of consumers and entrepreneurs.

The question that remains is to identify the links between prices and the quantity of money in the *General Theory*. Despite what many neoclassically-oriented economists claim, Keynes was deeply concerned with the 'supply-side' aspects of price determination as well as the monetary aspects. This is brought out in chapter 21 of the *General Theory* when Keynes examines the set of conditions which result in violations of the traditional quantity theory proportional price change theorem. These conditions were (1936, p. 296):

1. Effective demand will not change in exact proportion to the quantity of money.
2. Since resources are not homogeneous, there will be diminishing, and not constant, returns as employment gradually increases.
3. Since resources are not interchangeable, some commodities will reach a condition of inelastic supply whilst there are still unemployed resources available for the production of other commodities.
4. The wage-unit will tend to rise, before full employment has been reached.
5. The remunerations of the factors entering into marginal costs will not all change in the same proportion.

Keynes goes on to say (1936, pp. 296–7]:

> The Theory of Prices, that is to say, the analysis of the relation between changes in the quantity of money and changes in the price-level with a view to determining the elasticity of prices in response to changes in the quantity of money, must, therefore, direct itself to the five complicating factors set forth above.

This chapter is filled with brilliant elucidations of the relationship between changes in the quantity of money and the effects it may have on output, employment and prices. In the broadest sense, Keynes provided a 'general' framework for the analysis of price as well as output changes brought about by changes in the quantity of money conditioned by the realities of technology, resource constraints and profit motivations. It was the inability of the traditional Quantity Theory of Money's equations of exchange to handle the complications reality introduces which forced Keynes not to abandon the quantity tradition but rather to revitalize it by modifying the method of analysis and explication.

Anyone who doubts the link between the quantity theory and the *General Theory* need only to reread this work now while keeping in mind the arguments outlined above.

References
Keynes, J. M. (1913), *Indian Currency and Finance*, London: Macmillan.
Keynes, J. M. (1919), *The Economic Consequences of the Peace*, London: Macmillan.
Keynes, J. M. (1923), *A Tract on Monetary Reform*, London: Macmillan.
Keynes, J. M. (1930), *A Treatise on Money, 1. The Pure Theory of Money*, London: Macmillan.
Keynes, J. M. (1930), *A Treatise on Money, 11. The Applied Theory of Money*, London: Macmillan.
Keynes, J. M. (1936), *The General Theory of Employment, Interest and Money*, London: Macmillan.
Keynes, J. M. (1983), *Economic Articles and Correspondence: Academic*, London: Macmillan.
Keynes, J. M. (1973), *The General Theory and After: Part 1, Preparation*, London: Macmillan.
Keynes, J. M. (1977), *Activities: Treaty Revision and Reconstruction 1920–22*, London: Macmillan.
Keynes, J. M. (1982), *Social, Political and Literary Writings*, London: Macmillan.
Keynes, J. M. (1979), *The General Theory and After: A Supplement*, London: Macmillan.

PART III

MODERN ECONOMICS

9 On the history of neutral money

Hansjoerg Klausinger[1]

1. Introduction

In his monumental study of the history of economic analysis Schumpeter introduced the distinction between real and monetary analysis as signifying two opposing schools of economic thought in pre-classical economics (Schumpeter, 1954, p. 277). Thus the debate on the role of money has been on the scientific agenda from the beginning and controversy has continued up to the present. At the beginning of this century the neoclassical approach often comes close to examining value and monetary theory as belonging to two distinct branches of economics, interrelations between which can be neglected. Even the outstanding contribution of Wicksell makes some pedagogical use of this device when in the first volume of his *Lectures* he considers as a kind of 'first approximation ... production, distribution and exchange as if they were effected without the existence of money' (Wicksell, 1935, p. 5), while in the second volume 'actual conditions, in which money actually effects all exchanges and investments' (ibid., p. 6) are analysed. Yet ultimately Wicksell's analysis of the conditions of 'monetary equilibrium' and the monetarily-induced 'cumulative process' has challenged the propositions of real analysis which maintain a valid separation of the theories of value and money.[2] And in this context Wicksell (1936, p. 102) has coined one of the most ambiguous and controversial concepts of monetary theory – the concept of 'neutral money'.

The following inquiry attempts to evaluate critically some aspects of twentieth-century monetary thought by focusing on the history of the concept of 'neutral money'. It starts (section 2) by examining Hayek's use of this concept as the most fully developed analysis of pre-Keynesian monetary theory. It is the only explicit treatment of neutral money at that time, in which neutrality is related to a comparison of money and barter economies. The approach of the neoclassical synthesis (section 3) is different, ranging from the dichotomy between real and monetary economics and Patinkin's invariance theorem to propositions on the optimal quantity of money. These notions are then compared with the pre-Keynesian concept of neutrality. In section 4 the early discussion on money and growth is taken as an example of how the disappearance of the Hayekian neutrality notion contributed to confusion in evaluating the efficiency of monetary economies. Finally (section 5), the new classical (macro-) economics is interpreted as providing a rigorous foundation of Hayekian neutral money models. From an epistemological point of view there are seen to be some fundamental differences of how to use such a model.

2.   Hayek and the classical concept of neutral money

Wicksell's analysis of the conditions of monetary equilibrium and his distinction between the money and the natural rate of interest has provided a main source of development and controversy to monetary and business cycle theory in the first half of this century. In the discussion of the Wicksellian approach it is Hayek, who with a series of books and articles (Hayek, 1931a, 1933a, 1939, 1984)[3] returns to the fundamental question of the possibility of applying real analysis to a monetary economy, with the core of his analysis constituted by the analytical concepts of 'neutral money' and 'intertemporal equilibrium'.

According to Hayek the concept of neutral money implies comparing the results, that is, in allocation and distribution, of a monetary and a barter economy, where the latter corresponds to that type of an economy to which real analysis (or as Hayek sometimes (for example, 1933a, pp. 46, 104) calls it, 'static' or 'pure economic' analysis) applies. This barter economy is defined more precisely by Koopmans in a contribution to a book edited by Hayek as:

> the ideal type of an economy of pure barter, to which the laws of equilibrium theories apply . . . [Its subject is] a *hypothetical*, and in reality unthinkable state, where *simultaneously* the frictions which prevent full equilibrium because of the lack of a generally accepted medium of exchange are assumed to be absent, as well as those specific changes resulting from the actual introduction of such a medium of exchange' (Koopmans, 1933, pp. 228, 230; translated by the author)[4]

So it is clear that the monetary economy is not to be compared with an actual barter economy, but with the abstract type of an economy where money is not needed because there are no frictions or imperfections.[5]

The analytical device which Hayek develops for modelling such comparisons is the concept of intertemporal equilibrium. This concept relates to equilibrium for a whole time-period or sequence of points of time and does not presume conditions of stationarity. As Hayek contends, it is 'unjustified and inappropriate . . . to restrict the applicability of the equilibrium concept exclusively to systems which extend through periods of time within which all external conditions remain constant . . . Rather . . . it is only necessary to assume . . . that no deviation from the expected course of events takes place during the period' (Hayek, 1984, p. 85). So intertemporal equilibrium corresponds to equilibrium over time with perfect foresight.[6] Therefore equilibrium in an economy of frictionless barter is equivalent to perfect intertemporal coordination of individual plans such that plans are compatible with one another and therefore can be realized, and that expectations turn out to be correct. Now if an intertemporal equilibrium can be realized in a monetary economy rendering the same real characteristics as frictionless barter, then money (or the monetary system of this economy) is called neutral (Koopmans, 1933, p. 228; Hayek, 1984, p. 159). On the other hand, the monetary economy is in a state of intertemporal disequilibrium and money is said to be non-neutral if 'the prices established with the assistance of money do not correspond to the equilibrium prices of the hypothetical system which does not possess a medium of exchange, and therefore . . . must yield the same outcome as any other price structures inconsistent with equilibrium' (Hayek, 1984, p. 99) – the outcome being plans that cannot be realized and expectations that are not fulfilled.

Now two points should be emphasized. First, the intertemporal disequilibrium of Hayek is one generated by false prices – money prices diverging from the relations of barter equilibrium. As Hayek concludes (1939, p. 140), false prices induce expectations which will be disappointed. The most important of these (potentially false) prices is that which fundamentally links intertemporal decisions, that is the rate of interest. Following Hayek, that kind of disequilibrium which leads to business cycles is as a rule caused by a divergence of the money rate of interest from its natural or equilibrium value (Hayek, 1931a, p. 20f.; 1933a, p. 201f.). This overriding importance of the equality of the money and the equilibrium rate of interest derives from the possibility of creating and destroying money (and thereby purchasing power) especially in the market for credit, which is a unique feature of a monetary economy. So it is the elasticity of credit which enables intertemporal disequilibrium in a monetary economy to develop. Furthermore, a second point is clarified: only in a monetary economy do there exist endogenous forces responsible for a possible tendency away from intertemporal equilibrium, whereas without these monetary disturbances Hayek thinks the economy will 'operate according to the self-regulating principle of the economic system described by static theory' (Hayek, 1933a, p. 94).[7] Put in other terms, the adjustments generated by monetary disturbances are 'without any economic function' (Hayek, 1984, p. 99).

Therefore the prevalence of disequilibrium states in a monetary economy is a distinguishing feature of Hayek's approach.[8] It can be interpreted as reflecting the tension between the well-developed body of economic thought, valid within the boundaries of models of frictionless barter, and the necessity to apply it to phenomena which are genuinely monetary. Hayek's attempt to overcome this tension is not quite convincing. On the one hand, he concedes the possibility of valid real analysis, if money and equilibrium rates of interest coincide and perfect foresight is established. In this respect neutral money is to serve only as a fictitious point of reference with respect to which the actual evolution of the economy has to be measured. On the other hand, he makes clear in numerous passages that he considers the actual realization of intertemporal equilibrium in a monetary economy as highly improbable, especially if this economy is prone to injections of money and acts of hoarding:

> we must finally give up all thoughts of completely eliminating monetary influences by restricting money to the role of a passive mediator, so that the economy proceeds as if money were not employed in it. We will have to come to terms with the idea that money always exerts a determining influence on the development of the economy [and] that the principles derived for an economy without money can be applied to an economy with money only with substantial qualifications . . . (Hayek, 1984, p. 103)[9]

Interestingly enough, according to Hayek's writings in the 1930s there exists a conflict between attempts to neutralize money, for example by fixing its quantity, and the promotion of technical progress – an argument in line with Schumpeter's theory of entrepreneurial innovation and leading to the similar conclusion, that business cycles are to be considered the price of technical progress (for example, Hayek, 1928, p. 103; 1933a, p. 189).

Finally a crucial, if obvious, weakness of Hayek's monetary theory must be mentioned. He has no theory of why the equilibrium of the economy he analyses should be monetary in nature (Desai, 1982, p. 162). He does not explain what frictions are responsible for the existence of money and how, in the possible case of neutrality, these frictions can be completely overcome.

Hayek himself has stated as part of a future research agenda of monetary theory the desirability of examining the exact conditions of neutral money (Hayek, 1984, p. 159), so it is legitimate now to look at his approach retrospectively from the viewpoint of modern general equilibrium analysis. And it is surprising to what extent it seems to be capable of a neat translation into modern terms, which also renders some insights into the problems mentioned above.[10]

In re-examining the consistency of the Hayekian approach, it is straightforward to identify intertemporal equilibrium in an economy of frictionless barter with a general equilibrium of the Arrow–Debreu type, or more precisely with an analogous economy where future markets are perfectly substituted by perfect foresight and a sufficient number of distinct securities to span the whole space of dated commodities (Arrow, 1964; Nagatani, 1975). Neglecting problems concerning the uncertainty of states of nature, an efficient intertemporal coordination is thereby secured. Obviously here the natural or equilibrium rate of interest corresponds to that of an equivalent 'Arrow security' and can without difficulties be expressed in terms of some numéraire.

This reinterpretation sheds some light on the otherwise obscure debate between Sraffa (1932a, 1932b) and Hayek (1932).[11] There Sraffa attacked the concept of a natural rate of interest because there will always exist a multiplicity of equilibrium real (or 'own') rates each corresponding to arbitrary choices of commodity baskets whose exchange values are to be stabilised (Sraffa, 1932a, p. 50). But given a determinate path of money prices which preserves the price structure of equilibrium, the equilibrium *money* rate of interest is uniquely fixed. In this regard when staying within the boundaries of perfect foresight Hayek's analysis seems impeccable. A logical inconsistency lies elsewhere, namely in neglecting the proposition that neutral money is compatible with arbitrary movements of the price level and does not imply a determinate path of money prices – neither price-level stability, as Wicksell contended, nor a price level varying inversely with technical progress, as Hayek did (for example, Hayek, 1928).

General equilibrium analysis also makes it possible to tackle a main problem of Hayek's theory, namely how consistently to explain the existence of money. One feasible way is by taking account of transaction costs which inhibit the existence of future contracts or of a sufficient number of 'Arrow securities'. It is well known that since then plans cannot be coordinated once for all at the beginning of the time horizon, sequences of plans have to be formulated with trading at all points of time and also the one budget restriction relating to the whole time horizon has to be substituted by a sequence of restrictions. If these budget sequences are binding in barter equilibrium, there is a possible role for money in helping to consolidate these restrictions. Again assuming perfect foresight and a sufficient endowment of fiat money or costless transactions on forward markets for money (that is credit) the sequence restrictions can be completely overcome and an allocation corresponding to an Arrow–Debreu economy established. Following Hahn (1973) such a monetary economy is called 'inessential'. One has to agree with Desai (1982, p. 166f.) that this type of a monetary economy corresponds closely (if not exactly) to what Hayek may have had in mind when searching for the conditions of neutral money.

In summary, the view of monetary neutrality as stated by Hayek is foremost a proposition on the real characteristics of equilibrium in a monetary economy. Money is said to be neutral if the monetary economy reproduces the results of frictionless barter, thus validating the use of real analysis and upholding its propositions for a monetary economy, too.

3.   The neoclassical synthesis and neutral money

The classical view of neutrality was, if only implicitly, at the heart of the controversy between Keynes and the 'classics', confronting for example the question which Hayek had raised already earlier (Hayek, 1931, p. 270) whether monetary theory has to be constructed on a basis laid by real analysis. But with the success of the Keynesian revolution and its rejection of real analysis, implied for instance by the insistence on a monetary theory of interest or the so-called peculiarities of money,[12] the concept of neutral money disappeared from scientific discussion for some time. The approach of what came to be known as 'neoclassical synthesis' soon attempted to construct a generalized macro-model where the Keynesian and the classical version were nothing but two special cases. Therefore the classical case could create a narrow domain where real analysis and the classical concept of neutral money were to be reconstituted. As it turned out the notion of neutral money had changed its meaning during this process of reconstruction.

In this regard Modigliani's 1944 contribution is of paradigmatic importance. There neutrality is taken to mean the existence of a special case where the quantity theory is valid in so far as the system of equilibrium conditions can be classically dichotomized into a real and a monetary sector in a logically consistent way (ibid., 216f.). Then the real sector, comprising all commodity excess demand functions set equal to zero, will determine real variables, that is, quantities and relative prices, given the quantity of money and independently of the price level. The monetary sector, that is the condition of money market equilibrium, determines the price level.

As is now well known, this dichotomy between commodity and money market excess demand functions is invalid. The postulated homogeneity properties of the real-sector excess demand functions contradict the consistency restriction imposed by Walras's law. This was repeatedly demonstrated by Patinkin (for example, 1949, 1956). Similarly Hahn (1955, p. 59ff.) showed that accepting Walras's law, the validity of the procedure proposed by Modigliani implies Say's Law, which is incompatible with a monetary economy since it leaves money prices indeterminate. Patinkin had a positive solution to offer of how to capture consistently the classical proposition that money under some specified assumptions does not influence real variables. This is the present common definition of the 'neutrality of money' as a property not of equilibrium itself but of comparative statics, real variables being invariant to altering the quantity of money (Patinkin, 1956, 1965, pp. 72ff.). In the subsequent and somewhat notorious debate on the classical dichotomy some possibilities of how to model the classical position were clarified, especially the distinction between neutrality of short-run and long-run equilibrium (Archibald and Lipsey, 1958), but in general Patinkin's critique was not shaken.[13]

Another important proposition relating to Patinkin's analysis was elaborated by Samuelson (1968) and Friedman (1969). It established a special inefficiency of *laissez-faire* in a monetary economy, as even in a long-run equilibrium in the sense of Archibald and Lipsey there remains a discrepancy between the private and social costs of holding real balances. To the individual the opportunity cost of real balances is equal to the rate of return forgone on competing assets, whereas to society it is zero. Therefore a divergence between social costs and social benefits (which are supposed to equal private benefits) of holding real balances emerges. This leads to the so-called theorem of the optimal quantity of money. If – and it may be a big 'if' indeed – this is the only inefficiency of *laissez-faire*, it can be remedied by a policy of subsidizing real balances with an amount equal to the nominal rate of interest, subsidies being financed by lump-sum taxation. Generally this policy is compatible with any rate of inflation if a corresponding subsidy is chosen. The combination of no subsidy with deflating prices by a rate equal to that of the real return on capital is only a special case.[14]

Coming back to neutrality notions, what does this imply? First, it is clear now that an optimal money supply (that is, an optimal subsidy on cash) is a prerequisite for establishing an inessential monetary economy, or a neutral money of the Hayekian type. In the case where thereby global efficiency is achieved it is sufficient, too. It should be noted that this means that although there are frictions in this neutral money economy which differentiate it from an Arrow–Debreu economy, these can be completely undone by introducing money and subsidizing it optimally. As critiques have pointed out (for example, Hahn, 1971) the role of money according to this approach may seem rather contrived.

Second, both neutrality concepts employed within the neoclassical synthesis – the notion of a dichotomy into a real and monetary sector and the notion of neutrality as an invariance property of comparative statics – evidently are weaker than the classical concept of Hayek. For even when some dichotomization is valid, the monetary inefficiency of non-satiated real balances may persist and the real characteristics of equilibrium of frictionless barter and of monetary equilibrium diverge. Concerning Patinkin's definition of neutrality it leaves properties of the real charcteristics themselves out of discussion altogether, stating invariance only, so that any equilibrium allocation may be neutral provided it cannot be disturbed in a comparative static sense by altering the quantity of money.[15] From this point of view comparisons between barter and monetary economics seem useless, and indeed Patinkin's attempt to formulate such comparisons within his framework of analysis led to failure.[16]

Third, it was pointed out above – as the Hayek–Sraffa debate of the 1930s might have demonstrated to participants and commentators – that the classical notion of neutrality does not fix a unique path of the price level. On the contrary, it is compatible with any price level path to which economic actors have fully adjusted, including an optimal subsidy on real balances.

Finally, there is also a vital difference between Hayek and post-Keynesian neoclassicals concerning the mechanism by which money finds its way into the economy. In Hayek's analysis new money is created when the banks respond to an excess demand for loans by extending credit beyond the (real) limits imposed by public savings. So concomitantly with the injection of new money the equilibrium price structure is disturbed by a 'false' interest rate, leading to distortions of entrepreneurial investment.[17] On the other hand, in the Patinkin framework money is introduced simply as a lump-sum transfer to households, 'helicopter money' as Friedman (1969) termed it. Thereby the essential non-neutrality of money to which Hayek has pointed is reduced to a question of distribution effects, which are far too often neglected when it comes to the analysis of monetary policy.[18]

4.   Modelling growth and neutral money

The limited sense in which the term 'neutral money' has been used since Patinkin introduced his definition prevented comparisons between money and barter from playing a significant role in characterizing different approaches to monetary theory for some time, and if used made them a source of serious error sometimes. A point in case are early contributions to money and growth. Right from the start the examination of money and growth led to disturbing paradoxes when comparing the welfare of a representative actor in monetary and barter economies. So Tobin (1967, p. 71) concluded that introducing money does lower welfare compared with barter, as typically money works as a substitute for accumulating real capital. This was contested by Patinkin and Levhari (1968), who legitimately raised the question of why money then should be introduced (ibid., p. 208). They attempted a solution by considering not only the potentially negative effects on per capita output and consumption but also the additional utility derived from real balances, as a source of welfare absent in a barter economy. Unfortunately they arrived at a result that again seems paradoxical, namely that because of this utility of cash services, welfare of a monetary economy possibly exceeds that of barter (ibid., p. 214).

Evidently the solution to these puzzles consists, on the one hand, in defining correctly the transactions characteristics of the barter economy to which the monetary one is compared and, on the other hand, in clarifying what function money does fulfil in the latter. As a transactions technology is not specified in barter growth models like those of Solow (1956), the most sensible interpretation is that it is perfect[19] and Solow growth therefore reproduces a perfect foresight analogue of Arrow–Debreu. Now, to explain the existence of money one must take account of transaction frictions. The best money can achieve is completely to undo these frictions and again to replicate the results of frictionless barter. That is the Solow solution. Therefore the welfare of (frictionless) barter can at best be equalled but not exceeded; and if some of the money-generating friction remains effective the welfare of the monetary economy must fall short of barter. If the demand for real balances is satiated and its utility maximized by a regime of optimal money supply, then welfare may equal frictionless barter.

This analysis of the early literature on money and growth justifies the conjecture that by the reinterpretation of the neutrality concept, pre-Keynesian monetary theory was clarified but also some valuable insights were lost.[20]

5. Neutrality and New Classical Economics

The last task is to examine the relation between Hayek's approach to monetary theory and that of the new classical (macro-)economics.[21] Recent discussions have put the main question as follows: can the new classical economics be interpreted as formalizing basic insights which were already due to pre-Keynesian thought and were neglected primarily because of the failure to provide a rigorous model? Or in simpler terms: was Hayek a predecessor of Lucas?[22]

The models most suited to such a comparison are those of Lucas (for example, 1972, 1984, 1987) which are founded on the basis of microeconomic decision theory. These models come very close to models of neutral money. Looking at them from an analytical point of view their common approach can be seen to consist in the characterization of economies by rational expectations equilibrium.[23] In such economies there may exist a sufficient amount of securities to completely hedge against uncertainty which arises from shifts of tastes or technology. Yet this is accompanied by some (for example, monetary) source of 'noise', so that neither the current state of nature nor all market prices can be observed. Therefore, although equilibrium prices mirror the optimal use of available information they do not reveal the complex state of nature, real and monetary, fully. Put differently, noise inhibits the inversion of the function relating states of nature to equilibrium prices. Whereas rational expectations equilibrium in a case without noise corresponds to a full-information Arrow–Debreu equilibrium, in the situation typical of new classical (macro-) models signal confusion remains as a possible source of divergence.[24]

If new classical economics is to apply to a monetary economy, as it obviously is designed to, there is still the analytical problem of how to fit money into the model. Two possible procedures have been favoured up to now. One is the appeal to an overlapping generations friction (as by Lucas, 1972; and Wallace, 1980). The other is the introduction of a cash-in-advance constraint without further justifying it (for example, Lucas, 1982). In both frameworks a proper monetary policy can manage to realise Arrow–Debreu analogous equilibria if there is no noise. In the former case of overlapping generations an allocation can be reached with the efficiency properties of a well-behaved competitive equilibrium, although without money as an outside asset such an efficient equilibrium would not exist because a crucial condition concerning the connectedness of the endowments of different generations is violated. In the latter case of the cash-in-advance constraint proper monetary policy again is to eliminate the wedge between the returns on money and securities and to equalize the opportunity costs of cash goods and credit goods, respectively. So with an optimal subsidy on cash the monetary constraint might be completely eliminated.

Comparing new classical economics with Hayekian propositions on neutral money, *prima facie* the claim seems to be justified to consider new classical analysis as an internally consistent reconstruction of a neutral money economy along Walrasian lines. At the same time by introducing noise it allows the modelling of business cycles as temporary divergences from allocations which are efficient in the absence of expectational errors. Thus Hayek's programme to examine the conditions of neutral money rigorously seems satisfied. Nevertheless, looked at from an epistemological point of view there exists a vital difference, because the new classicals may put more faith in their construction than its inventor seemingly did. To Hayek neutral money, as shown above, served only as a fictitious point of reference. He surely never believed in the existence of a monetary economy where intertemporal coordination on the average could be taken for granted. At best the connection between 'pure economic theory' and monetary economics can be described as 'loosely joined'.[25] Yet the 'task of monetary theory', as Hayek (1931, p. 110) has seen it, is to go beyond the narrow limits imposed by the assumption of neutral money. Similarly, Hayek's concern with problems of information, especially the informational function attributed to markets and *market* prices (for example, Hayek, 1945), must have prevented him from postulating that economy-wide problems of pricing and coordination are to be solved within the head of each individual.[26] In this context the assumptions of perfect foresight or rational expectation do not seem to be less arbitrary than other so-called *ad hoc* assumptions.[27]

Summarizing this section leads to a somewhat paradoxical result: there is evidence of a close connection between Hayekian and new classical monetary analysis, because the aim of both was to establish a model of a monetary economy in intertemporal equilibrium. Thanks to the progress of technique, modern economists were successful where Hayek was not. Yet despite this common search of how to construct a model of neutral money, both approaches differ markedly in their intention of how it should be fruitfully applied and developed.

6. Summary

In the first part of this chapter different notions of the neutrality of money were contrasted. In particular Hayek's concept of neutral money was considered to be the most fully developed analysis to be found in pre-Keynesian monetary theory. It amounts to a comparison of the intertemporal equilibria of money and barter economies. Modern general equilibrium analysis was used to clarify some of the more vague aspects of Hayek's analysis; for example, the concept of an equilibrium rate of interest, and to supplement it with an explanation of why money exists at all. Furthermore, it was shown that the neutrality concepts developed within the framework of the neoclassical synthesis did not address the issue of comparing money and barter, and therefore proved both weaker and less fruitful.

In the second part two examples were presented in which use of the Hayekian concept of neutrality would have furthered insight. The first example is taken from early discussions of money and growth. It demonstrates that there was considerable confusion as to what has to be implicitly assumed in models in which there is no function attributed to money. Consequently, barter models often were misunderstood as relating to economies where transactions actually are carried out by barter methods instead as to those where the transaction technology is perfect (so that there is no task for money to perform). The second example deals with new classical economics. It is shown that it makes effective use, if unknowingly, of the Hayekian concept of neutral money, but there still exists in this regard a potentially valuable contribution to rediscover by following Hayek's sceptical evaluation of such neutral money-cum-rational expectations models.

Notes

1. I am grateful to Laurence S. Moss and Alfred Sitz for helpful comments on an earlier draft; as usual, responsibility for remaining errors is mine.
2. For a critical evaluation of Wicksell's monetary theory see Myrdal (1939).
3. It is worthwhile to note that just those works of Hayek which dealt most thoroughly with analytical concepts, namely Hayek (1928, 1933b), were published in German and not translated into English until recently (Hayek, 1984). Similarly, the more fundamental *Geldtheorie* and the application of its approach in 'Prices and Production' appeared in English in reverse order. So Hayek's monetary theory was presented to non-German discussion not very systematically.
4. When Hayek (1933b) commented on this definition, he on the whole accepted it, stressing only the additional assumptions of flexible prices and perfect foresight. Again it should be noted that Koopmans' contribution was not translated into English.
5. In contemporary monetary discussion, for example Barger (1935) and Rosenstein-Rodan (1936), often the 'wrong' comparison was made, whereas Robertson's (1940, p. 142) reference to neutral money is in the spirit of Hayek and Koopmans.
6. On this see Hayek (1928, p. 76; 1939, p. 139f.). Milgate (1979) establishes priority of Hayek's use of intertemporal equilibrium as against Lindahl and Hicks.
7. For instance Hayek remarks that 'the body of existing pure economic theory demonstrates that, so long as we neglect monetary factors, there is an inherent tendency toward an equilibrium of the economic system; and ... monetary factors may bring about a kind of disequilibrium in the economic system which could not be explained without recourse to these monetary factors' (1932, p. 238; for a similar statement see Hayek, 1928, p. 75). The mechanism whereby intertemporal disequilibrium eventually generates a crisis is some version of the Ricardo effect, see Moss and Vaughn (1986).
8. Disequilibrium in the sense used here does not preclude market clearing at any point of time but implies incompatibility of plans and expectations concerning the future. Intertemporal equilibrium of a monetary economy is therefore a much stronger condition than the monetary equilibrium of Wicksell and Myrdal.
9. Similar statements are to be found in Hayek (1931a, p. 109; 1933a, p. 190f.; 1933b).
10. This may be considered as implicit evidence on the existence of a methodological discontinuity between the equilibrium analysis of the early Hayek and the paradigm of market process employed by the late Hayek and the neo-Austrian school; this is contended for example by Hutchison (1981). It should also be noted that von Mises sceptically pointed out the fatal mistakes following from not using such barter fictions ('*Naturaltausch-Fiktionen*') with sufficient care (von Mises, 1940, 189f.).
11. Milgate (1979) shows that the critical misunderstanding as between the participants

of the controversy consisted in the confusion of conditions of intertemporal versus stationary equilibrium. For some views of the controversy dissenting from the following see Desai (1982), McCloughry (1982) and Lachmann (1986).

12. As the possibility of neutral money is outright rejected there is from the point of view of this study not much to say about Keynes as a monetary theorist. On his monetary analysis see Kohn (1986).
13. For a guide to this controversy see Mauer (1966).
14. This indeterminacy of the optimal rate of inflation is stressed by Riese (1986, p. 107ff.).
15. Strangely enough, neo-Austrian interpretations of Hayekian monetary theory as a rule take it for granted that there is nothing more to be learned from Hayek's concept of neutral money than can be captured within the Patinkin framework, for example O'Driscoll (1977, p. 50ff.). See Wonnacott (1958) for some early dissent.
16. Patinkin (1965, p. 75) identified a barter economy with the limit of a monetary economy where the nominal quantity of money has converged to zero. Obviously this does not make much sense; see Lutz (1969).
17. Thus fixing the effective circulation of money is a necessary condition for neutrality (Hayek 1984, p. 161). Having this in mind, it seems rather odd that some commentators were not able to find any differences between the neutrality concepts of Hayek and Patinkin (for example, Scheide, 1986, pp. 579, 589).
18. By the way, the Patinkin framework was also unhelpful in this regard to the Keynesian position, as it was easy to point out that the neutrality experiment merely described the effects of a change of the monetary unit which in any reasonable model should have no real effects.
19. Following Hahn (1969, p. 195).
20. If also this insight was negative, namely realising the narrow domain where real analysis can be consistently applied.
21. For an overview see Klamer (1984).
22. For some discussion of this connection see Kantor (1979), Laidler (1982), Butos (1985), Klausinger (1986), Scheide (1986) and also Lucas (1977, p. 215) himself.
23. Thereby the concept of rational expectations equilibrium is extended as now individuals not only have correct price forecasts conditional on states of nature (knowing the correct model) but also seek to extract from observed price signals a probabilistic forecast of current and future states of nature themselves. On this see Grossman (1981).
24. This account of new classical economics is given by Hahn (1980, p. 284ff.), who identifies equilibrium values (without noise) with the 'natural' values of monetarist theory. Of course, these are a long way from Friedman's definition of natural rates (Friedman, 1968), but evidently it is difficult to give this definition some analytical content otherwise.
25. Hayek (1941, p. 408); for an interesting interpretation see Garrison (1984).
26. An early exposition of the paradox of perfect foresight and theory absorption is given by Morgenstern (1935). For a similar critique of rational expectations see Frydman (1983).
27. Following Hayek (1937), perfect or coherent foresight cannot be inferred from the pure logic of choice, but necessarily belongs to the realm of empirical hypotheses. Therefore it seems to be not *ad hoc* only from the point of view of the model-building economist who, of course, has all the necessary information about structure and interdependence. See also Butos (1985).

References

Archibald, G. and Lipsey, R. (1958), 'Monetary and value theory: a critique of Lange and Patinkin', *Review of Economic Studies*, 26, pp. 1–22.

Arrow, K. J. (1964), 'The role of securities in the optimal allocation of risk-bearing', *Review of Economic Studies*, 31, pp. 91–6.

Barger, H. (1935), 'Neutral money and the trade cycle', *Economica*, n.s. 2, pp.429–47
Butos, W. N. (1985), 'Hayek and general equilibrium analysis', *Southern Economic Journal*, 52, pp. 332–43.
Desai, M. (1982), 'The task of monetary theory: the Hayek–Sraffa debate in a modern perspective', in M. Baranzini (ed.), *Advances in Economic Theory*, Oxford: Basil Blackwell, pp. 149–70.
Friedman, M. (1968), 'The role of monetary policy', *American Economic Review*, 58, pp. 1–17.
Friedman, M. (1969), 'The optimum quantity of money', in his *The Optimum Quantity of Money and Other Essays*, London: Macmillan, pp. 1–50.
Frydman, R. (1983), 'Individual rationality, decentralization, and the rational expectations hypothesis', in R. Frydman and E. S. Phelps (eds), *Individual Forecasting and Aggregate Outcomes*, Cambridge: Cambridge University Press, pp. 97–122.
Garrison, R. W. (1984), 'Time and money: the universals of macroeconomic theorizing', *Journal of Macroeconomics*, 6, pp. 197–213.
Grossman, S. (1981), 'An introduction to the theory of rational expectations under asymmetric information', *Review of Economic Studies*, 48, pp. 541–59.
Hahn, F. H. (1955), 'The rate of interest and general equilibrium analysis', *Economic Journal* 65: pp. 52–66; as reprinted in F. H. Hahn (1985), *Money, Growth and Stability*, Oxford: Basil Blackwell, pp. 56–74
Hahn, F. H. (1969), 'On money and growth', *Journal of Money, Credit and Banking*, 1, pp. 175–84; as reprinted in F. H, Hahn (1984), *Equilibrium and Macroeconomics*, Oxford: Basil Blackwell, pp. 195–213.
Hahn, F. H. (1971), 'Professor Friedman's views on money', *Economica*, 38, pp. 61–80; as reprinted in Hahn (1984), pp. 259–82.
Hahn, F. H. (1973), 'On transaction costs, inessential sequence economies and money', *Review of Economic Studies*, 40, pp. 449–61; as reprinted in Hahn (1985), pp. 105–27.
Hahn, F. H. (1980), 'Monetarism and economic theory', *Economica*, 47, pp. 1–17; as reprinted in Hahn (1984), pp. 283–306.
Hayek, F. A. (1928), 'Das intertemporale Gleichgewichtssystem der Preise und die Bewegungen des Geldwertes', *Weltwirtschaftliches Archiv*, 28, pp. 33–76; translated in Hayek (1984), pp. 71–117.
Hayek, F. A. (1931a), *Prices and Production*, London: Routledge.
Hayek, F. A. (1931b), 'Reflections on the pure theory of money of Mr. J. M. Keynes. Part I', *Economica*, 11, pp. 270–95.
Hayek, F. A. (1932), 'Money and capital. A reply', *Economic Journal*, 42, pp. 237–49.
Hayek, F. A. (1933a), *Monetary Theory and the Trade Cycle* (reprint 1966), New York: Augustus M. Kelley.
Hayek, F. A. (1933b), 'Über neutrales Geld', *Zeitschrift für Nationalökonomie*, 4, pp. 659–61; translated in Hayek (1984), pp. 159–62.
Hayek, F. A. (1937), 'Economics and knowledge', *Economica*, n.s. 4, pp. 33–54.
Hayek, F. A. (1939), 'Price expectations, monetary disturbances and malinvestments', in his *Profits, Interests, and Investment*, London: Routledge & Kegan Paul, pp. 135–56.
Hayek, F. A. (1941), *The Pure Theory of Capital*, London: Routledge & Kegan Paul.
Hayek, F. A. (1984), *Money, Capital and Fluctuations. Early Essays*, ed. R. McCloughry, London: Routledge & Kegan Paul.
Hutchison, T. W. (1981), 'Austrians on philosophy and method (since Menger)', in his *The Politics and Philosophy of Economics*, New York and London: New York University Press, pp. 203–32.
Kantor, B. (1979), 'Rational expectations and economic thought', *Journal of Economic Literature*, 17, pp. 1422–41.
Klamer, A. (1984), 'Levels of discourse in new classical economics', *History of Political Economy*, 16, pp. 263–90.
Klausinger, H. (1985), 'F. A. von Hayeks Theorie der Geldwirtschaft in neuerer Sicht', *European Journal of Political Economy*, 1, pp. 585–610.
Kohn, M. (1986), 'Monetary analysis, the equilibrium method, and Keynes' *General*

Theory', Journal of Political Economy, 94, pp. 1191–224.

Koopmans, J. (1933), 'Zum Problem des Neutralen Geldes', in F. A. Hayek (ed.), *Beiträge zur Geldtheorie*, Vienna: Julius Springer, pp. 211–359.

Lachmann, L. M. (1986), 'Austrian economics under fire: the Hayek–Sraffa duel in retrospect', in W. Grassl and B. Smith (eds), *Austrian Economics. Historical and Philosophical Background*, London: Croom Helm, pp. 225–42.

Laidler, D. (1982), 'On Say's Law, money, and the business cycle', in his *Monetarist Perspectives*, Oxford: Philip Allan, pp. 67–105.

Lucas, R. E. (1972), 'Expectations and the neutrality of money', *Journal of Economic Theory*, 4, pp. 103–24.

Lucas, R. E. (1977), 'Understanding business cycles', in K. Brunner and A. H. Meltzer (eds), *Stabilization of the Domestic and International Economy*, Carnegie-Rochester Series on Public Policy 5, Amsterdam: North-Holland, pp. 7–29.

Lucas, R. E. (1982), 'Interest rates and currency prices in a two-country world', *Journal of Monetary Economics*, 10, pp. 335–59.

Lucas, R. E. (1984), 'Money in a theory of finance', in K. Brunner and A. H. Meltzer (eds), *Essays on Macroeconomic Implications of Financial and Labour Markets and Political Processes*, Carnegie-Rochester Series on Public Policy 21, Amsterdam: North-Holland pp. 9–46.

Lucas, R. E. (1987), *Models of Business Cycles*, Oxford: Basil Blackwell.

Lutz, F. A. (1969), 'On neutral money', in E. Streissler (ed.), *Roads to Freedom: Essays in Honour of Friedrich A. von Hayek*, London: Routledge & Kegan Paul, pp. 105–16.

McCloughry, R. (1982), 'Neutrality and monetary equilibrium: a note on Desai', in M. Baranzini (ed.), *Advances in Economic Theory*, Oxford: Basil Blackwell, pp. 171–82.

Milgate, M. (1979), 'On the origin of the notion of "intertemporal equilibrium" ', *Economica*, 46, pp. 1–10.

von Mises, L. (1940), *Nationalökonomie. Theorie des Handelns und Wirtschaftens* (reprint 1980), Munich: Philosophia Verlag.

Modigliani, F. (1944), 'Liquidity preference and the theory of interest and money', *Econometrica*, 12, pp. 45–88; as reprinted in F. A. Lutz and L. W. Mints (eds) (1951), *Readings in Monetary Theory*, Homewood, Ill: Richard D. Irwin, pp. 186–239.

Morgenstern, O. (1935), 'Vollkommene Voraussicht und wirtschaftliches Gleichgewicht', *Zeitschrift für Nationalökonomie*, 6, pp. 337–57.

Moss, L. S. and Vaughn, K. I. (1986), 'Hayek's Ricardo effect: a second look', *History of Political Economy*, 18, pp. 545–65.

Myrdal, G. (1939), *Monetary Equilibrium* (reprint 1965), New York: Augustus M. Kelley.

Nagatani, K. (1975), 'On a theorem of Arrow', *Review of Economic Studies*, 42, pp. 483–5.

O'Driscoll, G. P. (1977), *Economics as a Coordination Problem*, Kansas City: Sheed Andrews and McNeel.

Patinkin, D. (1949), 'The indeterminacy of absolute prices in classical economic theory', *Econometrica*, 17, pp. 1–27.

Patinkin, D. (1956), *Money, Interest and Prices* (2nd edition 1965), New York: Harper & Row.

Patinkin, D. and Levhari, D. (1968), 'The role of money in a simple growth model', *American Economic Review*, 58, pp. 713–53; as reprinted in D. Patinkin (1972). *Studies in Monetary Economics*, New York : Harper & Row, pp. 205–42.

Riese, H. (1986), *Theorie der Inflation*, Tübingen: J. C. B. Mohr.

Robertson, D. H, (1940), *Essays in Monetary Theory* (reprint 1948), London: Staples Press.

Rosenstein-Rodan, P. N. (1936), 'The coordination of the general theories of money and price', *Economica*, n.s. 3, pp. 257–80.

Samuelson, P. A. (1968), 'What classical and neoclassical monetary theory really was', *Canadian Journal of Economics*, 1, pp. 1–15.

Scheide, J. (1986), 'New classical and Austrian business cycle theory: is there a difference?', *Weltwirtschaftliches Archiv*, 122, pp. 575–98.

Schumpeter, J. (1954), *History of Economic Analysis*, London: Allen and Unwin.
Sraffa, P. (1932a), 'Dr. Hayek on money and capital', *Economic Journal*, 42, pp. 42–53.
Sraffa, P. (1932b), 'A rejoinder', *Economic Journal*, 42, pp. 249–51.
Solow, R. M. (1956), 'A contribution to the theory of economic growth', *Quarterly Journal of Economics*, 70. pp. 65–94.
Tobin, J. (1967), 'The neutrality of money in growth models: a comment', *Economica*, 34, pp. 69–72.
Wallace, N. (1980), 'The overlapping generations model of fiat money', in J. H. Kareken and N. Wallace (eds), *Models of Monetary Economies*, Federal Reserve Bank of Minneapolis, pp. 49–82.
Wicksell, K. (1934), *Lectures on Political Economy: Vol I. General Theory*, London: Routledge & Kegan Paul. (First Swedish edition 1906.)
Wicksell, K. (1935), *Lectures on Political Economy: Vol. II. Money*, London: Routledge & Kegan Paul. (First Swedish edition 1906.)
Wicksell, K. (1936), *Interest and Prices*, London: Routledge & Kegan Paul. (First German edition 1898.).
Wonnacott, P. (1958), 'Neutral money in Patinkin's '*Money, Interest and Prices*', *Review of Economic Studies*, 26, pp. 70–1.

10 Dutch monetarism in retrospect

M. M. G. Fase

1. Introduction and background

Under the gold standard, on which the Netherlands was from 1875 until 1936 with an interruption for the period 1914–25, the main goal of Dutch monetary policy was to maintain the exchange rate of the guilder through purchases and sales of gold at agreed prices. The most important instrument for this policy was the Nederlandsche Bank's discount rate. When the free export of gold was suspended in 1914, monetary policy was divested of its generally accepted criterion. This does not mean that everyone agreed to the automatic link of the gold standard. G. M. Verrijn Stuart (1893–1969) was of the opinion that the gold standard prevailing before the First World War gave too much priority to the external value of the currency over its domestic value. In Verrijn Stuart's (1919, p. 184) view stabilization of the domestic price level should be the main target of monetary policy. In this context, he mentioned two problems. The first was the practical statistical question of how to devise a useful price index. Secondly, there was the institutional problem of the power and position to be afforded to the central bank.

In the mid-1920s, the place of monetary policy within the economic order was the subject of a polemic between Koopmans (1900–1958) and Posthuma (born 1900) in the Dutch journal *De Economist* (see Koopmans, 1925; Posthuma, 1926). This controversy was generated by a series of articles by J. Schumpeter in the Dutch weekly *ESB* of 1926 about the new theories on monetary policy proposed by J. M. Keynes. Schumpeter's critical remarks come down to three points. First, the aim of banking policy as advocated by Keynes should be the stabilization of the general price level. Schumpeter feared that this would systematically undermine the capitalist system. Secondly, Keynes assumed that price stabilization would dampen cyclical movements. In Schumpeter's opinion, however, unhampered cyclical fluctuations were indispensable for a healthy development of the economy. This is why he rejected Keynes' view on monetary policy. In the third place, Schumpeter disliked Keynes' preference for deliberate money control because he preferred an automatic system such as the gold standard to a discretionary policy pursued by the central bank.

Koopmans considered Schumpeter an advocate of the banking principle which he held to be outdated. In a reaction to Koopmans' criticism, Posthuma (1926) regarded the view held by Keynes and Koopmans as an example of 'physiocratic atavism' which equates the technical product and its value. Contrary to Koopmans in 1925, Posthuma was in favour of a monetary policy which ensured a completely neutral role for money. Several years later, in 1929, at the annual meeting of the Society for Economics and Statistics, Koopmans (1930) proposed the idea of an active banking policy bringing about a rate of interest ensuring that money did not exert a disturbing influence on profit. This meant that, under the impact of Posthuma's criticism of 1926, Koopmans accepted the principle of neutral money as the guideline for monetary policy and rejected the view of Verrijn Stuart of 1929 that the appropriate criterion for monetary policy should be the stability of the general price level.

The jewel in the crown of Netherlands thinking about monetary policy during the interwar period was no doubt the theory of neutral money developed by Koopmans from 1929 onwards. This theory provides the intellectual foundation of Dutch monetarism, which became predominant in the period 1946–67, when Dr Holtrop was president of the Netherlands Bank. The life-cycle of this Dutch view on monetary management, which spans more than 40 years, is marked by three rounds of discussion of great profundity from both a theoretical and a policy standpoint. The first round took place in the 1930s and started in 1929 with the above-mentioned view of Verrijn Stuart on the essence of price stabilization. The second round was prompted by the Bank's Annual Report for 1953, in which Dr Holtrop, then president of the Nederlandsche Bank, set out his method of monetary analysis for the first time. The third and final round was occasioned by the retired Dr Holtrop in 1971, when he attempted to summarize his monetary analysis in an econometric equation (see also Holtrop, 1972a, 1972b). This heavily criticized attempt prompted Selden (1975) to coin the term Dutch monetarism to summarize monetary thought in the Netherlands.

This chapter reports on the history of Dutch monetarism over its life-cycle. It is organized around the three debating rounds mentioned above. The chapter concludes with a final evaluation of this particular view in the perspective of present monetary thought.

2.   Koopmans' theory of neutral money

The concept of neutral money – which is older than the term itself – has its origins in the works of Ricardo, Menger and Mill. In the 1920s notably German-speaking economists such as Hayek used it in their analyses of the working of money. At the heart of the concept is the notion that, in principle, the result of the economic process may differ between a money-using economy and a pure barter economy. This difference arises because the use of money means that each barter transaction is split up into two parts, so that demand may fall short of, or exceed, commodity supply. As a consequence, disturbances of equilibrium may occur which are not conceivable in a non-monetary or barter economy.

Koopmans presented his analysis of neutral money in the essay 'Zum Problem des neutralen Geldes' published in 1933 in a volume edited by F. A. Hayek. This essay expounded on the criterion of neutral money and definitively established Koopmans' reputation as a monetary theorist. This contribution of 1933 may be viewed as a shortened version of his completed but never submitted dissertation. An important novelty of Koopmans' view was that he considered the narrow problem of monetary policy in the broader framework of welfare economics. This approach divested the criterion of neutral money of its *ad hoc* and *a priori* character that prevailed monetary thinking of the time. The underlying thought was that, as a guideline for economic policy, *laissez-faire* generates optimal welfare. Thus, neutral money is a necessary condition for the achievement of a Pareto optimum. According to Koopmans, however, *laissez-faire* does not mean refraining from intervention but promoting concurrence between reality and the ideal situation, as suggested by the concept of equilibrium. The latter provides the justification for the principle of neutral money in monetary policy, or in Koopman's words, 'a programme of managed currency' (1982, p. 54). Monetary policy is consequently fully compatible with the idea of *laissez-faire* which Koopmans chose explicitly as his working hypothesis. This implies – as recognized by Koopmans – that neutrality is no longer required if the optimum theorem is rejected as the guiding principle. Therefore Koopmans generalized the concept of neutrality and embedded it in a more general economic and welfare theoretical framework.

For Koopmans it was of great importance to have shown analytically that neutral money is not the same as price stability. He does not, however, provide a concrete guideline for monetary policy. Therefore it is not surprising that he concludes his theoretical analysis in the Hayek volume with the slightly disappointing observation that:

> die wissenschaftliche Grundlage für ein einwandfreies 'Management' der Geldversorgung bis auf weiteres fehlt. Insoweit bleibt mithin auch das

Endergebnis unserer Untersuchungen durchwegs negativ, und wir können an
dieser Stelle höchstens der Hoffnung Ausdruck geben, das die vorliegende
Arbeit vielleicht eine Anregung zu weiteren Untersuchungen auf diesem
Gebiete darstellen könnte. (1982, p. 431)

In other words, Koopmans resticts himself to showing just the conditions for money to be neutral for the course of the economy. He did
not, however, want to set forth concrete guidelines for monetary
management, as the above quotation illustrates.

G. M. Verrijn Stuart, who was a professor of economics in Rotterdam, a tireless researcher and a practical monetary theorist, regarded
this conclusion of Koopmans as totally unsatisfactory. While accepting
the principles of Koopmans' analysis, he continued to seek for a
concrete translation of the principle of neutral money to a norm for
monetary policy. In his farewell lecture, held on 8 October 1934 upon
leaving the Netherlands School of Economics in Rotterdam, Verrijn
Stuart attempted to shape Koopmans' idea to suit the practice of
monetary policy. Thus, he initiated the first round of discussion within
Dutch monetarism.

It began with an exchange of views between G. M. Verrijn Stuart and
Van Genechten (1895–1945), a lecturer from Utrecht University. G. M.
Verrijn Stuart (1934, 1935) held the view that neutrality of money is
desirable from the point of view of welfare. Unlike Koopmans, he
identified neutrality with stability of the intrinsic value of money – i.e.
'innere Geldwert' according to Menger's terminology. This is the value
of money governed by the ratio of the demand for to the supply of
money. This intrinsic value of money reflects the proper exchange
relationships of goods and services and is, hence, preferable to stabilization of the extrinsic value in exchange – i.e. 'aussere Geldwert' again
using Menger's terminology. This is the same as the general price level.
This emphasis on the stability of the intrinsic value of money led Verrijn
Stuart to the criterion of stable money flow or MV as the practical
yardstick for monetary policy. According to G. M. Verrijn Stuart, a
stable intrinsic value of money requires a stable money flow in addition
to a periodically re-weighted general price index, which also serves as a
point of reference. Van Genechten (1935, 1936) recognized the neutrality of money as the proper criterion, but opposed Verrijn Stuart's
choice of a general price index together with the MV index. Instead, he
proposed stabilization of the price index of marginal exports as a
supplementary criterion. For practical reasons G. M. Verrijn Stuart
expressed serious doubt about this solution. His father, the Emeritus
Professor C. A. Verrijn Stuart (1865–1948), also joined the debate by

advocating, like his son in 1929, stabilization of the general price index to the extent that full capacity utilization has not yet been achieved. In that case, C. A. Verrijn Stuart (1935, 1936) put forward, MV may increase. Tinbergen (born 1903) sided with Koopmans and his criterion of neutrality. It is noteworthy that Koopmans himself did not take part in this debate. However, Tinbergen also pointed out a general short-coming in the monetary approach adopted here, because in his view it took insufficient account of general economic interdependencies and completely ignored the policy instruments actually available. Conse-quently, Tinbergen (1936) found the approach of both the two Verrijn Stuarts and of Van Genechten too isolated and analytically incomplete. Unanimity was not achieved in this interesting debate and the concept of neutrality continued to hold the attention of Dutch monetarists, without having crystalized at the time into an operational criterion for monetary policy. A few years later, Keesing (1939), in his doctoral thesis for the University of Amsterdam, went indirectly into the concept of neutrality as part of his general equilibrium approach. In a critical analysis of Koopmans' views he concluded that the use of money exists only by virtue of uncertainty. Therefore the neutrality, as advocated by Koopmans, meant that the velocity of circulation of money would increase *ad infinitum*. The fact that – unlike Myrdal in the same volume – Koopmans did not take into account the importance of uncertainty and the consequences with regard to holding money is a serious flaw in Koopmans' analysis. The concept of neutrality did not meet with response in the Anglo-Saxon world either, as Koopmans' interesting and profound correspondence with Gregory and Robertson in the 1930s shows (see Fase, 1983). However, this does not alter the fact that Koopmans' pre-war monetary concept has had a prolonged fruitful impact on the evolution of postwar monetary thinking in the Nether-lands.

3. Holtrop's monetary analysis

While he was president of the Nederlandsche Bank, Dr Holtrop (born 1903) introduced a particular framework for the monetary diagnosis of the Dutch economy. The Bank's Annual Report of 1953 offers the first description of this method and caused an interesting monetary debate among Koopmans, Holtrop, Tinbergen and Witteveen (see Koopmans et al., 1955). This was followed by an interesting series of contributions by Goedhart (1955), De Jong (1954, 1973), De Roos (1954) and Polak (1957). This debate may be considered the second round of discussion on Dutch monetarism referred to earlier. The main result of the 1954 discussion was clarification and integration of the conceptual framework used by the Bank.

The starting point of Holtrop's policy analysis was the Wicksellian concern with monetary equilibrium and Koopmans' theoretical conditions for monetary neutrality (Holtrop, 1972b). In Koopmans' view neutral monetary influence or, following Myrdal's terminology, monetary equilibrium means an absence of either inflation or deflation. In other words, in such a situation there is neither excess aggregate demand (*reine Nachfrage*) nor a shortfall of aggregate demand (*Nachfrage Ausfall*). Therefore, the basic source of any monetary disturbance is to be found in an inflationary or deflationary process. An inflationary process is caused by spontaneous or *ex ante* money-creation and dishoarding. Inversely, a deflationary process is caused by spontaneous money cancellation or hoarding. Thus a necessary and sufficient condition for the occurrence of any monetary equilibrium is that the algebraic sum of spontaneous inflationary and deflationary disturbances should be zero.

The main purpose of Dr Holtrop's method of monetary analysis is to locate inflationary and deflationary disturbances. As money that is anywhere must be somewhere it is necessary to distinguish logically between autonomous and induced monetary actions such as hoarding and money-creation. Holtrop's analysis is based on the contention that careful observation and measurement enables the Bank to calculate approximately the size of autonomous hoarding (or dishoarding) and money cancellation (or creation) for particular broad sectors of the economy such as the government sector, the private sector, the financial sector and the foreign sector. The result of this calculation is the liquidity surplus or deficit of each sector. This is supposed to reflect the amount of net deflationary or inflationary financing in the sector considered. As this was the heart of the Bank's monetary approach, it became the main issue in the debate of 1954.

Holtrop's analysis has three totally different sides. First, there is the question of the *location* of inflationary and deflationary disturbances. This localization is not just geographic in the sense of foreign versus domestic. To the extent that the disturbances are domestic, attempts are made to allocate them to the various sectors distinguished. The second side, and this concerns both the sectors individually and the classification into domestic and foreign, relates to the fundamental distinction of inflationary or deflationary disturbances into autonomous *impulses* and induced reactions, two concepts which are, incidentally, closely related to the concepts spontaneous and induced as used by the English economist Robertson in the 1920s. The third feature is that, in addition to M1, Holtrop also takes potential or *near money* into consideration as a possible source of monetary disturbances. In the 1950s this was no doubt a new development.

The first question is mostly a statistical measurement problem with, at least in Holtrop's approach, a high normative bias. The second question is mainly analytical in nature and leaves scope for a free interpretation of the facts.

The discussion induced by Holtrop's Annual Report for 1953 covered each of the aspects mentioned here and led to a further elaboration of the method of analysis and a deepening of insight. A major problem, however, is to determine statistically to what extent the observed monetary disturbances are autonomous or spontaneous events rather than induced responses. As a matter of fact this requires a set of additional hypotheses to approximate the autonomous monetary impulses empirically.

Holtrop's principal criterion is the liquidity surplus or deficit. The sector with a liquidity surplus causes monetary circulation to stagnate and, hence, gives rise to deflation. In his critique, Koopmans (1955) does not regard this as the most relevant criterion and, furthermore, has reservations, like Goedhart (1955), about the logic of near money or secundary liquidity in this imputation. Notably, Koopmans prefers the financial rather than the narrow monetary flow as the criterion. The principal difference is the fact that Koopmans also takes capital market and credit transactions into consideration. Other criticisms of Koopmans, Tinbergen, Witteveen and Polak concern the method of determining the autonomous impulses. Notably, Witteveen advocates a combination with the Keynesian approach, as worked out later by Bos (1956) and Kessler (1958). The precise definition of monetary equilibrium itself was also the subject of discussion by Goedhart, Witteveen, De Jong and De Roos. Of these authors, notably Goedhart – an associate of Holtrop in the 1940s – succeeded in giving a clear-cut description of the condition for monetary equilibrium in a dynamic economy. Unlike the other authors, he did so without necessarily equating it with full-employment equilibrium, which is only one of the many situations of monetary equilibrium, as Zijlstra (1948) – Holtrop's successor as president of the Bank – indicated earlier in a theoretical study of Koopmans' monetary analysis in a stationary economy.

The importance of the method of Holtrop or the Bank as a practical tool of monetary analysis was its diagnostic value. It enables the Bank to recognize the origin and character of monetary disturbances in the Dutch

economy and to delineate the responsibilities approximately. Therefore, the method has a strong normative emphasis and was used as a
policy tool.

4. Holtrop's econometric evaluation

As indicated above, the cornerstone of Holtrop's monetary approach is
that any disturbance of monetary equilibrium is caused by inflationary
or deflationary monetary impulses. In an open economy such as that of
the Netherlands these impulses are either of domestic or of foreign
origin. Domestic monetary impulses, D, are brought about by either
liquidity creation, Lcr, or spontaneous liquidity activation, Lact. The
latter is, in Holtrop's terminology, identical with a decline in the desire
for liquidity. The autonomous external monetary impulse, E, is basically the balance of payments surplus adjusted for induced changes in
imports. This view results in a relationship explaining nominal income
change, ΔY, by domestic and external monetary impulses, i.e.

$$\Delta Y = \alpha + \beta D + \gamma E$$

which may be seen as sort of a reduced-form equation implied by the
fully specified monetary model of Dr Holtrop. This idea leads Dr
Holtrop to an econometric evaluation of his model by regressing
nominal percentage income change on both domestic liquidity creation,
Lcr, as proxy for internal monetary impulses, and external monetary
impulses. Using yearly figures for the sample period 1954–69 Holtrop
(1971, 1972a) presented the following estimated equation:

$$\frac{\Delta Y_t}{Y_{t-1}} = 2.50 + 0.32 \frac{Lcr_t}{Lcr_{t-1}} + 0.43 \frac{E_t}{E_{t-1}}$$
$$(1.39) \quad (0.10) \qquad\qquad (0.08)$$

with standard errors in parentheses, $R^2=0.69$, DW=1.58 while all
variables are measured as percentage changes with respect to the
preceding year. The estimates support Holtrop's monetarist view and
indicate that for the sample period changes in nominal income are
dominated by foreign impulses.

Holtrop's econometric verification has been seriously criticized by
several scholars for a variety of reasons. This debate of the early 1970s
may be considered as the third and concluding round in the discussion of
Dutch monetarism. In an interesting essay, Selden (1975) examined
Holtrop's monetary analysis and econometric exercise from the Ameri-

can monetarist perspective and took an ambivalent view. On the one hand, he admired 'the obstinate insistence' with which the importance of money had been defended by Dr Holtrop and the central bank. On the other hand, he had serious doubts about Holtrop's empirical testing of his own theory. He criticized the suppression of the money stock in explaining income and doubted the focus on credit, particularly because this is a central feature of the Keynesian rather than the monetarist approach. Secondly, he had difficulties in accepting that the composition of credit matters, because this is contrary to the quantity theory tradition which is also the starting point of Holtrop's model. Finally he criticized the empirical work because of the assumed absence of time-lags, feedback mechanisms and any lack of stability analysis. Selden supports this econometric critique by offering statistical evidence and additional empirical results based on alternative specifications estimated using the same data-set as Holtrop.

Apart from criticism in the international literature, Holtrop's statistical verification called forth critical comments by the Dutch authors Engering (1972) and Kuipers and Wilpstra (1973), which were published shortly after the Dutch version of Holtrop's study appeared. Engering criticizes Holtrop's approach because in fact he runs a regression of an identity, which should, on *a priori* grounds, produce a perfect correlation and regression coefficients equal to one. He attributes the fact that this is not found in the statistical verification to the assumptions used for constructing the data on the external impulse and to the use of money creation as a proxy for the domestic monetary impulse. In fact, Holtrop's exercise is nothing more than the statistical verification of an identity. In spirit, however, it resembles the reduced-form approach of the monetarists of the Federal Reserve Bank of St Louis as Holtrop seems to indicate.

Completely different is the criticism of Kuipers and Wilpstra which is, incidentally, levelled in part at Engering's attack. They consider Engering's critique not well founded and recognize that statistical verification of the identity implied by the Holtrop model is not very meaningful. Therefore, they wish specification of the entire model and estimation of the reduced-form equation which can be derived from it. Furthermore, like Polak (1957) many years earlier, they plead for more attention for the dynamic properties of the model. In contrast to Selden's econometric examination the regression results of Kuipers and Wilpstra confirm Holtrop's econometric findings. A problem totally ignored by Kuipers and Wilsptra, however, is the fact that Holtrop's model is not a structural model in the usual sense. It is a model without behavioural equations and does not, as a matter of fact, easily fit into the common set-up of a structural macroeconomic model. As argued by Kessler (1972), it was never designed to be that. Therefore he describes the Holtrop model as a condition model, i.e. a diagnostic rather than a causal model and one may wonder if in this view econometric estimation is appropriate.

Reviewing the final round, as described here, of the debate about Dutch monetarism, Den Butter (1979) in a detailed empirical analysis pointed out the analogy with the famous St Louis equation of Anderson and Jordan. He further examined the Holtrop equation econometrically and found a high degree of instability of Holtrop's empirical results for varying sample periods. The same conclusion was reached before by Selden in his critique on Dutch monetarism. Nowadays, the discussion about Holtrop's model has subsided and the impulse analysis as a tool of monetary diagnosis has disappeared from the Bank's Annual Reports.

5. Conclusion

According to Kuhn (1970), theories or paradigms very often disappear from the scientific scene not because of refutation or falsification, but primarily because the questions to be answered change. Consequently, the associated theories or conceptual frameworks become obsolete. Then they fade away to become history. Dutch monetarism seems to be a case in point.

A striking feature of the Holtrop model is its notable lack of behavioural relationships and its absence of feedback between the monetary and real sectors of the economy. Consequently, proper hypothesis formulation and empirical testing, typical characteristics of modern macroeconomics, are almost absent in the Holtrop approach. Instead, abstract theorizing and empirical classification are the predominant features of Dutch monetarism. Therefore, it does not fit very well in the modern approach to monetary theory. This is much more integrated in macroeconomics than the Wicksellian or Koopmansian concern about monetary equilibrium, which was typical of the pre-Keynesian era. There the roots of Dutch monetarism are to be found. With the slow shift of the frame of reference to the novel apparatus of macroeconomics, monetary analysis, too, altered dispensing with the need for profound deliberations on monetary equilibrium.

References

Bos, H. C. (1956), *A Discussion on Methods of Monetary Analysis and Norms for Monetary Policy*, Rotterdam: Netherlands Economic Institute.

Butter, F. A. G. den (1979), *An Empirical Analysis of Dutch Monetarism*, paper presented at the European Meeting of the Econometric Society, Athens, 04/07–09–1979 (mimeo).

Engering, F. A. (1972), 'De monetaire multiplier en het monetaire model', *Maandschrift Economie*, vol. 36, 11, pp. 521–49.

Fase, M. M. G. (1983), 'The 1930 correspondence between Koopmans, Robertson and Gregory', *De Economist*, vol. 131, pp. 305–43.

Genechten, R. van (1935), 'Antwoord aan G. M. Verrijn Stuart: De maatstaf der geld voorziening? *De Economist*, vol. 84, pp. 707–16, 721–6.

Genechten, R. van (1936), 'Aanteekeningen over de relativiteit der geldwaarde', *De Economist*, vol. 85, pp. 643–7.

Goedhart, C. (1955), 'Monetair evenwicht in een dynamische volkshuishouding', I, II, *De Economist*, vol. 103, pp. 161–202, 272–312.

Holtrop, M. W. (1971), *Over de Doeltreffendheid van de Monetaire Politiek: Nederlandsche ervaringen 1954–1969*, Amsterdam: North-Holland.

Holtrop, M. W. (1972a), 'On the effectiveness of monetary policy: the experience of the Netherlands in the years 1954–1969', *Journal of Money, Credit, and Banking*, vol. 4, 2, pp. 283–311.

Holtrop, M. W. (1972b), *Money in an Open Economy: Selected Papers on Monetary Policy, Monetary Analysis and Central Banking*, Leiden: Stenfert Kroese.

Jong, F. J. de (1955), 'Monetair evenwicht en inkomensevenwicht', I, II, *De Economist*, vol. 103, pp. 142–455, 505–34.

Jong, F. J. de (1973), *Developments of Monetary Theory in the Netherlands*, Rotterdam: Rotterdam University Press.

Keesing, F. A. G. (1939), *Het Evenwichtsbegrip in de Economische Literatuur*, Purmerend: J. Muusses.

Kessler, G. A. (1958), *Monetair Evenwicht en Betalingsbalansevenwicht*, Leiden: Stenfert Kroese.

Kessler, G. A. (1972), Monetary analysis and monetary policy, in: *Money in an Open Economy: Selected Papers on Monetary Policy, Monetary Analysis and Central Banking*, Leiden: M. W. Holtrop, Stenfert Kroese, pp. xxv–xxlvi.

Koopmans, J. G. (1925), 'De zin der bankpolitiek: (Schumpeter contra Keynes)', *De Economist*, vol. 74, pp. 798–818.

Koopmans, J. G. (1982 [1930]), 'Geldvoorziening en conjunctuur', in *Neutraal Geld: een keuze uit de geschriften van prof. mr. J. G. Koopmans*, ed. M. M. G. Fase et al. Leiden/Antwerpen: Stenfert Kroese, pp. 19–28.

Koopmans, J. G. (1933), 'Zum problem des neutralen Geldes', in *Beiträge zur Geldtheorie*, ed. von F. A. Hayek, Wien: Julius Springer, pp. 211–359.

Koopmans, J. G. (1982), 'Geldvoorziening en economisch evenwicht: een bijdrage tot de problemen van neutraal geld en managed currency', in *Neutraal geld*, op. cit., pp. 29–205.

Koopmans, J. G. et al. (1955), *Monetaire Uiteenzettingen, Overdruk uit Economisch-Statistische Berichten 1954–1955*.

Kuhn, T. S. (1970), *The Structure of Scientific Revolutions*, 2nd edn., Chicago: University of Chicago Press.

Kuipers, S. K. and Wilpstra, B. S. (1973), 'Over Holtrops monetaire theorie', *Maandschrift Economie*, vol. 37, 11, pp. 489–507. Met een naschrift door F. A. Engering, pp. 507–11.

Polak, J. J. (1957), 'Monetary analysis of income formation and payments problems', *International Monetary Fund, Washington D. C., Staff Papers*, vol. 6, 1, pp. 1–50.

Posthuma, S. (1926), 'De zin der bankpolitiek', *De Economist*, vol. 75, pp. 423–58.

Roos, F. de (1954), 'Condities voor monetair evenwicht', *De Economist*, vol. 102, pp. 321–38.

Schumpeter, J. (1925), 'Oude en nieuwe bankpolitiek', I, II, III, *Economisch-Statisitsche Berichten*, vol. 10, no. 496 t/m 498.

Selden, R. T. (1975), 'A critique of Dutch monetarism', *Journal of Monetary Economics*, vol. 1, 2, pp. 221–32.

Tinbergen, J. (1936), 'Conjunctuurpolitiek en prijsstabilisatie', *De Economist*, vol. 85, pp. 443–56.

Verrijn Stuart, C. A. (1935), 'Waardevast of neutraal geld?', *De Economist*, vol. 84, pp. 872–82.

Verrijn Stuart, C. A. (1936), 'Waardevast versus neutraal geld', *De Economist*, vol. 85, pp. 648–654.

Verrijn Stuart, G. M. (1919), *Inleiding tot de leer der Waardevastheid van het Geld*, 's-Gravenhage: Martinus Nijhoff.

Verrijn Stuart, G. M. (1965 [1934]), 'De Waardevastheid van het Geld', in *Verspreide opstellen 1922–1965*, Haarlem: G. M. Verrijn Stuart, De Erven P. Bohn, pp. 83–96.

Verrijn Stuart, G. M. (1935), 'De maatstaf der geldvoorziening', *De Economist*, vol. 84, pp. 695–707, 716–21, 726.

Zijlstra, J. (1948), *De Omloopsnelheid van het Geld en Zijn Betekenis voor Geldwaarde en Monetair Evenwicht,* Leiden: Stenfert Kroese.

11 Patinkin and the *real* real-balance effect

Paul B. Trescott[1]

The second edition of Don Patinkin's *Money, Interest, and Prices* (1965) has achieved a well-deserved place in the literature of monetary economics. In addition to being a rigorous scholarly analysis of monetary theory, the book is also a formidable contribution to the history of economic thought. A series of appendices addresses issues of doctrinal history directly, with particular reference to Walras, Wicksell, Fisher, Cassell and Keynes.[2]

The central concept of Patinkin's book is the celebrated 'real-balance effect', which he describes as the '*sine qua non* of monetary theory' (1965, p. 21). He introduced the real-balance effect with the same passage in both editions:

> [I]f the individual's initial [real money] balances are . . . increased above the level which he considers necessary, he will seek to remedy this situation by increasing his amounts demanded of the various commodities, . . . thereby drawing down his balances. On the other hand, should they [money holdings] be decreased below the level he considers necessary, he will seek to remedy the situation by decreasing his amounts demanded, thereby decreasing his planned expenditures, and thereby building up his balances. (1956, pp. 20–1; 1965, pp. 18–19)

Of course, excess money holdings could be directed into the bond market as well as the market for commodities, as conventional Keynesian analysis emphasized.

To Patinkin, the critical importance of the real-balance effect arose from its role in the determination of the equilibrium price level. Analysis of this problem evolved through the famous price-flexibility debate of the 1940s and 1950s. Pigou, Haberler and Scitovsky had argued that a decline in the price level would increase the real value of those forms of individual wealth with fixed money values, most notably cash. Increase in real wealth would stimulate increased consumption at any given level of real income.

To the profession, much of the importance of the real-balance effect is attached to its role in the adjustment process through which a change in the money stock would affect the macro-economy. In Keynesian macrotheory, increased money enters the economy through financial markets, lowers interest rates, stimulates investment, and raises income through multiplier effects. However, empirical studies in the 1960s began to display monetary effects on nominal GNP which were too large and too rapid to be explained by plausible applications of the Keynesian adjustment apparatus. The real-balance effect provided a possible supplement to the Keynesian view.

However, systematic incorporation of real-balance effects into the mainstream of monetary analysis has been hampered by ambiguity in defining and applying the concept. In truth, there are two very different versions of the real-balance effect. Ironically, they can be fairly well identified with the two editions of Patinkin's book. The bulk of this chapter shows the difference between the two versions, points out the important implications of the differences, relates them to Patinkin's history of economic thought, and links them with the general debate over the monetary adjustment process.

Wealth-induced real-balance effect

The best-known version of the real-balance effect is the one which has been so carefully crafted in Patinkin's second edition. We term this the wealth-induced real-balance effect (WRBE). In this view, real money balances are considered to be a component of national wealth. Wealth in turn is a determinant of consumption. An increase in real money balances which raises wealth would tend to stimulate consumption (1965, pp. 19–21). In many sources, the terms 'wealth effect' and 'real-balance effect' are used interchangeably.

Analysis in this mode is consistent with the thrust of the price-flexibility debate and can incorporate the wealth-saving-consumption analysis of Metzler and Modigliani–Brumberg–Ando. The WRBE can be presented in terms of a relatively rigorous microeconomic theory of individual optimization.

However, the limitations of the WRBE approach are substantial. They include the following:

1. The WRBE applies only to 'outside' money, as noted by Kalecki (1944). Bank deposits, the chief form of money in a modern economy, cannot be counted as a component of wealth for the economy as a whole, because deposits which are an asset to depositors are also liabilities owed by the banks. Even if one concedes the Pesek-Saving (1967) claim that deposits are not liabilities for the banks, increase in bank deposits is usually matched *pari passu* by incresase in debts owed to the banks.

2. Even transactions which increase the volume of outside money may not increase national wealth. If the central bank buys government securities in the open market, and if government securities as well as cash are considered full components of national wealth, then the open-market purchase does not raise wealth directly. (Patinkin, 1948, p. 551)

3. Since outside money is, at best, only a small component of national wealth, and since the marginal propensity to consume out of wealth is not very large, the empirical magnitude of WRBE is likely to be quite small. (Patinkin, 1965, p. 21)

4. The WRBE is primarily concerned with consumption. However, we may find it productive to develop a real-balance effect for investment as well. (Gramm and Timberlake, 1969)

5. In the long run, the wealth of the household is endogenous – it is one more decision variable. (Niehaus, 1978, p. 91)

Thus it does not appear that the WRBE contributes much to explaining why a monetary expansion initiated by open-market purchases and extended by bank lending and deposit creation should generate a large and rapid expansion of expenditures for goods and services.

Patinkin has been at pains to show precedents in the history of economic thought for recognition of real balance effects, citing especially Fisher and Wicksell. However, as we shall show, the historical precedents do not rely on wealth in forming the link between real money balances and expenditures.[3]

Disequilibrium real-balance effect
The second version of the real-balance effect, which (after Fischer, 1981) we term the disequilibrium real-balance effect (DRBE), is quite traditional. It simply involves the proposition that when people's actual money holdings exceed their desired holdings, they will tend to use the excess money to buy goods and services directly, as well as to acquire financial assets or repay debts. The quotation above, in which Patinkin introduces the real-balance effect, is perfectly consistent with the DRBE. The DRBE does not involve wealth at all. It can be viewed as arising because of the unique character of money as the medium of payments (Yeager, 1968).

The contrast between these two types of real-balance effects was clearly recognized by Mishan (1958) and discussed by Patinkin (1965, pp. 433–9). Mishan termed the WRBE the 'asset-expenditure' effect, and showed it could be represented by $C = C_1 (Y, r, M_s/P)$. However, the contrast can be enhanced if we write $C = C(Y, r, w, . . .)$ where

$$w = K + \frac{M_b + \alpha B_g}{P}.$$ That is, consumption is a function of real income, real wealth, and interest rates, where wealth is the sum of real capital and the real value of base money (M_b) and some fraction α of government bonds Bg.

Mishan termed the DRBE the 'cash balance effect' which

> comes into operation when the cash available to the community for transactions purposes . . . diverges from the amount of cash that the community desires to hold for this purpose. The effect itself takes the form of *attempts* to change the quantity of cash – either (a) to add to it by reducing current expenditure below current income, an attempt which in general issues in a decline in aggregate money income, or (b) to reduce it by increasing current expenditure above current income . . . (p. 107)

He wrote the DRBE as $C = C_1 (Y, r, [M_s - M_d])$ (p. 10), to which we need to add the qualification that $M = CU + DD + \ldots$ In the DRBE it is the difference between desired and actual money which stimulates expenditures. In equilibrium, this effect disappears. Mishan noted that the two real-balance effects are not mutually exclusive, and consumption and investment functions could be written which would include both effects.

Patinkin's first edition (1956) relies primarily on the DRBE. Considering the attention devoted to wealth by Pigou, Metzler, and by Patinkin himself in articles prior to 1956, the lack of a wealth emphasis in the 1956 edition is striking. The term 'wealth' does not appear in the index, though it is used occasionally in the text. In 1956, after introducing the real-balance effect with the paraphrase of Wicksell quoted above, Patinkin went on to say 'this new effect measures the influence on demand of a change in real balances, other things being held constant' (1956, p. 21).

In 1956, Patinkin acknowledged 'the necessity of distinguishing between the degrees of liquidity and illiquidity of various types of assets and liabilities' (1956, p. 204). In the basic algebraic functions for his macro-model, Patinkin 1956 entered the real value of government bonds and money holdings separately, thus allowing the two to have differing effects on demand for commodities, bonds and money (1956, p. 205; 1965, p. 669). In the 1965 edition, he constrained the effects to be the same for both components (1965, pp. 289–90). Several reviewers of the 1956 volume attributed the DRBE to Patinkin.[4]

Besides Mishan, the contrast between the two versions of the real-balance effect has been noted by Niehans (1978), Rush (1980) and Fischer (1981), but without elaborating all the implications. Significant differential characteristics of DRBE include the following:

1. The DRBE operates for all types of money, including bank deposits. It is not necessary to make distinctions between inside and outside money, or to try to establish whether the process of changing the money supply changes wealth or not.
2. Emphasis on DRBE makes it clear that a fall in nominal income resulting from a non-monetary disturbance can create a positive real-balance effect by decreasing the demand for nominal money, regardless of whether the decrease occurs in prices or in real output (Mishan, 1958, pp. 110, 113). Thus price flexibility is not crucial for the self-correcting tendency of the system.
3. While Patinkin's exposition of WRBE applies primarily to consumption, it seems to be relatively easy to incorporate DRBE into the investment function as well (Mishan, 1958, pp. 110, 113; Patinkin, 1965, pp. 208–9).
4. While the empirical significance of WRBE is likely to be small, no such conclusion is apparent for DRBE. DRBE thus appears a much more likely candidate to help explain the apparent large and rapid adjustment of expenditures to monetary growth.

Patinkin's shift of emphasis is easy to understand. He was not concerned with empirical or policy aspects of the monetary process, but primarily with theoretical rigour, stressing optimization and equilibrium.[5] The DRBE is almost too simple. It can be stated in a sentence or two. The more rigorous one's analysis of consumption and investment decisions, the harder it is to fit it in.[6] The recent literature stressing 'liquidity constraints' represents one possible rigorous approach.

Wicksell, Fisher and Keynes
In both editions of his book, Patinkin reproduced with high praise passages from Wicksell and Fisher giving their explanations of the real-balance effect.[7] In neither passage is there any reference to wealth nor is such a relationship offered elsewhere in their work. A careful inspection of the quoted passages indicates that each is an admirable statement of the disequilibrium real-balance effect.

Keynes' analysis of real-balance effects (though without that terminology) in the *General Theory* is well known and received much attention from Patinkin.[8] Keynes' brief statement makes no reference to wealth and, of course, assumes that all the excess supply of money will flow into the bond market (see Patinkin, 1965, pp. 634–7).

In contrast to his numerous references to Keynes' *General Theory*, Patinkin's two editions do not deal very much with Keynes' earlier writings. Patinkin acknowledges that the Cambridge economists 'do at

various points indicate their recognition of this [real-balance] effect'
(1956, p. 438; 1965, p. 604). Patinkin notes that Keynes (1923) had
stated, 'When people find themselves with more cash than they require,
. . . they get rid of the surplus by buying goods or investments, or by
leaving it for a bank to employ, or possibly by increasing their hoarded
reserves.'[9]

Patinkin criticized the Cambridge economists, including the earlier
Keynes, because 'they frequently failed to provide a systematic dynamic
analysis of the way in which the monetary increase generated real-
balance effects in the commodity markets . . .' (1956, p. 100; 1965, p.
167).

Surprisingly, in all these discussions, Patinkin never referred to the
very clear and detailed exposition of real-balance effects in Keynes'
Treatise on Money.

The section in the *Treatise* has several significant features. One is the
repeated use of the term 'real-balances'. The second is an explicit
statement of the mutual determination of cash holdings and commodity
purchases, as follows:[10]

> Every decision by an individual as to whether *at the existing price levels* he
> desires to buy, to sell, or to do neither is, in effect, a decision as to whether
> he desires to decrease, increase or leave unchanged his real-balances. (1930,
> I, p. 225; emphasis in original)

It is worth quoting Keynes' exposition at some length, since it meets so
completely Patinkin's complaint that the link with commodity markets
was not generally articulated:

> In a state of equilibrium between the amount of Real-balances required, the
> amount of Cash-balances outstanding and the Price-level, the normal flow of
> purchases and sales has no tendency either to alter the relative aggregate
> volumes of Cash-balances and Real-balances or to modify the Price-level. If,
> however, at any moment the pressure of the individuals who wish to diminish
> their Real-balances . . . exceeds that of those who wish to increase their
> Real-balances . . ., the greater eagerness of the buyers than of the sellers at
> the existing price-level creates a tendency for the price-level to rise. The
> price-level will rise until there is again an equilibrium between the eager-
> nesses of the two parties. The causation of the price-change is in the form of
> an *increase in demand* at the existing price-level, and the articles to which the
> additional buying pressure has been directed rise in price. (1930, I, pp.
> 225–6)

Keynes then describes the adjustment process involving increased
spending, higher prices, and the effects on real balances:

> . . . the recent sellers, finding themselves with an increment, not only of
> cash-balances, but also of real-balances, become, in their turn, additional
> purchasers. Thus an endless chain of additional purchasing at something

above the old price-level . . . is set up, affecting commodity after commodity, until equilibrium is brought about by a new and higher price-level being established at which the aggregate holdings of real-balances are diminished by the exact amount by which the original set of depositors, who turned buyers of goods, had decided to diminish their real-balances. (1930, I, pp. 226–7)

Keynes reiterated the link between cash position and demand for goods:

Whenever depositors as a whole take steps to diminish the amount of their real-balances, their behaviour can only take the form of *an increased demand on their part at the existing level of prices*, which must result in a tendency for the price-level to rise. Thus the price-level . . . is the balancing factor which brings into appropriate relation the volume of real-balances which result from the collective decisions of the depositors and the volume of money-balances which results from the collective decisions of the depositors and the volume of money-balances which result from the collective decisions of the bankers. (1930, I, p. 228; emphasis in original)

Keynes' discussion, which occupies most of six pages, does not appear inferior to those of Wicksell and Fisher. Like their analyses, Keynes' exposition is clearly in the style of disequilibrium real-balance effects.[11] Keynes' example makes clear that the decreased desire for real balances which initiates the price rise flows into the goods market and not the bond market – a striking contrast to his analysis in the *General Theory*.

At the end of his exposition of the real-balance effect, Keynes indicated he himself did not find it a fruitful approach:

Formerly I was attracted by this line of approach. But it now seems to me that the merging together of all the different sorts of transactions – income, business and financial – which may be taking place only causes confusion, and that we cannot get a real insight into the price-making process without bringing in the rate of interest and the distinctions between incomes and profits and between savings and investment. (1930, I, p. 229)

This evidence of Keynes' familiarity with disequilibrium real-balance effects makes even more striking his treatment of the topic in the *General Theory*. It seems to me that an important part of Keynes' discontent with the traditional Cambridge approach was its apparent tendency to limit changes in demand for goods and services to two sources – changes in the stock of money and changes in people's demand schedule for money. A major achievement of the *General Theory* was to show that changes in someone's propensity to spend could change total income (shift the IS curve) even when neither M_s nor the M_d schedule shifted (LM curve stays fixed).

Money and spending – the broader discussion
Clark Warburton, whose name does not appear in Patinkin's index, was

one of the first US economists to recognize an important link between the quantity of money and consumer spending:

> The monetary approach asks the question: What is the usual or expected relation of consumers' expenditures to their cash balances or of cash balances to expenditures? . . .
>
> Individuals . . . have little influence over the total volume of money in the economy. They can change the proportion of the total which they hold only by spending at an abnormal rate, or by hoarding, and then only when their changed rate of use of money is not matched by a similar change in the rate of use of money by other holders thereof (business or government). If they do not change their rate of spending for consumption they will, when adjusting their scale of living to larger incomes, make that adjustment at such a rate as will keep their cash balances in proportion to their increased consumption expenditures. (1944, p. 303, pp. 308–10)

Warburton repeatedly referred to the adverse effects on consumption of the decrease in the money stock in 1930–3, a significant part of which was a windfall decrease reflecting bank failures: 'Individuals and enterprises were faced with the necessity, as their cash balances dwindled, of attempting to conserve them by postponing as many expenditures as possible' (1945, p. 117; also 1944, p. 320).

Many of the pioneering econometric studies of expenditure behaviour in the 1940s and 1950s experimented with using money-stock measures in consumption and investment functions (see Schotta, 1964, p. 622; Meyer and Kuh, 1957, pp. 239–43). Often this was done without much systematic theoretical framework.[12]

None of these empirical studies displayed large monetary effects. And certainly none had an impact on monetary economics comparable to the 1963 research study by Friedman and Meiselman (FM). Using a great variety of time periods, but a simple single-equation reduced-form specification, they presented evidence that the money stock had a much more significant influence on consumption than did 'autonomous' expenditures. Details of the infighting which resulted from this study are well known (Poole and Kornblith, 1973) and need not concern us here. Suffice to say that the Friedman–Meiselman study forced the profession to acknowledge that money had a large and rapid influence on total demand for goods and services.

With this recognition came the inevitable questions: why and how? The FM results were not those to be expected from a Keynesian view of the adjustment process. What alternative view of the adjustment process could be presented, which would account for the dramatic results?[13]

Friedman's *Theory of the Consumption Function* had presented only brief and vague suggestions that the money stock might have any influence on consumption (1957, pp. 5, 17). The need for some

explanation was thus urgent. In both the FM study, and in a contempor-
aneous article with Anna Schwartz (1963), Friedman put forth essentially the same view of the monetary adjustment process.

That view can be termed an 'augmented portfolio balance' view.
Money is viewed as one of many forms of wealth held by households;
the other forms include financial assets, housing, stocks of consumer
durables and storables, and human capital. Monetary changes disturb
the balance, and in the adjustment, say, to a rise in the stock of money,
households increase their demands for real as well as financial assets.
Friedman and his associates ingeniously argued that changes in relative
prices would lead to stimulation of demand for consumer services as
well as goods (FM, 1963, pp. 218–20).

The general reaction, however, was that, first, Friedman's statement
of the adjustment process was very similar to the views of Keynesians
such as James Tobin and Arthur Okun, and second, the large and rapid
impacts of money on income did not appear to be explained by the
Friedman adjustment progress.[14] Indeed, Friedman had referred to the
same adjustment model in 1961 in arguing that the lags in response to
monetary policy were long and variable.[15] It is significant that the
pejorative term 'black box' came into use *after* 1963, indicating the
general feeling that the monetarist analysis lacked a persuasive and
coherent view of the adjustment process (see Morgan, 1978, pp. 7, 79,
83, 93; Clower, 1971, p. 27).

Although Modigliani (1963) acknowledged the potential role of
Patinkin-type real-balance effects on wealth, they played a minor role in
his theoretical structure and virtually none in the econometric model.

Pesek and Saving (1967) presented a potentially revolutionary analysis which redefined wealth in such a manner that ordinary increase in
cheque deposits could be shown to have a large impact on wealth and
spending. They claimed that cheque deposits were not really bank
liabilities, and were therefore net wealth. This analysis failed to deal
with the tendency for indebtedness to banks to match deposit increases.
Ultimately, their analysis was not accepted by the profession.[16]

Several empirical studies dealt directly with the DRBE. Crockett
(1964) recognized the likelihood of 'an asset disequilibrium effect' (p.
122). Consumption might respond disproportionately to a decline in
transitory income 'if only because asset and credit resources for
consuming in excess of income are limited' (p. 111). She found a
significant time-series impact on consumption for $(L-L_n)$ for 1929–41 and
1951–60, where L was actual liquid assets and L_n represented desired
holdings estimated from permanent income and a time trend (p. 127).

A similar study by Zellner, Huang and Chau (1965) found econometric support when 'the real balance effect was formulated in such a way as to permit an *imbalance* in the liquid asset position of consumers to be corrected by an adjustment of consumption expenditures'.[17]

Meiselman and Simpson (MS, 1971) remedied many of the alleged deficiencies of the earlier Friedman–Meiselman study. MS used quarterly data for various measures of the money stock including the monetary base to estimate polynomial distributed lag regressions explaining total consumption and a number of its components, as well as expenditures on residential housing. They reiterated a view of consumer adjustment much like that of FM, but with more emphasis on sequence. They argued that 'the more durable any class of expenditures, the shorter the lag. . . . A change in the stock of money first leads to a relatively large increase in expenditures for housing construction, then expenditures for consumer durables, then consumer nondurables, and lastly consumer services' (p. 232). Such a sequence would, of course, support the underlying logic of the augmented portfolio approach (compare Friedman and Schwartz, 1963, p. 61). However, non-durables and services showed responses of sufficient size, rapidity and goodness of fit to suggest the possibility of DRBE.

In the series of interchanges concerning Friedman's monetary framework (Gordon, 1974), the issue of the adjustment process was argued still further. In his explanatory text, Friedman reiterated the essence of the augmented portfolio view (pp. 28–9). In other portions of his exposition, however, he relied on the DRBE (pp. 2–3, 51). Writing an algebraic expression for the change in nominal income, he included terms reflecting the difference between money demand and supply. The accompanying verbal description stated that a discrepancy between money supply and money demand 'will be manifested primarily in attempted spending, hence in the rate of change in nominal income.'[18]

Patinkin cited the last sentence as evidence of 'the crucial role that Friedman assigns to the real-balance effect . . . ' (Gordon, 1974, p. 119). Friedman denied the contention, stating 'I believe the real balance effect plays a negligible role in the process. The substitution effect between money and other assets is, I believe, the key factor' (p. 175).

Both he and Patinkin have apparently concluded that the DRBE can be viewed as a shorthand expression for the dynamic adjustments arising out of a portfolio balance model.[19] However, Park (1972) questioned whether a portfolio model is likely to display a large and rapid increase of demand for goods and services in response to an increase in the money supply. Park also showed that the sequence analysis presented in Friedman–Scwartz (1963) and Meiselman–Simpson (1971) was inconsistent with the view that real goods are close substitutes for either money or the open-market asset purchased (pp. 24, 27–8, 32–6). Thus it appears that Friedman's frequent identification of DRBE with a portfolio-adjustment model is unwarranted.

In any event, there followed a steady flow of empirical studies using the disequilibrium real-balance effect. Paul E. Smith (1972) and Smith and Jan Kmenta (1973) used a DRBE approach for the consumption sector of condensed macroeconomic models. Leonall Andersen (1975) presented a model of nominal income determination for the US in which discrepancy between money supply and money demand was the driving force changing nominal income. P. D. Jonson (1976) developed a macro-model for the United Kingdom derived from the analysis of Archibald and Lipsey (1958). He found 'a powerful and significant disequilibrium real balance effect on a broad expenditure aggregate . . .' (p. 982). Jonson and Taylor (1978) developed an econometric model of Australia in which consumer spending adjusted to the gap between actual and desired money balances. They used a separate equation to estimate desired money holdings, and then used that to derive DRBE (pp. 294, 314). Carr and Darby (1981) used assumptions about disequilibrium between desired and actual money holdings to aid in estimating demand schedules for money.

We have suggested that Patinkin recoiled from using the DRBE and preferred the WRBE because of his desire for a rigorous analysis consistent with mainstream micro theory (see Patinkin, 1965, pp. 436–9). In a conventional textbook exposition of household behaviour, the purchase of each product is uniquely determined by real income and relative prices. Patinkin extended this by adding wealth to the constraint variable. It is worth asking, how can holdings of money have any influence in such a system, beyond the role of money as wealth? Clower (1967) suggested that money holdings are a constraint on purchase in a special fashion, since we live in an economy in which 'money buys goods and goods buy money, but goods do not buy goods' (p. 208). Income and wealth are not merely sources of 'value' available as purchasing power; they are also sources of spending money.[20]

For households which spend less than their income, this distinction between 'value' and spendable money is unimportant. But once we accept a theory (permanent income, life-cycle) according to which the optimum current consumption of individual households may be greater than their current income, then the households' cash position becomes important (Crockett, 1964). This view is stressed in recent analysis of 'liquidity constraints'. Thus we find Tobin (1978) arguing that:

> many households, mainly the young and the poor, are at corners of maximum current consumption; they would borrow more and spend more today if they

could. . . . Liquidity-constrained consumers behave as if they have short horizons, measured in weeks or months or years rather then decades or lifetimes. They will spend any increment of liquid resources within those short horizons. . . . That is why monetary policies and events which relax or tighten liquidity constraints are especially powerful . . . (p. 427)

Fischer (1981) stressed the role of real balances in the intertemporal analysis of consumption.

By a similar line of reasoning, it is easy to incorporate DRBE into investment analysis. Niehans (1978) suggested that one could plausibly write an investment function which contained a term for the difference desired and actual capital (traditional in the capital stock adjustment analysis) and another for the difference between desired and actual money holdings (p. 92). Money holdings do not affect the desired capital stock, but can speed up or slow down the rate at which the firms' capital approaches the desired level.[21]

Conclusion

There are two versions of the real-balance effect, a fact noted initially by Mishan (1958). The best-known version, based on wealth, is impressively derived in Patinkin's second edition (1965). It does not appear to have antecedents in the history of economic thought outside of the price-flexibility debate initiated by Pigou and Haberler. Patinkin's citations from Wicksell and Fisher make no reference to wealth. This is true also for the impressive passages of Keynes' *Treatise*, which were neglected by Patinkin.

The other version, the disequilibrium real-balance effect, is very traditional, having been well stated by Wicksell, Fisher and Keynes. It is the version stressed (though not exclusively) in Patinkin's first edition (1956) and in much of Milton Friedman's work since 1963. Surveys of the literature on the monetary adjustment process have generally neglected the DRBE (Park, 1972; Spencer, 1974; Laidler, 1978) but it appears a potentially valuable analytical tool. The DRBE helps to explain why monetary changes affect many types of spending forcefully and rapidly even when changes in interest rates and other credit indicators are insignificant. The DRBE appears especially important for analysis of monetary behaviour in less-developed countries. The DRBE also appears helpful in explaining how bank failures in 1930–3 could have a powerful deflationary effect on total spending.

Notes

1. The author is grateful for helpful comments from David Kleykamp, Axel Leijonhufvud and Don Patinkin.

2. Patinkin (1956, pp. 373–476; 1965, pp. 527–650). Only minor revisions were made in these passages for the second edition.
3. Patinkin's disclaimer in the second edition appears relevant: 'It is inevitable . . . that there have remained undetected various passages which continue to reflect ways of thinking since superseded . . . ' (1965, p. xv).
4. Mishan's view is that 'unawares, [Patinkin] sometimes invokes the one effect, sometimes the other' (pp. 106–7, 117). In my view, the WRBE is less well-developed in the first edition than in the articles on the price-flexibility debate.
   Reviews of Patinkin which stressed DRBE include Archibald and Lipsey (1958, pp. 339, 365); Christ (1957, p. 349). However, the three empirical applications of Patinkin's first edition stress variations of 'net liquid financial wealth' (Mayer, 1959; Galloway and Smith, 1961; Schotta, 1964).
5. Patinkin (1965, pp. 436–9) deals directly with DRBE and rejects it on the grounds that the desired level of money holdings cannot appropriately be a term in the demand function and that the DRBE form 'does not reflect the dependence on total wealth which characterizes a demand function derived in the usual manner from utility maximization' (p. 437).
6. Dornbusch and Mussa (1975) developed a theoretical basis for DRBE based on optimization over time, but only on the assumption that there is no 'alternative asset which bears a rate of return and which the household can trade for stocks of cash balances at a point in time without transactions costs' (p. 420).
7. The passages quoted by Patinkin are as follows:
   Now let us suppose that for some reason or other commodity prices rise while the stock of money remains unchanged, or that the stock of money is diminished while prices remain temporarily unchanged. The cash balances will gradually appear to be too small in relation to the new level of prices (though in the first case they have not on the average altered in absolute amount. It is true that in this case I can rely on a higher level of receipts in the future. But meanwhile I run the risk of being unable to meet my obligations punctually, and at best I may easily be forced by shortage of ready money to forgo some purchase that would otherwise have been profitable.) I therefore seek to enlarge my balance. This can only be done – neglecting for the present the possibility of borrowing, etc. – through a reduction in my demand for goods and services, or through an increase in the supply of my own commodity (forthcoming either earlier or at a lower price than would otherwise have been the case), or through both together. The same is true of all other owners and consumers of commodities. But in fact nobody will succeed in realizing the object at which each is aiming – to increase his cash balance; for the sum of individual cash balances is limited by the amount of the available stock of money, or rather is identical with it. On the other hand, the universal reduction in demand and increase in supply of commodities will necessarily bring about a continuous fall in all prices. This can only cease when prices have fallen to the level at which the cash balances are regarded as adequate. (In the first case prices will now have fallen to their original level.) Wicksell (1936 [1898], pp. 39–40); Patinkin (1956, p. 420; 1965, pp. 581–2).
   Suppose, for a moment, that a doubling in the currency in circulation should not at once raise prices, but should halve the velocities instead; such a result would evidently upset for each individual the adjustment which he had made of cash on hand. Prices being unchanged, he now has double the amount of money and desposits which his convenience had taught him to keep on hand. He will then try to get rid of the surplus money and deposits by buying goods. But as somebody else must be found to take the money off his hands, its mere transfer will not diminish the amount in the community. It will simply increase somebody else's surplus. Everybody has money on his hands beyond what experience and convenience have shown to be necessary. Everybody will want to exchange this relatively useless extra money for goods, and the desire so to do must surely drive

up the price of goods. No one can deny that the effect of every one's desiring to spend more money will be to raise prices. Obviously this tendency will continue until there is found another adjustment of quantities [of money] to expenditures, and the V's are the same as originally. That is, if there is no change in the quantities sold (the Q's), the only possible effect of doubling M and M' will be doubling of the p's; for we have just seen that the V's cannot be permanently reduced without causing people to have surplus money and deposits, and there cannot be surplus money and deposits without a desire to spend it, and there cannot be a desire to spend it without a rise in prices. In short, the only way to get rid of a plethora of money is to raise prices to correspond.

Fisher (1911, pp. 153–4); Patinkin (1956, p. 435; 1965, p. 599).

8. Keynes duly noted that 'reduction in the wages-bill, accompanied by some reduction in prices and in money-income generally, will diminish the need for cash . . . ; and it will therefore reduce *pro tanto* the schedule of liquidity preference for the community as a whole. *Cet. par.* this will reduce the rate of interest and thus prove favourable to investment' (1936, p. 263; see also pp. 266–7). In writings subsequent to 1965, Patinkin has argued that these passages did not develop a real-balance effect (1969, pp. 1158–9).

9. Patinkin (1974, p. 16), which also points out the sloppiness of Keynes' statement as regards 'hoarded reserves'.

10. Compare Patinkin's statement that 'to say that an individual adjusts his money balances so as to maintain a desired relationship between them and his planned expenditures on commodities is at the same time to say that he adjusts these expenditures so as to maintain a desired relationship between them and his money balances' (1956, p. 20; 1965, p. 18).

11. Keynes does refer to changes in the distribution of wealth attending these price changes, but total wealth is not altered. (1930, I, p. 228). In correspondence, Patinkin pointed out that the Keynes passage does not deal with a change in the supply of money.

12. In his 1965 edition Patinkin summarized a dozen time-series econometric studies of consumption functions in which some measure of real money balances was included. Having noted that most of them found significant influence of money on consumption, Patinkin correctly pointed out that 'none of [these] studies . . . really tests the real-balance effect in the manner implied in this book. . . . First, they define real balances as liquid assets, and not as net financial assets of fixed money value . . . Second . . . they give the impression that it is real balances *per se* which influence consumption, instead of real balances as a component of total wealth' (p. 655).

Patinkin presented a set of his own regressions using a measure of household net worth and also subdividing this to isolate those net assets of fixed money value. His results allow the possibility that the two components of net worth have different effects.

13. Patinkin (1965) suggested that, in FM (1963), their 'interpretation of their findings in terms of the predominance of 'monetary' as distinct from 'credit' effects . . . is in part an alternative statement of the hypothesis that there exists a real-balance effect on the commodity market' (p. 644n).

14. Arthur Okun commented: 'I was surprised to find that the transmission mechanism described by Friedman and Schwartz was similar to the one I visualize . . . ' (1963, p. 74). However, Okun warned that 'If monetary factors have the leverage on income that Friedman and Schwartz expect, they must have a better fulcrum than the general equilibrium asset model implies' (1963, p. 74). Nearly a decade later, Tobin remarked, 'The puzzle is how Friedman could think that his account of the transmission mechanism supports monetarist conclusions' (Gordon, 1974, p. 89). (See also Gurley 1969, p. 1191; Park, 1972; Spencer, 1974; Laidler, 1978.)

15. Friedman's (1961) article on lags was actually written after FM (1963) and makes explicit reference to the results of that study. His summary of the adjustment process is asserted to be the same as that in the FM article. However, the 1961 article stresses

the slowness of the process, a theme which is absent in the 1963 version (1961, pp. 462–3). Friedman (1964) also stressed that the process was slow 'indirect and complicated' (p. 6).

16. Patinkin (1969); Park (1972, pp. 5–9); Smith (1970).

17. Ironically, the authors citied Friedman's testimony before the Joint Economic Committee as revealing 'most lucidly the potential importance of a real-balance effect in the process of adjusting from a position of disequilibrium toward equilibrium' (p. 573). Schotta (1962) had also attributed real-balance effects to Friedman's earlier writings (p. 621n).

18. Gordon (1974, p. 119). In their *Monetary Trends* (1982), Friedman and Schwartz reproduce much of the presentation given in *Monetary Framework*. The portfolio analysis is summarized at pp. 57–8, whereas DRBE implications are clear at p. 62. The argument that Keynesians overemphasize 'first-round effects' of money creation, while quantity theorists downplay them (pp. 29–31), and the claim that their own image of adjustment is more 'direct' than the Keynesian image (p. 57) seem more consistent with DRBE than with a portfolio model.

19. It is significant that two major studies of the monetary adjustment process deal *only* with portfolio models (Park, 1972; Laidler, 1978). In addition, Thomas Mayer characterized the monetarist view of the transmission process as one in which, 'if the public finds itself with excess balances it will reduce them by increasing expenditures, presumably on both goods and bonds' (Mayer 1978, pp. 7, 15). Yet his detailed analysis of the adjustment process is entirely in portfolio terms. Zincone (1967) suggested that the term 'real-balance effect' be defined to include 'all changes in spending behaviour resulting from a change in the real stock of money' (p. 693).

20. As Harry Johnson (1970) put it, discussing Clower, 'Economic actors have to be considered as constrained in their choices, not by the potential worth of their initial endowments of goods and money, but as purchasers by their initial cash balances . . .' (p. 18).

Clower's idea has evolved into the 'cash-in-advance' models; see Lucas (1980); Sargent (1987, chapter 5). Intuitively, one can also see affinity between the DRBE and the concept of unanticipated money growth.

21. Investment models which involve credit rationing usually imply the existence of DRBE for investment. Examples of such models are in Stiglitz and Weiss (1981); Fazzari and Athey (1987). However, these do not discuss DRBE directly.

References

Andersen, Leonall (1975), 'A monetary model of nominal income determination', *Review*, Federal Reserve Bank of St Louis, 57:6 (June), pp 9–19.

Archibald, G. C. and Lipsey, Richard G. (1958), 'Monetary and value theory: a critique of Lange and Patinkin', *Review of Economic Studies*, 26:1 (October), reprinted in *Monetary Theory and Policy*, (1976) ed. Richard Thorn, New York: Praeger, pp. 339–65.

Carr, Jack and Darby, Michael R. (1981), 'The role of money supply shocks in the short-run demand for money', *Journal of Monetary Economics* 8:2 (September), pp. 183–99.

Christ, Carl F. (1957), 'Patinkin on money, interest, and prices', *Journal of Political Economy*, 65:4 (August), pp. 347–54.

Clower, Robert W.. (1971), 'Theoretical foundations of monetary policy', in *Monetary Theory and Monetary Policy in the 1970s*, ed. G. Clayton, J. C. Gilbert and R. Sedgwick, London: Oxford University Press, pp 15–28.

Clower, Robert W. (1967), 'A reconsideration of the microfoundations of monetary theory', *Western Economic Journal*, 6: (1967), pp. 1–9, reprinted in *Monetary Theory* (1970), ed. Robert Clower, Baltimore, MD: Penguin Books.

Crockett, Jean (1964) 'Income and asset effects on consumption: aggregate and cross section', in National Bureau of Economic Research, *Models of Income Determination*, Princeton, NJ: Princeton University Press, pp. 97–132.

Dornbusch, Rudiger and Mussa, Michael (1975), 'Consumption, real balances and the hoarding function', *International Economic Review*, 16:2 (June), pp. 415–21.

Fazzari, Steven M. and Athey, Michael J. (1987), 'Asymmetric information, financing constraints, and investment', *Review of Economics and Statistics*, 69:3 (August), pp. 481–7.

Fischer, Stanley (1981), 'Is there a real balance effect in equilibrium?', *Journal of Monetary Economics*, 8:1 (July), pp. 25–39.

Fisher, Irving (1911), *The Purchasing Power of Money*, New York: Macmillan.

Friedman, Milton (1957), *A Theory of the Consumption Function*, Princeton, NJ: Princeton University Press.

Friedman, Milton (1961), 'The lag in effect of monetary policy', *Journal of Political Economy* 69:5 (October), pp. 447–66.

Friedman, Milton (1964), 'Post war trends in monetary theory and policy', *National Banking Review*, 2:1 (September), pp. 1–9.

Friedman, Milton and Meiselman, David (1963), 'The relative stability of monetary velocity and the investment multiplier in the United States, 1897–1958', in *Commission on Money and Credit, Stabilization Policies*, New York: Prentice-Hall.

Friedman, Milton and Schwartz, Anna J. (1963), 'Money and business cycles', *Review of Economics and Statistics*, XLV:1 (February supplement), pp. 32–64.

Friedman, Milton and Schwartz, Anna J, (1982), *Monetary Trends in the United States and the United Kingdom*, Chicago: University of Chicago Press.

Galloway, Lowell and Smith, Paul E. (1961), 'Real balances and the permanent income hypothesis', *Quarterly Journal of Economics*, 75:2 (May), pp. 302–13.

Gordon, Robert J. (ed.) (1974), *Milton Friedman's Monetary Framework*, Chicago: University of Chicago Press.

Gramm, W. P. and Timberlake, Richard H., Jr (1969), 'The stock of money and investment in the United States, 1897–1966', *American Economic Review*, 59:5 (December), pp. 991–6.

Gurley, John G. (1969), Review of Friedman, *Optimum Quantity of Money*, in *Journal of Economic Literature*, 7:4, pp. 1188–92.

Johnson, Harry G. (1970), 'Recent developments in monetary theory', in *Money in Britain, 1959–1969*, ed. David R. Croome and Harry G. Johnson, Oxford, reprinted in *Monetary Theory and Policy* (1976), ed. Richard Thorn, New York: Praeger, pp. 7–32.

Jonson, Peter D. (1976), 'Money and economic activity in the open economy: The United Kingdom, 1880–1970', *Journal of Political Economy*, 84:5 (October), pp. 979–1012.

Johnson, Peter D. and Taylor, John C. (1978), 'Inflation and economic stability in a small open economy: a systems analysis', in Karl Brunner and Allan Meltzer (eds), *The Problem of Inflation*, Amsterdam: Elsevier/North-Holland, pp. 289–323.

Kalecki, Michael (1944), 'Professor Pigou on the 'Classical Stationary State' – a comment', *Economic Journal* 54:1 (April), pp. 131–2.

Keynes, John Maynard (1923), *Tract on Monetary Reform*, London: Macmillan.

Keynes, John Maynard (1930), *Treatise on Money*, London: Macmillan.

Keynes, John Maynard (1936), *The General Theory of Employment, Interest, and Money*, London: Macmillan.

Kmenta, J. and Smith, P. E. (1973), 'Autonomous expenditures versus money supply: an application of dynamic multipliers', *Review of Economics and Statistics*, 55:3 (August), pp. 299–307.

Laidler, David (1978), 'Money and money income: an essay on the 'transmission mechanism', *Journal of Monetary Economics*, 4:2 (April), pp. 151–91.

Lucas, Robert E., Jr (1980), 'Equilibrium in a pure currency economy', *Economic Inquiry*, 18:2 (April), pp. 203–19.

Mayer, Thomas (1959) 'The empirical significance of the real balance effect', *Quarterly Journal of Economics*, 73:2 (May), pp. 275–91.

Mayer, Thomas (1978), *The Structure of Monetarism*, New York: W. W. Norton.

Meiselman, David and Simpson, Thomas D. (1971), 'Monetary policy and consumer expenditures: the historical evidence', in *Consumer Spending and Monetary Policy:*

The Linkages, Federal Reserve Bank of Boston, pp. 229–78.

Metzler, Lloyd A. (1951), 'Wealth, saving and the rate of interest', *Journal of Political Economy*, 59:2 (April), pp. 93–116.

Mishan, E. S., (1958), 'A fallacy in the interpretation of the cash balance effect', *Economica*, n.s. 25, 98 (May), pp. 106–18.

Modigliani, Franco (1963), 'The monetary mechanism and its interaction with real phenomena', *Review of Economics and Statistics*, 45:1 (February Supplement), pp. 79–107.

Morgan, Brian (1978), *Monetarists and Keynesians: Their Contributions to Monetary Theory*, New York: John Wiley.

Niehans, Jurg (1978), 'Metzler, wealth, and macroeconomics: a review', *Journal of Economic Literature*, 16:1 (March), pp. 84–95.

Okun, Arthur (1963), 'Comments on Friedman and Schwartz', *Review of Economics and Statistics*, 45:1 (February Supplement), pp. 72–7.

Park, Yung Chul (1972), 'Some current issues on the transmission process of monetary policy', *IMF Staff Papers*, 19:1 (March), pp. 1–43.

Patinkin, Don (1948), 'Price flexibility and full employment', *American Economic Review*, 38:3 (September), pp. 543–64.

Patinkin, Don (1956), *Money, Interest, and Prices*, 1st edn, White Plains, NY: Row Peterson.

Patinkin, Don (1965), *Money, Interest, and Prices*, 2nd edn, New York: Harper & Row.

Patinkin, Don (1969), 'Money and wealth: a review article', *Journal of Economic Literature*, 7:4 (December), pp. 1140–60.

Patinkin, Don (1974), 'Keynesian monetary theory and the Cambridge School', in *Issues in Monetary Economics*, ed. H. G. Johnson and A. R. Nobay, London: Oxford University Press, pp. 3–30.

Pesek, Boris and Saving, Thomas R. (1967), *Money, Wealth and Economic Theory*, New York: Macmillan.

Poole, William and Kornblith, Elinda (1973), 'The Friedman–Meiselman CMC Paper: new evidence on an old controversy', *American Economic Review*, 63:5 (December), pp. 908–17.

Rush, Mark (1980), 'A comment on two specifications of the real balance effect', Working Paper no. 104, University of Pittsburgh, Department of Economics.

Sargent, Thomas J. (1987), *Dynamic Macroeconomic Theory*, Cambridge, Mass.: Harvard University Press.

Schotta, Charles Jr (1964), 'The real balance effect in the United States, 1947–1963', *Journal of Finance*, 19:4 (December), pp. 619–30.

Smith, Paul E. (1972), 'Lags in the effects of monetary policy: comment', *American Economic Review*, 62:1 (March), pp. 230–33.

Smith, Warren L. (1970), 'On some current issues in monetary economics: an interpretation', *Journal of Economic Literature*, 8:3 (September), pp. 767–82.

Spencer, Roger W. (1974), 'Channels of monetary influence: a survey', *Review*, Federal Reserve Bank of St Louis, 56:11 (November), pp. 8–26.

Stiglitz, Joseph E. and Weiss, Andrew (1981), 'Credit rationing in markets with imperfect information', *American Economic Review*, 71:3 (June), pp. 393–410.

Tobin, James (1978), 'Monetary policies and the economy: the transmission mechanism', *Southern Economic Journal*, 44:3 (January), pp. 321–31.

Warburton, Clark (1944), 'Monetary expansion and the inflationary gap', *American Economic Review*, XXXIV (June), pp. 303–27.

Warburton, Clark (1945), 'Monetary theory, full production, and the Great Depression', *Econometrica*, 13 (April), 114–28, reprinted in *Depression, Inflation, and Monetary Policy* (1966), Baltimore, MD: Johns Hopkins University Press.

Wicksell, Knut (1936 [1898]) *Interest and Prices*, trans. R. F. Kahn, London: Macmillan.

Yeager, Leland (1968), 'Essential properties of the medium of exchange', *Kyklos*, 21:1, reprinted in *Monetary Theory* (1973), ed. R. W. Clower, Baltimore, MD: Penguin Books.

Zellner, Arnold, Huang, David and Chau, L. C. (1965), 'Further analysis of the short-run consumption function with emphasis on the role of liquid assets', *Econometrica*, 33:3 (July), pp. 571–81.

Zincone, Louis (1968), 'The real-balance effect: aspects and evidence', *Journal of Finance*, 23:4 (September), pp. 693–4.

12 A rational reconstruction of the rational expectations revolution

Shyam J. Kamath[1]

1. Introduction

The last fifteen years have seen the transformation of macroeconomics by an idea that began twenty-five years ago. The 'New Classical' economics of the Rational Expectations (RE) School has created considerable controversy in the macroeconomics profession and chaos among believers in received pre-REH macroeconomic theory. Many economists have seen it as the beginning of the end of Keynesian macroeconomics and policy activism, and as a much-needed reinstatement of the rationality postulate and 'microfoundations' in the macroeconomics literature. Some have gone so far as to declare that 'it has triumphed decisively'.[2] The REH literature has become a growth industry (though this industry shows signs of having stabilized) and has been filling up the pages of the major economic journals. The REH-critique industry has also been a beleaguered but thriving sector of the economics profession. The debate has been a heated one with greater effects on the intellectual temperature than in the lighting, as is wont in such debates.

The RE programme was launched by Muth (1961) because, in his own words, 'dynamic economics models do not assume enough rationality'. Muth was dissatisfied with the way in which expectations were incorporated into economic models and with the view that the rationality assumption in economics was inadequate to explain observed economic phenomena. He proposed and appropriated the name for the Rational Expectations Hypothesis (REH) which he then proceeded to apply to price fluctuations and inventory behaviour in the context of the microeconomists' well-known 'cobweb problem' in agricultural markets. The REH, as Muth first proposed it, was predicated on the assertion that 'expectations, since they are informed predictions of future events, are essentially the same as the predictions of the relevant economic theory . . ., that expectations of firms (or, more generally, the subjective probability distribution of outcomes) tend to be distributed,

217

for the same information set, about the prediction of the theory (or the "objective" probability distribution of outcomes)' (1961, p. 316). It is part of the folklore of the macroeconomics literature and an unresolved issue for historiographers of economics that the REH was ignored for over ten years until Lucas (1972a, 1972b, 1973), Sargent (1971, 1973) and Sargent and Wallace (1973) resuscitated and rejuvenated it to take centre-stage in macroeconomic theory and policy. As Lucas (1981), who is generally credited with the introduction of the REH into macro-models, puts it, the objective of applying the REH in such models was almost exclusively to attempt to discover a useful theoretical explanation for observed business cycles.[3]

In this chapter, I examine the RE programme and the claims of its critics so as to understand and criticize the claims made by both sides. The approach adopted attempts to (a) understand the RE programme by analysing the problem situation facing RE theorists (i.e. the objectives, their logical interrelations and the situational context); (b) analyse the problem situation of their critics; and (c) criticize the adequacy of the theory and the arguments of the critics in solving the theorists' and critics' problem situation. The methodological adequacy of both the REH programme and that of its critics will thus be critically analysed. The claim of success for the programme and the success (or lack of success) of the many critiques will be identified to the extent necessary since inadequate programmes and misdirected criticisms are likely to hinder rather than help our understanding of theory development in economics. This task of understanding a theory (or its critiques) fundamentally involves the reconstruction of the problem situation of the theorist (or critic) as he saw it and to show that in his opinion the theory (or criticism) was a satisfactory solution to the problem. The method used is called Rational Reconstruction – hence the title of this chapter.[4]

Section 2 discusses the problem situation confronting RE theorists. A rational reconstruction of the critiques of the RE programme is contained in section 3. A critique of the critiques is attempted in section 4. Section 5 assesses the RE programme in terms of its objectives and the problem situation and presents some conclusions.

2.   The problem situation of the RE programme

The problem situation confronting RE theorists can be characterized quite briefly. The major macroeconomic theories of the neo-Keynesian era were predicated on the assumption that markets do not clear and that activity at the aggregate level is characterized by a state of perpetual disequilibrium.[5] Economic agents were either perceived to be 'irrational' in the sense of suffering from money illusion and inelastic expectations or even if rational in the sense of being maximizers (as in the majority of the non-market-clearing literature), they were not able to conclude trades that would clear markets because of informational discrepancies or the existence of constrained under-employment equilibria. Consequently, policy activism in moving the economy to equilibria that clear markets became a dominant prescriptive feature of the non-monetarist models of the post-Keynesian era. Economists and policy-makers held the view that variations in government spending, taxes and the national debt were necessary to stabilize both the price level and the real economy.

While the monetarists led by Friedman (1968, 1970) emphasized the stability of the market economy and argued against policy intervention, even their models depicted economic agents as biased or irrational in their expectations as, for example, with models of inflation where economic agents were shown as forming expectations of future inflation rates adaptively on the basis of past rates causing them to underestimate the inflation rate when it is accelerating and overestimate it when it is decelerating (e.g. Cagan, 1956; Friedman, 1968). (However, Friedman and other proponents of the natural rate hypothesis argued that anticipations of price and wage changes would eventually catch up to realized changes. This may be considered a precursor of the weak form of the REH.) While monetarist models were not 'policy-activist' in the Keynesian sense, they also focused on policy objectives such as the well-known Friedman constant money-growth rule.

It was in this neo-Keynesian context that Muth (1961) proposed the REH. The basic thrust of the REH of Muth was the introduction of rationality in economic and econometric models. However, as already noted, Muth did not apply the REH to macroeconomic models and essentially confined himself to showing how the REH radically altered the nature of results in microeconomic models.

In the early 1970s, economists began to tackle the problem of finding adequate 'microfoundations' for macroeconomic theories. The Phelps volume (1970) contained a collection of papers that attempted to do this. A primary focus of the volume was to examine labour market micro-behaviour, information and expectations in general equilibrium terms and provide a foundation for observed business cycles and theoretical constructs like the NRH. It was a direct result of the search for such micro-foundations that the REH was first applied to the problem of explaining business cycles.[6] The problem situation confronting Lucas (and in the subsequent work of Thomas Sargent, Neil Wallace, Robert Barro, himself and others) can be characterized by his statement:

> The first theoretical task indeed, the central theoretical problem of macro-economics is to find an analytical context in which [output fluctuations] can occur and which does not at the same time imply the existence of persistent, recurrent, unexploited profit opportunities. (1975, p. 1114, brackets added)

The REH theorists then proceeded to demonstrate the existence of the business cycle in the presence of rational expectations. In a policy context, rational expectations applied to the theory of economic policy meant that policy-makers could not fool the public all the time, especially not with the same policy. In its most extreme version, rational economic agents were assumed to know the 'true' underlying model of the economic process and were assumed to incorporate the policy parameters of the system in the formation of their expectations. Forecasting errors were thus deemed to be independent of all endogenous variables including policy parameters.

In its less extreme version, and as it is usually used in the literature, the REH was proposed as a hypothesis regarding the economic use of information. Transactors make the best use of available information, in the sense that additional information is collected up to the point where the extra benefits of the information collected no longer exceed their costs. In other words, the formation of rational expectations was founded on a straightforward application of Stigler's (1961) ideas on the 'economics of information'. Perfect knowledge was not assumed and this view was consistent with error. However, rational expectations which were incorrect would be correctly incorrect. Thus, by this view, economic actors could act correctly given the probabilities and yet there could exist serially correlated errors. The existence of these 'correct' serially correlated errors could then be used to explain the existence of the business cycle. 'Rationality' was therefore no longer equated with the assumption that market expectations were true mathematical expectations conditional on all information.

Most rational expectations models followed the lead of Lucas (1972, 1975) in explaining the existence of serially correlated movements of real output about trend by imposing rationality and identifying unsystematic monetary-fiscal shocks as generating these movements. The effects of the fiscal-monetary shocks were said to be distributed through time because of informational lags (and sometimes an accelerator effect). Agents rationally perceived these recurrent cycles which distorted perceived rates of return but based their actions on balancing the risk of incorrectly responding to spurious price signals due to the transitory nature of the real investment opportunities created against the risk of failing to respond to meaningful signals.

The RE explanations of the business cycle had embedded in them the

REH propositions regarding macroeconomic stabilization policy. The extreme REH policy-related proposition was that of Sargent and Wallace (1975) that in a textbook Keynesian model with rational expectations, no systematic stabilization policy would be able to change the variance of fluctuations in real income. This implied that activist, countercyclical stabilization policy was ineffective whether it was anticipated or not. Advocates of conventional policy implicitly assumed that it could take the economy by surprise. But the RE view implied that it pays economic agents to anticipate policy, consequently any policy actions and their effects, even if minimally regular, were incorporated into economic agents' expectations and plans, resulting in the policy being rendered impotent.

To summarize then, the problem situation of the RE programme was to explain the occurrence of business cycles and other related economic phenomena and theoretical constructs such as the Natural Rate Hypothesis (NRH) and the neutrality of activist policy in an equilibrium context, eschewing non-market-clearing models and *ad hoc* explanations such as the downward rigidity of wages and prices, adaptive expectations, persistence of decision errors and other types of 'irrationality', underemployment equilibria, and market coordination and informational failures. The theoretical aim of the RE theorists was to explain observed macroeconomic phenomena in equilibrium-maximizing terms.

The situational constraints or background on which the primary aims were formulated were to explain all economic phenomena in terms of (a) individualism, (b) the postulate of rational behaviour, i.e. that individuals do not leave any opportunity unutilized to improve their decisions, (c) the postulate of market-clearing prices, and (d) the use of the most modern mathematical and econometric methods.[7] The analysis that follows will examine whether the RE programme was an adequate solution to the problem situation of RE theorists, and whether the situational constraints were met in achieving the purported solution.

The RE programme was challenged from many quarters. The critiques were aimed at various assumptions, conclusions and implications of the programme with only an exception or two examining its logical foundations. These critiques are examined next before proceeding to an assessment of the methodological adequacy of the programme.

3. Major critiques of the RE programme – a reconstruction
The purpose of this section is to discuss selectively the major critiques of the RE programme which purport to have a methodological basis in the sense of criticizing the inadequacy of the theoretical methods employed by REH theorists, rather than critiques that pick on specific technical or

methodologically 'peripheral' issues. This is being done so as to understand fully the criticisms before critiquing them in turn.

The criticisms of the RE programme can be broadly categorized under the following headings:

The irrefutability critique

Buiter (1980) and Tobin (1980a) argue that the REH is an irrefutable hypothesis since it is a joint hypothesis, it being necessary to incorporate the Muth rationality hypothesis with some other hypothesis about economic behaviour incorporating observable magnitudes; thus natural rate-cum-REH, term structure-cum-REH, interest rate parity-cum-REH models are usually tested in the literature. Conflicting empirical evidence can only show that the conjunction of these hypotheses is refuted. There is no way of being sure that it is one or more of the auxiliary hypotheses that are responsible for the conflicting test results rather than the REH.[8] Buiter argues that as a result:

> the hypothesis appears to be in danger of being consistent with any conceivable body of empirical evidence, because the assumption of optimal use of the available information cannot be tested independently of an assumption about the available information set. . . . By suitable redefinition of the information set conditioning the forecast, any pattern of serial correlation in the endogenous variables of a model can be rationalized as consistent with Muth-rational expectations. By becoming irrefutable, the hypothesis would cease to belong to the realm of scientific (i.e. positive or empirical) theory as defined by Popper. (1959, 1980, p. 38)

Others (e.g. Buck, 1982; Lovell, 1986) review tests of RE models in the conventional confirmationist mould and argue that the evidence is not 'consistent' with the REH. The tests and their critiques however do not deal adequately with the irrefutability issue and proceed as if the REH is in fact refutable by conventional empirical testing.

The lack of realism critique

Many economists have argued that the REH is not 'realistic' in that it ignores real-world rigidities such as institutional constraints, sluggish price response and lags in adjustment and, in particular, the existence of wage contracts of greater than one time period in length. Franklin Fisher (1972) argues that it is unrealistic to assume that individuals can make the necessary calculations implied by the REH since economists themselves do so with great difficulty. Arrow (1972) levels a similar criticism when he states that: 'in the rational expectations hypothesis, economic agents are required to be superior statisticians, capable of analyzing the future general equilibrium of the economy' (1978, p. 160).

R. J. Gordon (1976), Modigliani (1977), Akerlof (1979), Simon (1979) and Tobin (1980b) argue that the REH is inconsistent with the statistical evidence and hence unrealistic. The principal evidence they cite is:

(a) The existence of the business cycle, particularly the period of prolonged unemployment during the Great Depression of the 1930's.
(b) Statistics showing that most persons currently unemployed have been in unemployment for a long time which cannot be blamed on misinformation regarding real wages or utility maximization.
(c) The existence of lags in the relationship between inflation and change in money growth, between monetary surprises and unemployment and other lags in price adjustment.

Fischer (1977), Taylor (1980), McCallum (1983) and others have argued that long-term labour contracts exist in the real world which prevent wages (and in some models, prices) from adjusting rationally so that in fact policy-makers are provided with an informational advantage and consequently the extreme policy-neutrality implications of the REH do not hold. The literature on stabilization policy in REH models with contracts of more than two-period length has been advanced by the pro-policy school as sufficient grounds for ignoring the policy-neutrality implications of RE models and for advocating the efficacy and desirability of stabilization policy.

O'Driscoll (1979), Haberler (1980), Frydman (1982), Machlup (1983) and Ebeling (1986) have also criticized RE models for being 'as if' models where the problem is assumed away before it is solved. According to these critics and other economists of the Austrian School, the RE programme assumes away the process by which expectations are formed and changed and how market coordination finally emerges.[9]

A number of post-Keynesian economists, such as Colander and Guthrie (1980–1), Cherry, Clawson and Dean (1981–2), Handa (1982), Gomes (1982), Davidson (1982–3) and Wible (1982–3, 1984–5) have similarly argued about the lack of realism or relevance of the REH to the real world. According to this line of criticism 'the REH analogy is misleading as a description of crucial decision-making by entrepreneurs' (Davidson, 1982–3, p. 183) and 'its real world relevance is, at best, minimal' (Colander and Guthrie, 1980–1, p. 227). Colander and Guthrie (1980–1) have also criticized the RE programme for implicitly assuming away the possibility of beneficial government stabilization in a model with rational, optimizing individuals. By adopting a radical, neo-

Coasian perspective and making stabilization a public good, they claim that the policy neutrality critique of the REH school is invalidated.

Others like Arrow (1978), Solow (1979, in Klamer 1983), Tobin (1980a, 1980b), Hahn (1980) and Blinder (1983) have criticized the RE programme for its 'unsubstantiated' use of the assumption of market-clearing wages and prices which they claim is responsible for the policy-neutrality results. According to these economists, the REH by itself is not objectionable but only its use in conjunction with the assumption of market-clearing prices is.

The information and learning critiques

The major critique of models incorporating the REH have been that these models impose extreme information assumptions and do not incorporate explicit models of learning behaviour. Poole (1976), Shiller (1978), O'Driscoll (1979), Benjamin Friedman (1979) and Buiter (1980) have criticized the REP for assuming 'perfect knowledge' as in neoclassical models of perfect competition. Benjamin Friedman points out that, while the *information exploitation* assumption (that economic agents efficiently utilize whatever information is available) is hardly objectionable, it is the *information availability* assumption (that the information sets available to economic agents are sufficient to permit them to form expectations characterized by conditional subjective distributions of outcomes that are equivalent to the conditional objective distributions of outcomes indicated by the relevant economic theory) which is highly objectionable.

Benjamin Friedman (1975, 1979) also heads the list of critics (others include Modigliani, 1977, Simon, 1979; O'Driscoll, 1979; and Buiter, 1980) who argue that the omission of an explicit learning model in the REH framework begs the whole question of how rational expectations are really formed. They therefore conclude that without such a learning model, the REH models are essentially long-run in nature and have no significance for short-run behaviour or policy.

Shiller (1978), O'Driscoll (1979), Frydman (1983), and Runde and Torr (1985) specifically examine the convergence aspects of the information and expectations problem and conclude that there is no guarantee of convergence and also that there is a problem of a multiplicity of conceivable convergence solutions. Shiller also argues that even if a model does converge eventually on an RE equilibrium it may take so long to do so that due to intervening changes a RE equilibrium may never be reached.

A related criticism of the REH (see Machlup, 1983; Frydman and Phelps, 1983; and Runde and Torr, 1985) is that a RE equilibrium not only requires that every economic agent know the true values of the parameters of the 'actual' model but also entails the perceived and actual unanimity of beliefs and economic world-views across all agents. According to this view, divergent expectations about the 'true' economic model cannot be accommodated within the RE programme and consequently typical RE results are obtained by assuming away the problems of information gathering and expectations formation that are alleged to be fundamental to economic phenomena.

The equivalence critique

Benjamin Friedman (1975, 1979) has argued that the REH is equivalent to the adaptive expectations hypothesis in the long run. However in the short run, the Adaptive Expectations Hypothesis (AEH) does not exhibit the error orthogonality property of REH models so that there is a role for macroeconomic stabilization policy in short-run contexts. Friedman argues that the AEH is the more 'credible' hypothesis in the short run while being consistent with the REH in the long run. Therefore the 'New Classical' macroeconomic results no more obtain and policy matters.

Methodological critiques

The RE programme has been examined from a number of different perspectives to assess its methodological foundations. One set of papers attempts to examine the programme in terms of some preferred model of the philosophy of science. Maddock (1984) assesses the RE macro-programme as an example of a Lakatosian (1970) programme in terms of the tenets of the MSRP (Methodology of Scientific Research Programmes). He concludes that in terms of his Lakatosian reconstruction, the programme is immature and underdeveloped but nevertheless able to 'generate some novel facts and to attract limited support for certain of them' (p. 308). Klamer (1983, 1984) and McCloskey (1985) examine the programme (the latter limits his examination to Muth's seminal article) from the viewpoint of successful rhetoric (see McCloskey, 1983, 1985) and conclude that the RE programme has been successful in the art of persuading its audience, though Klamer discusses both the issues and the subsets of the audience that have been unconvincing or unconvinced.

The second set of papers in this group has more critically examined the methodological foundations of the RE programme. Boland (1982) and Rogers (1982) identify the conventionalist/inductivist foundations of the programme and argue that there is a failure on the basis of the philosophical and logical problems associated with these methodologies.[10]

Two other lines of methodological criticism need to be mentioned. Wible (1984–5) criticizes the RE programme for not having epistemic foundations – the programme's fundamental defect is seen as the failure to provide a theory of how information is produced. He also accuses the RE programme of involving an infinite regress of informationally–based optimization theories and then attempting to terminate the regress by adopting the methodological viewpoint of instrumentalism which is then deemed to be repudiated by the Popper–Kuhn–Lakatos growth-of-knowledge view of science. Davidson (1982–3), on the other hand, criticizes the RE programme for being logically inapplicable to economic decision-making in time since such 'crucial' decision-making is known to be non-ergodic and characterized by pure uncertainty *à la* Knight–Hicks–Shackle, and thus incapable of being captured by any kind of statistical distribution. This criticism is tantamount to denying the possibility of induction and will be discussed in detail in the next section.

4.   Critique of the critiques – a rational reconstruction
This section attempts to complete the task of understanding the REP by trying to analyse the adequacy of the programme as a solution to the problem situation posed in section 2. While doing this we examine the critiques of the REP discussed in section 3 to facilitate our understanding of the programme's adequacy. This procedure is predicated on the conviction that any criticism of a theory is founded on an understanding of the theory and that by criticizing the criticism we can (a) see where the criticisms are valid so that the affected parts of the theory can be identified and consequently replaced (this way we simultaneously examine the adequacy of the theory as a solution to the problem it was meant to solve); and (b) point out invalid criticisms so that misguided criticisms, which by their failure add apparent credibility to the criticized theory and are therefore worse than the absence of criticism, can be weeded out and the sources of misunderstanding that led to the invalidation of the criticism can be identified.

The first set of criticisms that have been identified in the previous section have been grouped under the heading of the Irrefutability Critique. There are three kinds of methodological issues involved here. At one level are the difficulties involved with testing joint hypotheses. At another level, the statistical problems of empirical refutation present many difficulties. And third, the status of the REH as a refutable hypothesis on purely logical grounds needs to be examined.

The problem with testing joint hypotheses discussed briefly above can be summarized as follows. As a matter of logic, testability cannot be verifiability.[11] This is because it is impossible to verify or demonstrate the truth of a statement or theory since it is impossible to show that a strictly universal statement is true even if it is true.[12] For example, the universal statement 'all ravens are black' can be verified only if we can guarantee that no future raven will be non-black. Since there is no inductive logic by which we can guarantee this, verifiability is rendered impossible. And since every theory must contain as an assumption at least one strictly universal statement, theories of this type cannot be verified.[13] Since this consideration does not preclude 'falsifiability' or 'refutability' (since we can demonstrate that such a statement is false by showing that at least one counter-example exists), this criterion is adopted instead of 'verifiability' in economics (and in the other social and natural sciences). This then brings us to the problem with joint hypotheses. If refutability is adopted as the criterion for choosing theories, then a joint hypothesis becomes very difficult to refute since if it is rejected we can conclude that:

(a)   the hypothesis under examination (in our case the REH) is false,
(b)   the accompanying joint hypothesis (e.g. the term structure theory or the interest rate parity theory) is false, or
(c)   both (a) and (b) are false.

This difficulty arises because of the way in which refutation works. Proving one of the conclusions of a theory false does not tell us which of our assumptions (hypotheses) was false.[14] Consequently, a proponent of the REH can always argue that it was not the REH that was falsified but rather the accompanying hypothesis and thus insulate the hypothesis from being refuted. In this sense the Buiter–Tobin critique is quite valid but there are other considerations which make matters even worse for the majority of economists who are prone to testing theories to justify their 'truth' status.

The problems with refutability of any non-joint hypothesis have been identified by Boland (1977) and Jensen, Kamath and Bennett (1987). Typically, theories (or hypotheses) are tested by building models of the theories. Models in turn are typically conjunctions of three sets of assumptions:

(i)   A set of behavioural assumptions about people and/or institutions, the conjunction of all of which traditionally constitutes a 'theory'.
(ii) A set of simplifying assumptions about the relationships contained in (i) so as to make the theory testable (e.g. assuming linearity of demand curves).

(iii)   A set of assumed parametric specifications about values of parameters created in (ii). These assumptions are always needed when building applied economics models.

As already stated, the problem is that even when a prediction or conclusion of a model is falsified we are not able to identify specifically which of the above three sets of assumptions was falsified, i.e. whether it was one of the basic assumptions of the theory or the additional assumptions introduced in the model's construction. Thus, even if the REH could be tested as a non-joint hypothesis it would be impossible to reject it (or for that matter any other hypothesis) since we could never know whether it was the hypothesis or the accompanying additional assumptions that were falsified. The point is that in order to show that a theory is false by empirical testing, the tester must show that *all* possible models of the theory are false. Since there are an infinite number of ways in which the basic behavioural assumptions (the REH in our case) can be combined with all possible sets of simplifying assumptions and parametric specifications, the requirement that all possible models be shown to be false is impossible for the same reason that verification is impossible. This may then lead us to conclude that falsification and consequently testing of any economic theory is impossible.[15]

The above may seem a drastic and dismal conclusion for most, if not all, economists. But there is no reason to throw up one's hands in despair. By pointing out the problems with our testing methods, methodologists can provide an impetus for improvement. Bennett's (1981) testing method provides just such a means of improving our testing methods.[16] This procedure involves testing a model of the theory and a model of a counter-example of the theory with the same data, confirmation methods and tests (i.e. subjecting them to similar empirical definitions, conventions, data and rules of evidence).

The last issue that remains is to examine the status of the REH on purely logical grounds. It was argued that the REH consists of a set of behavioural assumptions of which the information exploitation assumption was a strictly universal statement. The underlying behavioural principle of the REH is the rationality principle that all economic agents are maximizers in that they do not leave any opportunities for gains from trade unexploited. This view amounts to the same as the neoclassical maximization principle that 'all consumers maximize something'. Boland (1981) has recently argued that the logical form of the neoclassical maximization principle renders it untestable. He argues that it is not a strictly universal statement or a tautology but an existential metaphysical statement which is the last item on the rank-ordered list of assumptions which is deliberately placed beyond question and hence rendered untestable.

If Boland's view of the maximization principle is accepted and our characterization of the nature of the REH is correct, then the REH is logically rendered untestable and we can argue that no test or logical criticism of the REH can ever convince an RE theorist that his position is wrong.

Thus we may conclude our critique of the Irrefutability Critique by saying that the Buiter–Tobin criticism does not go far enough. In fact, the problem of refutability runs deeper and extends to the very foundations of neoclassical methodology itself. If our analysis is correct, it is futile to criticize the REH just as it is futile to criticize the maximization hypothesis.[17]

The second set of criticisms against the REH can be discussed under what has been called the Lack of Realism Critique sub-heading. According to this line of criticism, the REH is either 'unrealistic' in the assumptions it makes or simply does not conform to the statistical evidence. Lack of realism of assumptions presents no problems if one adopts an instrumentalist position regarding the REH.[18] For instrumentalists, the falsity (or nonconformity to evidence) of the assumptions is of no concern as long as the conclusions or predictions 'work'. Friedman's (1953) famous 'as if' methodology is the paradigm example of an instrumentalist approach whereby so long as the hypothesized effect is observed, and this would be the effect if in fact economic agents behave as assumed, then the behavioural assumption could be used even when it is false. Thus the Franklin Fisher (1972), Arrow (1972), O'Driscoll (1979) and Benjamin Friedman (1979)–type critiques can be easily handled as irrelevant if a specifically instrumentalist position was adopted.

Nevertheless, most policy-oriented economists (with the exception of O'Driscoll and other Austrians, who can be characterized as anti-interventionist) object to the unrealistic assumptions of REH models. From this it may be concluded that they do not espouse an explicitly instrumentalist methodology. However, the economics profession can be characterized as being conventionalist rather than instrumentalist.[19] Among others who would be dissatisfied with instrumentalist views of the REH would be the empiricists who require that the truth of one's conclusions or predictions rest solely and firmly on the demonstrable truth of the premises; and the prescription that one must so justify every claim for the truth of one's conclusions or predictions. As had been pointed out, empiricists do not see a problem of induction.

A number of problems can be seen to exist even if one adopts a conventionalist/empiricist perspective. A conventionalist methodology is self-defeating since it does not adequately with the fundamental problem of induction since it involves induction in the long run and the choice of conventionalist 'truth' criteria themselves can be considered *ad hoc*. [20] Similarly, empiricism is problematic because of the inability to deal with the problem of induction and other methodological difficulties. [21]

A fundamental problem that exists with the endeavour to establish the truth of one's assumptions is that of an infinite regress. Only contingent proofs of the truth of one's assumptions are feasible since the establishment of their truth would depend on a prior establishment of the truth of observation statements on which the assumptions are predicated which would in turn depend on the truth of a prior theory on which this observation statement is dependent which in turn would require proven observation statements which . . . *ad infinitum*. All this would be possible on the basis of the existence of a valid reverse *modus ponens*, which is a complete fiction. [22] All one can do is try to falsify one's conjectured assumptions though it may never be established that in fact they are true. [23] The REH does not claim that it is an unrealistic hypothesis and its realistic status can only be resolved by attempting to falsify it by repeated tests. But then, once again, the problems of refutability mentioned above need to be squarely confronted.

With regard to the existence of the business cycle and the existence of labour contracts, proponents of the REH have met this criticism head on by arguing that these can be rationalized as equilibrium phenomena in the presence of rational expectations. If the REH were literally true then as a logical conclusion we would not expect to see a business cycle since all markets would clear and all opportunities for unexploited gains would be exploited. However, as discussed in section 2, RE theorists as epitomized by Lucas (1980, 1981) set their original goal as trying to rationalize economic fluctuations in a maximizing general equilibrium framework and the RE programme can be seen as an attempt to explain the business cycle and the related phenomena as a consequence of optimizing behaviour in the presence of government policy intervention.

A major rationale for the existence of the business cycle given by RE theorists like Lucas (1975) is that cyclical movements in business activities are generated by unsystematic monetary-fiscal shocks, the effects of which are distributed through time due to information lags and an accelerator effect. This rationale is problematic since such models, by positing information lags artifically, constrain the amount of intertemporal information transmitted and beg the question as to why the information is so constrained. If rational economic agents perceived such lags and fluctuations as being constraining they would find means (e.g. an economy-wide bond market) to overcome these constraints. An RE rebuttal to this criticism would be that if people choose not to overcome informational lags and other 'constraints' it is because doing so is too expensive so that in fact the existence of the business cycle reflects people's rational choice.

The RE programme's attempt to explain the existence of the business cycle can thus be characterized as *ad hoc*. The New Classical economists' rejection of the Keynesian macroeconomic programme is predicated on the *adhoc*ery of its stylized facts such as rigid money wages, imperfect information and the existence of money illusion. While overcoming such *adhoc*ery through the postulate of rational expectations and market-clearing (at least from a conventionalist perspective), the introduction of island parables, imperfect information and confusions between aggregate and relative price shocks can be considered equally arbitrary and *ad hoc*.

It is pertinent to note here that while the RE explanation of the business cycle leaves something to be desired, alternative explanations which rely on systematic error or irrationality are even more hard-pressed since explanations need to clarify why agents continue to make systematic errors.

The policy neutrality conclusions of the REH have been brought into question by the contractual theories of labour markets and the empirical phenomenon of the existence of such contracts in the real world. In this context, Kantor (1979) has tried to counter this criticism with the argument that the existence of such contracts is taken as given and not explained. Secondly, he points out that the manner in which contractual arrangements would alter if the authorities attempted to make use of the apparent rigidities implied by contracts is also not indicated. Thirdly, he points out that to the extent that the periods for which individual firms and workers contracts overlap, there is a degree of flexibility imparted to the price level in general that may not be true of an individual price or wage. His fourth criticism is that rational economic agents 'will find it imperative to take a position on stabilization policy precisely because reversing position in these markets is costly over the forecast span. Moreover, given such anticipations, there can be no presumption that the impact of stabilization policy will be under rather than overestimated' (1979, p. 1437).

Kantor's first three criticisms are easily dealt with. There is a large literature providing a rationale for the existence of contracts under the title of Implicit Contract Theory. Secondly, the shortcomings of the

Fischer (1977) analysis where contract length is exogenous have been overcome by McCallum's (1983) analysis of endogenous contract length. This analysis provides a means of determining the effect of a change in policy on contractual arrangements. Kantor's third point in any case concedes that stabilization policy will be effective, albeit in a reduced manner.

It is the fourth criticism that merits some attention. As has been pointed out by Boland (1982), the REH and its critics base their epistemology on the view that true knowledge requires inductive proofs, and learning is constrained by the fact that inductive proofs are impossible so that knowledge is only 'true' according to some degree of probability. Consequently, conventionalist neoclassical models like the REH recognize limited or 'imperfect' knowledge and economic agents are presumed to act on the basis of optimum information, given the costs and availability of information. Though information may be imperfect in a global sense it is optimal in a maximizing sense so that even fixed contracts can be rationalized as being 'rational', leaving open the question of whether the anticipated impact of stabilization policy will be under- or overestimated in drawing up such contracts. Thus, though stabilization policy may be feasible it may not be desirable.[24] With regard to the desirability of stabilization policy, the critics are wrong in that in the absence of an inductive logic, governments can be wrong just as individuals can be, even in the presence of rational expectations.

With regard to the critique of the Austrians and the Post- Keynesians that the REH assumes away the process by which expectations are formed and therefore does not reflect real-world 'crucial' decision-making, this criticism is itself implicitly predicated on an acceptance of inductivism which is itself problematic.[25] The neo-Keynesian criticism that RE policy-neutrality results are the consequence of the assumption of market-clearing and not the REH indicate a confusion regarding the joint-testing problem and the instrumentalist methodology of most RE theorists.

The most celebrated critiques of the RE programme are the criticisms of the information and learning assumptions of RE models. The basic thrust of these critiques is that RE models do not incorporate a theory of learning and therefore they argue that such models do not address the question as to how economic agents acquire the necessary information to form rational expectations. This argument is then extended to conclude that therefore RE models have nothing to say about the efficacy of policy in the short run.

The concern with how the individual acquires the true knowledge of his or her circumstances dates back to Friedrich Hayek's seminal paper (1937). His concern was that since such knowledge was necessary for explaining any stable equilibrium it becomes imperative for the theorist to explain how economic agents gain their knowledge in order to explain how the economy changes over time. Hayek recognized that there was a major problem here since there is no inductive way of showing how any individual could ever acquire true knowledge. According to Boland (1978), while Hayek admitted defeat, neoclassical theorists were more optimistic since they adopted conventionalism to get around the problem of induction. Boland argues that the RE hypothesis represents their solution to the problem of induction.

This purported solution can be summarized as follows. The REH has a conventionalist theory of learning which is not explicitly discussed because it is presumed that everyone understands and implicitly accepts such a theory. The conventionalist theory of learning recognizes the problem of induction in that there is really no way to collect enough facts to absolutely prove the truth of any explanation. By positing that knowledge can be 'true' only according to some degree of probability, economists argue that learning takes place whenever the probability of one's knowledge is increased, e.g. when the degree of confirmation of a theory has increased. Thus, absolute proofs of our knowledge are not required and the attempt is to maximize the quantity of facts collected or improve their quality. Over this conventionalist theory of learning is imposed the 'economics of information acquistion' *à la* Stigler (1961) wherein rational agents acquire information to the point where the marginal benefit from collecting one additional bit of information just matches the marginal cost of acquiring that information. The REH states precisely that information is exploited up to the point where it is economical to do so and expectations are formed on this basis. Therefore the contention that the REH has no theory of learning associated with it is just plain wrong.[26]

The accompanying criticism of RE models such as those of Friedman (1979), O'Driscoll (1979), and others that these models, by assuming *information availability*, are perfect knowledge models is also logically incorrect. Most RE models do not assume perfect knowledge; only that knowledge is acquired up to the point where it is economical to do so (i.e. where MB = MC). However, as Boland (1982) argues, models which employ some form of 'imperfect' knowledge constitute a form of conventionalism which demands the attainment of an inductive proof before anyone's knowledge is considered perfect. Since inductive proofs are impossible, perfect knowledge is deemed impossible. Boland argues that this view of knowledge is not warranted since one's knowledge can be true even if it cannot be proved to be true. He also argues that all conventionalist theories of knowledge are self-contradictory and should be rejected on their own terms since they deny truth status to theories, but the denial is itself a theory which is asserted to have true status.

A valid criticism of the information assumptions of RE models and also all models that incorporate the 'economics of information' (in the sense of Stigler, 1961) relates to the assumption that economic agents acquire information up to the point where MB = MC. Such a process begs the question as to where and how information on the costs and benefits of information search was obtained in the first place. This can lead to an infinite regress which cannot be terminated on instrumentalist or conventionalist grounds.

The convergence and 'time taken to final-convergence' critique of Shiller (1978) is important only to those who espouse a conventionalist theory of learning.[27] However for anyone who does not accept the conventionalist methodology these problems may be irrelevant.

As regards the 'disparate' expectations critique of Machlup (1983), Frydman and Phelps (1983) and Runde and Torr (1985), basically their criticism is well directed since, as already discussed, RE models must account for the process by which information is gathered and a unanimity of beliefs/expectations achieved. There is no logical reason why expectations should converge to a stable equilibrium in the presence of disparate expectations except perhaps by accident. As Runde and Torr (1985) show, attempts to incorporate divergent expectations into RE models have been *ad hoc* and often demonstrate stability by assuming that either agents are irrational or such expectations are transient. However, to the extent that these critics require an inductivist/conventionalist demonstration of the 'truth' of RE equilibria, their criticism is misdirected since this is clearly an impossible task. Quite clearly, RE models do have an implicit theory of conventionalist learning and criticizing them for not incorporating such a theory is incorrect. However, the theory of learning itself is methodologically inadequate.

Another major criticism against the RE programme is that included under what we have titled the equivalence critique. Boland (1982) is quite right in his criticism of the supposed equivalence relation. His conjecture is that since the equivalence claim is supposed to be a criticism this suggests that there is something wrong with adaptive expectations. And to him what is wrong with adaptive expectations is that its explanation is *ad hoc*. While rational expectations are formed economically (if one accepts conventionalism), adaptive expectations are formed arbitrarily in the sense that the adjustment parameter (by which each subsequent expectation is adjusted based on the previous error), even if chosen to conform to standard statistical criteria, is necessarily arbitary since the number of trials (representing the quantity of information needed to predict 'properly') is arbitary. Thus, while the number of trials can be chosen on the same basis as MB = MC in information acquisition in RE models, it is not necessary that this be so, so that adaptive expectations and rational expectations are not necessarily the same even in the long run. Boland argues that while the adaptive learning model of Friedman accurately portrays the conventionalist theory of learning, the rational expectations approach is definitely superior and logically consistent if one accepts conventionalism.

Lastly, it is necessary to consider the other methodological critiques of the REH. Maddock's (1984) Lakatosian reconstruction of the RE programme is a conventional application of the MSRP to the RE Revolution. A recent meta-methodological assessment of the applicability of the MSRP to economic theory by Hands (1985) concludes that the methodology itself is deficient since it fails to account for progress in economics on its own internal criteria of increasing empirical content and empirical success. Application of Hands' analysis to Maddock's assessment of the programme reveals reasons for a more negative appraisal than that of the latter. Maddock's claim is that the RE programme represents a progressive programme because it predicted two novel facts: the ineffectiveness of stabilization policy even in the short run and the deviation of output from its natural rate in any period should be independent of data which were available at the moment of prediction. As regards the first 'novel' fact, neutrality propositions have a long history in monetary theory and the assertion of short-run (monetary) policy neutrality is not new to economics.[28] In any case, the super-neutrality proposition is foreshadowed by the strong form of the Efficient Markets Hypothesis (EMH) put forward by Samuelson (1965) and Fama (1970), where policy can be viewed as the 'news' instantly factored into goods and asset prices rendering it ineffective.[29] Similarly, the second 'novel' fact was also well known in the EMH literature albeit in a different context and is equivalent to the proposition that price changes are random and independently distributed of each other and data that were available at the time of the change. It is also not clear that each step in the development of the RE programme entailed an increase in empirical content as required by the MSRP (see Hands. 1985) since it is not clear that the programme had any falsifiable empirical content because of the manner in which it was tested (as discussed earlier) and the fact that others (e.g. Fischer, 1977; Taylor, 1980) demonstrated that models with REH could generate a stabilizing role for policy.

With regard to Klamer (1983, 1987) and McCloskey's (1985) assessment of the rhetorical success of the RE programme, a methodological
critique of the 'rhetoric of economics' will not be attempted here.
Nevertheless, there is little doubt that the REH has (perhaps unwarran-
tedly) been successful in changing the 'level of discourse' in macroeconomics.

The most cogent methodological critique of the RE programme is
that of Boland (1982). He correctly argues that the critics of the REH on
the information and learning, policy intervention and equivalence issue
are wrong because of the logical problems of conventionalism and the
problem of induction (the view taken in this chapter is similar). As
Boland points out, the epistemological basis of the REH is a
conventionalist theory of knowledge which requires inductive proofs
and is therefore *unrealistic* because it would take an unrealistic (read
impossible) amount of time to provide the presumed necessary inductive proof of 'perfect knowledge'. However, models of 'imperfect
knowledge' are equally nihilistic since they also adopt a form of
conventionalism which demands inductive proofs. The problem with the
REH, as well as its more conventional critiques, is that both are
founded on the same self-contradictory methodology of conventionalism. While conventionalism may be suited for the solution of some
kinds of problems (see Boland, 1982), it is not of much help in the long-
term enterprise of searching for true theories. Thus, because of the
inherent problems associated with its underlying methodological
perspective, the debate over the RE programme is likely to remain a
sterile family dispute about the (in)adequacy of conventionalism to
solving real theoretical problems in economics.

Finally, the Austrian and Post-Keynesian critiques need to be
considered. The basic thrust of these criticisms is valid since the RE
programme is applicable to situations of Knightian risk but not to those
of Knight–Hicks–Shackle uncertainty where economic events are
unique. Hicks (1979) and Kamath and Jensen (1985) discuss the
methodological basis and implications of this view and show that
theorizing about such situations requires a non-inductive methodology.

5.   Did the rational expectations revolution succeed? An evaluation and conclusions

Having considered the major critiques of the RE programme, it is
necessary to assess whether the original objectives of this programme
outlined in section 2 were achieved and whether the programme has
been a success or a failure.

With reference to the ostensible objectives of the RE programme we may note the following points:

(a) The RE programme has to a large extent been successful in meeting its primary objective of reinstating rationality into macroeconomic models and macroeconomics in general. Its success is borne out by the virtual disappearance from the major economic journals of other expectation adjustment hypotheses such as adaptive expectations, partial adjustment, Koyck distributed lags, etc. It has also made its impact in intermediate macroeconomic textbooks which now incorporate rational expectations as an integral element in their contents. Another indicator of the success of the RE programme is the fact that it has placed the onus on those who profess obstacles to rational expectations equilibria (such as Keynesian disequilibrium theorists) to come up with convincing explanations of why economic agents should be consistently wrong in their expectations.

(b) With respect to another proximate objective, namely that of trying to rationalize business cycles in a general equilibrium framework, the RE programme can be characterized as having failed. As had been argued in section 4, RE models have been hard-pressed to express economic fluctuations without imposing artificial *ad hoc* constraints such as information lags, isolated markets or lack of specific markets. The extreme RE programme position has been characterized as rationalizing the business cycle as a reflection of people's 'rational' choice. This rationale can be criticized on a number of counts.

(c) The attempt to show that standard macroeconometric models are of doubtful value for policy simulation purposes has been successful in one sense and a failure in another. The Lucas critique of standard models has widely come to be accepted and most economists concede that agents' behaviour is not invariant to alternative policy rules and macroeconometric models with policy-invariant parameters are quite inadequate for policy simulation. However, the extreme policy-neutrality implications of the early RE models have been tempered by the literature on contracts. The existence of contracts of greater than one-period length has provided a logical demonstration of the feasibility of short-run macroeconomic stabilization policy. Its desirability is however, questionable.

As regards the methodological foundations, Boland's (1982) conclusion that the REH is the only logically adequate solution to the problem of conventions is correct.[30] The REH by not requiring knowledge to be perfect (true) but merely 'adequate' in the sense of acquiring information economically provides a superior and logically consistent circumvention of the problem of induction as compared to any other hypothesis. We may note however that methodologically this is no great recommendation for adopting the hypothesis since conventionalism as a methodological doctrine is limiting. The conventionalist foundations of the RE programme bring its very basis (and that of its critics) into serious question. As long as the REH is predicated on a conventionalist theory of learning, it is self-contradictory and does not qualify on its own terms since such a theory denies truth status to theories, but this denial is itself a theory asserted to have truth status.

It would be far more rewarding to reconstruct the RE programme and its problem situation by showing the feasibility of rational expectations equilibria without adopting a conventionalist methodology. A solution to this problem would entail the use of a non-justification theory of knowledge that demonstrates that one's knowledge *can* be perfect (true) even though it cannot be shown that it actually *is* true. It would also require an emphasis on the *process* of (disparate) expectations formation rather than on mathematical formalism and 'scientistic' rigour. Such a programme awaits construction.

In conclusion, it may be conjectured that the REH will continue to occupy centre-stage in the unresolved debates in neoclassical economics as long as the predominant conventionalist methodology continues to dominate. This is ironic since the REH presents the only logically consistent solution to the problem of conventions but will not be seen as such by both protagonists and antagonists. If economists were to give up their self-contradictory methodology the REH would be radically altered. But this would be part of a massive revolution in neoclassical economics the details or outcome of which cannot yet be conjectured. Certainly there is likely to be no lack of work for 'rational' economists who are dissatisfied with their present methodology.

Notes

1. I would like to thank Larry Boland, John Chant and Chris Jensen for comments on some early ideas. An earlier version of this paper was presented at the HES meeting at Harvard University in June 1987. Participants of California State University, Hayward's Economics Workshop, particularly Chuck Baird, Greg Christainsen, Jim St. Clair and Steve Shmanske, provided useful comments. The usual disclaimer applies.
2. Barro (1984, p. 179). Klamer (1984) also endorses, albeit tentatively, the success of REH 'discourse'.

3. Lucas (1981) discusses this focus in his Introduction. See also the Lucas interview in Klamer (1983), especially pp. 37–46.
4. The method of rational reconstruction is developed in Popper (1945, 1957, 1968), Latsis (1972) and Wong (1978). Hands (1985) discusses some problems with Popper's development of the method.
5. For discussions of the Keynesian Revolution see Keynes (1936, 1937), Hicks (1937), Clower (1965) and Leijonhufvud (1968). The modern disequilibrium macroeconomics literature is contained in Barro and Grossman (1971), Benassy (1975) and Drazen (1980).
6. See the Introduction and pp. 213–39 of Lucas (1981) for a discussion of the problem situation and series of events that led to the incorporation of the REH in equilibrium models of the business cycle. See also the Lucas interview in Klamer (1983).
7. The last constraint is explicitly mentioned by Lucas (1981) in the Introduction and by him and Sargent in Klamer (1983).
8. This problem has been recognized in the economics literature but has not been given sufficient emphasis until recently. Boland (1977), Roll (1977), Cross (1982) and Kamath, Jensen and Bennett (1985) discuss this issue. This problem is called the Duhem–Quine problem or thesis.
9. The Austrian critique of the REH and much of neoclassical economics is based on Hayek's (1937) alternative conception of market coordination and equilibrium. For problems in the Hayekian market coordination view see Boland (1977), Vanberg (1985) and Ebeling (1986).
10. Conventionalism is the methodology by which theories are viewed as being catalogues or filing systems which are not either true or false and which are to be appraised by such 'conventional' criteria of convenience as simplicity, generality, goodness of fit, etc. Instrumentalism is the methodological view that theories are useful instruments for generating successful predictions or conclusions. The truth status of theories are irrelevant for practical purposes and all that matters is whether the conclusions that are logically derived from the theories 'work' (see Friedman, 1953). For a discussion of these and other methodological viewpoints see Boland (1979, 1982).
11. See Karl Popper (1963, chapters 1 and 4). For a comprehensive discussion of the methodological difficulties of testing in economics see Boland (1977, 1982), Bennett (1981), and Jensen, Kamath and Bennett (1987).
12. Universal statements are of the type all X's have property Y. In the theory of market prices for example, a universal statement is 'all demand curves are downward sloping'. Note however that there is a class of universal statements that can be verified. These are universal statements that limit (in terms of time or space) the class of X's to a finite size.
13. The universal statement of the REH is that 'all people exploit information until the point at which its marginal product equals its marginal cost.' (This is what Benjamin Friedman (1979) calls the information exploitation assumption of the REH.) A verification of this assumption would entail establishing that every individual, past, present and future, has the desired characteristic of exploiting information up to the point where MB = MC. Obviously this cannot be done because of what is called the problem with induction in that there is no inductive logic with which to connect the theory with positive evidence and still provide the logical assurances of deductive logic.
14. This is the attribute of the mode of argument called *modus tollens* where one can argue against the truth of one's assumptions from the falsity of one's conclusions. Specifically even though one of the assumptions used is false, there is no means by which one can identify *which* one of the assumptions is false. This is called the Duhem–Quine thesis (see Harding, 1976; Boland, 1977; and Cross, 1982).
15. It should be pointed out here that this conclusion is unavoidable on grounds of logic alone. Most economists adopt the conventionalist criterion of degrees of confirmation (e.g. hypotheses are retained on the basis of their 'goodness of fit' and other

conventional criteria such as t-values, robustness, etc.). For a discussion of these and other 'conventionalist' criteria and the methodological problems involved see Kamath, Jensen and Bennett (1986).

16.   See Bennett (1981) and Jensen, Kamath and Bennett (1987).

17.   Mongin (1986) argues that 'all-and-some' statements are in principle falsifiable and neoclassical theory can be shown to be false. His demonstration fails because it is the *manner* in which the neoclassical maximization postulate is used which renders it unfalsifiable. The point is that it is the use of an immunizing strategem which renders
.   the postulate as irrefutable regardless of whether it is in principle falsifiable. (I thank Larry Boland for personal correspondence on this issue.)

18.   See Boland (1979) for a discussion. Klamer's (1983) interviews with Lucas, Sargent and Townsend clearly indicate that these RE theorists espouse the instrumentalist position put forward in Friedman (1953).

19.   See Boland (1979, 1982) for a discussion. It should be pointed out here that conventionalists may argue about the nature or the possibility of determining the 'appropriate or probable truth' of theories so that they are concerned with the realism of assumptions.

20.   The problem of induction is that of finding a general method of providing an inductive proof of anyone's claim to empirical knowledge. See Boland (1970, 1982) for a discussion of the methodological shortcomings of inductivist and conventiona-list methodologies.

21.   See Caldwell (1982, chapters 2 and 3) for a discussion of the shortcomings of the empiricist methodology.

22.   *Modus ponens* involves the mode of arguing from the truth of one's conclusions on the basis of the truth of one's assumptions. There is no valid reverse *modus ponens* by which one can argue from the truth of one's conclusions to the truth of one's assumptions.

23.   See Popper (1963, 1968) for a discussion.

24.   See Beenstock (1980) for a neoclassical defence of the anti-policy view which separates the issue of the feasibility of intervention from its desirability in a world with rational expectations.

25.   Inductivism is the methodological doctrine that says that all theories can be true and all true theories (or assumptions) are the result of applying inductive logic to observations. This doctrine flounders on account of Hume's (1748, 1955) famous problem of induction discussed earlier.

26.   It should be noted here that a number of REH models with explicit 'theories of learning' have been developed. These include those in the 1982 *Journal of Economic Theory* issue on RE models (see particularly the Introduction by Blume, Bray and Easley, 1982) and those contained in Frydman and Phelps (1983). All these learning models are inductive and most often yield non-convergent, non-unique solutions.

27.   This line of criticism is also adopted by Rogers (1982), the critics in Klamer (1983), Frydman (1983), Runde and Torr (1985), and is admitted to be valid by Sargent in Klamer (1983).

28.   For a discussion of money neutrality propositions, see Patinkin (1965).

29.   Kantor (1979) and Sheffrin (1983, chapter 4) discuss the parallels between the REH and EMH literature.

30.   The problem of conventions is the problem of finding generally acceptable criteria on which to base any contingent, deductive proof of any claim to empirical knowledge.

References

Akerlof, George (1979), 'The case against conservative macroeconomics – an inaugural lecture', *Economica*, 46 (August), pp. 219–37.

Arrow, Kenneth J. (1978), 'The future and present in economic life', *Economic Inquiry*, 16 (April), pp. 157–69.

Barro, Robert J. (1984), 'Rational expectations and macroeconomics in 1984', *American*

Economic Review, 74 (May), pp. 179–82.

Barro, Robert J. and Grossman, Herschel I. (1971), 'A general disequilibrium model of income and employment', *American Economic Review*, 61 (March), pp. 82–93.

Beenstock, Michael (1980), *A Neoclassical Analysis of Macroeconomic Policy*, Cambridge: Cambridge University Press.

Benassy, J. P. (1976), 'Neo-Keynesian disequilibrium in a monetary economy', *Review of Economic Studies*, 43, pp. 69–81.

Bennett, Robert E. (1981), *An Empirical Test of Some Post-Keynesian Income Distribution Theories*, unpublished PhD Dissertation, Simon Fraser University, Burnaby, B.C.

Blinder, Alan S. (1983), 'Conversations with neo-Keynesian economists: The "younger generation" – Alan S. Blinder' in Arjo Klamer, *Conversations With Economists*, Totowa, NJ: Rowman & Allanheld.

Blume, Lawrence E., Bray, Margaret M. and Easley, David (1982), 'Introduction to the Stability of Rational Expectations Equilibrium', *Journal of Economic Theory*, 26, pp. 313–17.

Boland, Lawrence A. (1970), 'Conventionalism and economic theory', *Philosophy of Science*, 37, pp. 239–48.

Boland, Lawrence A. (1977), 'Testability in economic science', *South African Journal of Economics*, 45, pp. 93–105.

Boland, Lawrence A. (1978), 'Time in economics vs. economics in time: The "Hayek Problem" ', *Canadian Journal of Economics*, 11, pp. 240–62.

Boland, Lawrence A. (1979), 'A critique of Friedman's critics', *Journal of Economic Literature*, 17, pp. 503–22.

Boland, Lawrence A. (1981), 'On the futility of criticizing the neoclassical maximization hypothesis', *American Economic Review*, 71 (March), pp. 1031–6.

Boland, Lawrence A. (1982), *The Foundation of Economics Method*, London: Allen and Unwin.

Buck, Andrew (1985), 'An empirical note on the foundations of rational expectations', *Journal of Post-Keynesian Economics*, 7 (Spring), pp. 311–23.

Buiter, Willem (1980), 'The macroeconomics of Dr. Pangloss: A critical survey of the New Classical Macroeconomics', *Economic Journal*, 80, pp. 34–50.

Cagan, Phillip (1956), 'The monetary dynamics of hyperinflation' in *Studies in the Quantity Theory of Money*, ed. M. Friedman, Chicago: University of Chicago Press.

Caldwell, Bruce J. (1982), *Beyond Positivism: Economic Methodology in the Twentieth Century*, London: Allen & Unwin.

Cherry, Robert, Clawson, Patrick and Dean, James W. (1981–2), 'Microfoundations of macrorational expectations models', *Journal of Post-Keynesian Economics*, 4 (Winter), pp. 214–30.

Clower, Robert W. (1965), 'The Keynesian counterrevolution: A theoretical appraisal', in the *Theory of Interest Rates*, ed. F. H. Hahn and F. P. R. Brechling, London: Macmillan: New York: St Martin's Press.

Colander, David C. and Guthrie, Robert S. (1980–1), 'Great expectations: What the dickens do rational expectations mean?', *Journal of Post-Keynesian Economics*, 3 (Winter), pp. 219–34.

Cross, Rodney (1982), 'The Duhen–Quine thesis, Lakatos and the appraisal of theories in macro-economics', *The Economic Journal*, 92, pp. 320–40.

Davidson, Paul (1982–3), 'Rational expectations: A fallacious foundation for studying crucial decision-making processes', *Journal of Post-Keynesian Economics*, 5 (Winter), pp. 182–98.

Drazen, Allan (1980), 'Recent developments in macroeconomic disequilibrium theory', *Econometrica*, 2 (March), pp. 283–306.

Ebeling, Richard M., 'Towards a hermeneutical economics: Expectations, prices and the role of interpretation in a theory of the market process', in Israel M. Kerzner (ed.), *Subjectivism, Intelligibility and Economic Understanding*, New York: New York University Press.

Fama, E. Ugene F. (1970), 'Efficient capital markets: A review of theory and empirical work', *Journal of Finance*, 25, pp. 383–423.

Fischer, Stanley (1977), 'Long-term contracts, rational expectations and the optimal money supply rule', *Journal of Political Economy*, 55 (February), pp. 191–205.

Fisher, F. (1972), 'Comment on paper by R. Lucas', in *The Econometrics of Price Determination*, ed. Otto Eckstein, Washington, D. C.

Friedman, Benjamin M. (1975), 'Rational expectations are really adaptive after all', *Harvard Insitute of Economic Research Discussion Paper No. 430*, Cambridge, Mass.

Friedman, Benjamin M. (1979), 'Optimal expectations and the extreme information assumptions of rational expectations macromodels', *Journal of Monetary Economics*, 5 (January), pp. 23–41.

Friedman, Milton (1953), 'Methodology of positive economics', in *Essays in Positive Economics*, Chicago: University of Chicago Press.

Friedman, Milton (1968), 'The role of monetary policy', *American Economic Review*, 58 (March), pp. 1–17.

Friedman, Milton (1970), 'A theoretical framework for monetary analysis', *Journal of Political Economy*, 78 (April/May), pp. 193–238.

Frydman, Roman (1982), 'Towards an understanding of market processes: Individual expectations, learning and convergence to rational expectations equilibrium', *American Economic Review*, 72 (September), pp. 652–68.

Frydman, Roman and Phelps, Edmund S. (1983), *Individual Forecasting and Aggregate Outcomes*: *'Rational Expectations' Examined*, Cambridge: Cambridge University Press.

Gomes, Gustavo M. (1982), 'Irrationality of "Rational Expectations" ', *Journal of Post Keynesian Economics*, 5 (Fall), pp. 51–65.

Gordon, Robert J. (1976), 'Recent developments in the theory of inflation and unemployment', *Journal of Monetary Economics*, 2, pp. 185–219.

Haberler, Gottfried (1980), *Notes on Rational and Irrational Expectations*, Washington: American Enterprise Institute.

Handa, Jagdish (1982), 'Rational expectations: what do they mean? – Another view', *Journal of Post-Keynesian Economics*, 4 (Summer), pp. 558–64.

Hands, Douglas W. (1985), 'Karl Popper and economic methodology: a new look', *Economics and Philosophy*, 1 (April), pp. 83–100.

Hands, Douglas (1985), 'Second thoughts on Lakatos', *History of Political Economy*, 17, pp. 1–16.

Hahn, Frank (1981), *Money and Inflation*, Cambridge, Mass: MIT Press.

Hahn, Frank (1986), 'Review of Arjo Klamer's conversations with economists', *Economics and Philosophy*, 2 (October), pp. 275–81.

Harding, Sandra (1976), *Can Theories be Refuted? Essays on the Duhem-Quine Thesis*, Dodrecht-Holland: D. Reidel.

Hayek, Friedrich A. (1937), 'Economics and knowledge', *Economica*, 4 (ns), pp. 33–54.

Hicks, John R. (1937), 'Mr. Keynes and the Classics: a suggested interpretation', *Econometrica*, 5 (April), pp. 147–59.

Hume, David (1748/1955), *An Inquiry Concerning Human Understanding* (reprint), Indianapolis: Bobbs-Merrill.

Kamath, Shyam J. and Jensen, K. Christian (1985), 'Liquidity, error and decision-making in economics', mimeo.

Kamath, Shyam J., Jensen, K. C. and Bennett, R. E. (1985), 'The empirical appraisal of economic theories: some problems and an alternative test procedure', *Dolhousie School of Business Discussion Paper, No. 38*.

Jensen, K. Christian, Kamath, S. J. and Bennett, R. E. (1987) 'Money in the production function – alternative test procedure', *Eastern Economic Journal*, July–September, pp. 259–69.

Kantor, Brian (1979), 'Rational expectations and economic thought', *Journal of Economic Literature*, 17 (December), pp. 1422–41.

Keynes, John M. (1936), *The General Theory of Employment, Interest and Money*, New York: Macmillan.

Keynes, John M. (1937), 'The general theory of employment', *Quarterly Journal of Economics*, 51, pp. 209–23.

Klamer, Arjo (1983), *Conversations with Economists*, Totawa, NJ: Rowman & Allanheld.

Klamer, Arjo (1984), 'Levels of discourse in New Classical Economics', *History of Political Economy*, 16, pp. 263–90.

Lakatos, Imre (1970), 'Methodology of scientific research programs', in Imre Lakatos and Alan Musgrave (eds), *Criticism and the Growth of Knowledge*, Cambridge: Cambridge University Press.

Latsis, Spiro (1972), 'Situational determinism in economics', *British Journal for the Philosophy of Science*, 23, pp. 207–45.

Leijonhufvud, Axel (1968), *On Keynesian Economics and the Economics of Keynes: A Study in Monetary Theory*, New York: Oxford University Press.

Lovell, Michael C. (1986), 'Tests of the rational expectations hypothesis', *American Economic Review*, 76 (March), pp. 72–81.

Lucas, Robert E. Jr (1972a), 'Econometric testing of the natural rate hypothesis', in Otto Eckstein (ed.), *The Econometrics of Price Determination Conference*, Washington, D.C.: Board of Governors, Federal Reserve System.

Lucas, Robert E. Jr (1972b), 'Expectations and the neutrality of money', *Journal of Economic Theory*, 4 (April), pp. 102–24.

Lucas, Robert E. Jr (1973), 'Some international evidence on output-inflation tradeoffs', *American Economic Review*, 63 (June), pp. 326–34.

Lucas, Robert E. Jr (1979), 'An equilibrium model of the business cycle', *Journal of Political Economy*, 83 (December), pp. 1113–44.

Lucas, Robert E. Jr (1980), 'Methods and problems in business cycle theory', *Journal of Money, Credit, and Banking*, 12 (November), pp. 696–715.

Lucas, Robert E. Jr (1981), *Studies in Business Cycle Theory*, Cambridge, Mass: MIT Press.

Machlup, Fritz (1983), 'The rationality of rational expectations', *Kredit und Kapital*, 16, pp. 172–83.

Maddock, Rodney (1984), 'Rational expectations macrotheory: A Lakatosian case study in program adjustment', *History of Political Economy*, 16, pp. 291–309.

McCallum, Bennett T. (1980), 'Rational expectations and stabilization policy', *Journal of Money, Credit and Banking*, 12 (November), pp. 716–46.

McCallum, John C. P. (1983), 'Stabilization policy and contracts under rational expectations', *American Economic Review*, 73 (June), pp. 414–19.

McCloskey, Donald M. (1983), 'The rhetoric of economics', *Journal of Economic Literature*, 31 (June), pp. 434–61.

McCloskey, Donald M. (1985), *The Rhetoric of Economics*, Madison, Wisconsin: University of Wisconsin Press.

Modigliani, Franco (1977), 'The monetarist controversy, or, should we forsake stabilization policies?' *American Economic Review*, 67 (March), pp. 1–19.

Mongin, Philippe (1986), 'Are "all-and-some" statements falsifiable after all? The example of utility theory', *Economics and Philosophy*, 2 (October), pp. 185–96.

Muth, John F. (1960), 'Optimal properties of exponentially weighted forecasts', *Journal of the American Statistical Association*, 55 (June), pp. 299–306.

Muth, John F. (1961), 'Rational expectations and the theory of price movements', *Econometrica*, 29 (July), pp. 315–35.

O'Driscoll, Gerald P. Jr (1979), 'Rational expectations, politics and stagflation', in *Time, Uncertainty and Disequilibrium*, ed. Mario J. Rizzo, Lexington: D. C. Heath.

Phelps, Edmund S. (ed.) (1970), *Microeconomic Foundations of Employment and Inflation Theory*, New York: Norton.

Popper, Karl R. (1963), *Conjectures and Refutations: The Growth of Scientific Knowledge*, New York: Harper and Row.

Popper, Karl R. (1968), *Logic of Scientific Discovery*, New York: Science Editions.

Rogers, C. (1982), 'Rational expectations and neoclassical economics: The methodology of the New Classical Economics', *South African Journal of Economics*, 50, pp. 318–39.

Roll, Richard (1977), 'A critique of the asset pricing theory's tests, Part I: On past and future testability of the theory', *Journal of Financial Economics*, 3, pp. 129–76.
Runde, J. and Torr, C. (1985), 'Divergent expectations and rational expectations', *South African Journal of Economics*, 53, pp. 217–25.
Samuelson, Paul A. (1965), *Foundations of Economic Analysis*, New York: Athenaeum.
Sargent, Thomas J. (1971), 'A note on the accelerationist controversy', *Journal of Money, Credit, and Banking*, 8 (August), pp. 721–5.
Sargent, Thomas J. (1973), 'Rational expectations, the real rate of interest, and the natural rate of unemployment', *Brookings Papers on Economic Activity*, 2, pp. 429–80.
Sargent, Thomas J. and Wallace, Neil (1973), 'Rational expectations and the dynamics of hyperinflation', *International Economic Review*, 14 (June), pp. 328–50.
Sargent, Thomas J. and Wallace, Neil (1975), 'Rational expectations, the optimal monetary instrument, and the optimal money supply rule', *Journal of Political Economy*, 83 (April), pp. 241–54.
Sheffrin, Steven M. (1983), *Rational Expectation*, Cambridge: Cambridge University Press.
Shiller, Robert J. (1978), 'Rational expectations and the dynamic structure of macroeconomic models', *Journal of Monetary Economics*, 4, pp. 1–44.
Simon, Herbert A. (1979), 'Rational decision making in organizations', *American Economic Review*, 69 (June), pp. 493–513.
Solow, Robert M. (1979), 'Alternative approaches to macroeconomic theory: a partial view', *Canadian Journal of Economics*, 12, pp. 339–54.
Stigler, George (1961), 'The economics of information', *Journal of Political Economy*, 69 (June), pp. 213–25.
Taylor, John B. (1980), 'Aggregate dynamics and staggered contracts', *Journal of Political Economy*, pp. 1–23.
Tobin, James (1980a), 'Are New Classical models plausible enough to guide policy?' *Journal of Money, Credit and Banking*, 12 (November), pp. 788–99.
Tobin, James (1980b), *Asset Accumulation and Economic Activity*, Chicago: Chicago University Press.
Vanberg, Viktor (1985), 'Spontaneous market order and social rules: a critical examination of F. A. Hayek's theory of cultural evolution', *Economics and Philosophy*, 2 (April), pp. 75–100.
Wallace, Neil (1976), 'Microeconomic theories of macroeconomic phenomena and their implications for monetary policy', in *Rational Expectations and the Theory of Economic Policy; Part II: Arguments and Evidence*, Thomas J. Sargent and Neil Wallace, (eds) Minneapolis: Research Department, Federal Reserve Bank of Minneapolis.
Wible, James R. (1982–3), 'The rational expectations tautologies', *Journal of Post Keynesian Economics*, 5 (Winter), pp. 199–207
Wible, James R. (1984–5), 'An epistemic critique of rational expectations and the neoclassical macroeconomic research program', *Journal of Post Keynesian Economics*, 7 (Winter), pp. 269–81.
Wong, Stanley (1978), *The Foundations of Paul Samuelson's Revealed Preference Theory*, London: Routledge and Kegan Paul.

Author Index

Subject Index